GRAHAM KERR is one of the country's most popular food personalities. Since his days as the Galloping Gourmet, Kerr has evolved a unique approach to healthy cooking: Minimax™. His first two books featuring Minimax—*Graham Kerr's Smart Cooking* and *Graham Kerr's Minimax™ Cookbook*—were immediate commercial successes. And the *Minimax™ Cookbook* won the I.A.C.P. award for the best cookbook in the health and diet category. Through syndication and rebroadcast on Discovery, his 1990 television series "The Graham Kerr Show" introduced this innovative style to millions of fans, old and new. His new show, "Graham Kerr's Kitchen," is seen nationally on PBS. Kerr lives on Camano Island, Washington.

Other books by Graham Kerr

Graham Kerr's Minimax™ Cookbook

Graham Kerr's Smart Cooking

GRAHAM KERR'S

◆

Creative Choices Cookbook

A Minimax™ Cookbook

A PERIGEE BOOK

A Perigee Book
Published by The Berkley Publishing Group
200 Madison Avenue
New York, NY 10016

Book design by H. Roberts

G. P. Putnam's Sons edition: October 1993
First Perigee edition: October 1994
Perigee ISBN: 0-399-52135-6

Minimax is a trademark of the Treena and Graham Kerr Corporation.

Nutrient calculation was performed on the Minnesota Nutrition Data System (NDS),
software developed by the Nutrition Coordinating Center,
University of Minnesota, Minneapolis.

The Library of Congress has catalogued the G. P. Putnam's Sons edition as follows:

    Kerr, Graham.
    [Creative choices cookbook]
    Graham Kerr's creative choices cookbook.
        p. cm.
    Includes index.
    ISBN 0-399-13896-X
    1. Cookery. 2. Low-fat diet—Recipes. I. Title.
TX714.K478   1993   93-1989   CIP
641.5′ 638—dc20

Printed in the United States of America
1   2   3   4   5   6   7   8   9   10

This book is printed on acid-free paper.

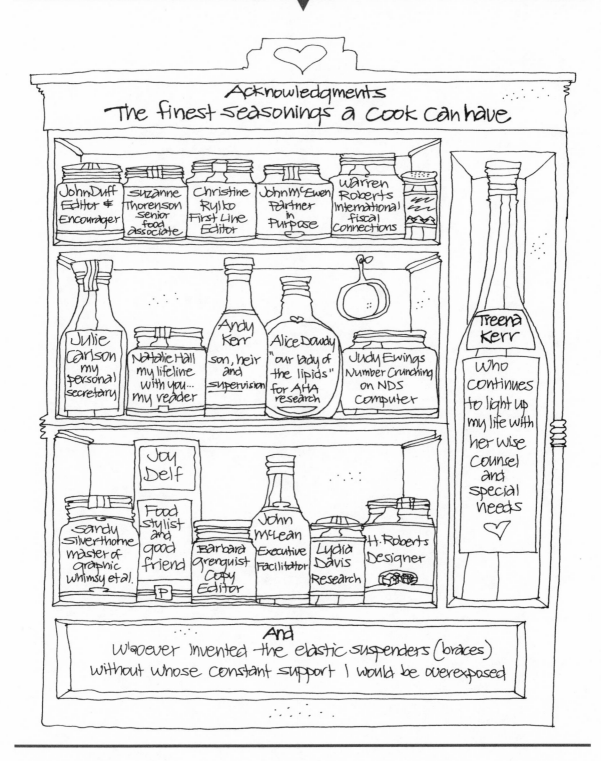

Acknowledgments
The finest seasonings a cook can have

And
Whoever invented the elastic suspenders (braces)
without whose constant support I would be overexposed

Dear Friend,

I want to urge you, as a friend — hence this personal note — to find out how you are affected by the food you eat.

Perhaps you or your loved ones are overweight, have high cholesterol, heart disease, cancer, or diabetes, or even suffer from exhaustion. Whatever your needs, it's a great idea to have some simple tests arranged by a sympathetic physician, and then to take the results to a registered dietitian who can explain, in practical terms, just how unique you are.

Once you fully understand your individual situation, it is then my job to help you create style, within limits, and have fun while you're doing it!

I believe that there is no loss of freedom in choosing to give up on risk, especially when there is still time to make a real difference. The sooner you choose, the more positive the result.

Now let's create together!

Contents

Graham Kerr's
Creative Choices Cookbook

Introduction

I consider myself a world authority on change; one way or another, I've seen and experienced a great deal of it in my working years since 1949. I've dined with Claude Terrial at the Tour d'Argent in Paris and eaten with the poorest of the poor in Central America. My wife, Treena, and I have set our own table at one time with plastic plates and at another with French porcelain. High on the hog or sitting in the dust . . . we've *been* there.

We've also made a change in the way we eat: we've chosen to eat less fat, fewer refined carbohydrates (sugars), and less sodium. We eat small amounts of flesh protein, red meat, as well as "white" poultry, and seafood; and large amounts of fresh fruit and vegetables, cereals, beans and other legumes. All these I season and garnish with fresh herbs and spices, wine, fruit vinegars, and all manner of aromatic, colorful foods that carry very little risk.

I made the change because I married a "high risk" individual. Treena is a demographic disaster. She comes from a family with a history of early death from heart problems. Her untreated cholesterol is 300 plus. She has hypertension and is a borderline diabetic. She reacts adversely to large doses of niacin (a simple way for some folk to reduce cholesterol). She is slightly overweight and used to be a smoker. Her HDL ("good" cholesterol) is low and her LDL ("bad" cholesterol) high . . . as is the little-*a* apoprotein factor, which is the worst of all.

As if all this weren't enough, she has already had a stroke and a heart attack and is a typical "A" type personality who simply refuses to see herself as one who is at risk.

I first changed my own diet in 1972 and eventually reduced my blood cholesterol level from 265 to 160. I lost weight and still enjoy excellent health. Treena did not accept my ultrarestrictive life-style, which left her, she often complained, with "nothing to eat."

It was fifteen years later, in 1987, that the stroke and the heart attack brought her long list of risks to the surface. I had understood the potential results of her high-fat diet but I had failed to grasp that the solution wasn't to ban everything in sight but rather to *enhance* what sensible quantities and manner of food could be eaten.

I began this process of discovery in 1987, and I've been fully occupied in its development ever since. Quite simply, you will find in these pages a record of a personal journey of *change*—a change that has proven to be lasting, enjoyable, and healthy for ourselves and our family, as well as for many good friends.

My three *Minimax* books can be neatly reversed. I began with *Smart Cooking* in 1991, which revisited some of the world's best-known classic dishes that I had previously cooked in the *Galloping Gourmet* days, heedless of any health factors.

The *Minimax Cookbook* was the second book, published in 1992. It dealt with techniques that could be used in day-to-day cooking that would result in less fat, sugar, and sodium and much more aroma, color, and texture. *Creative Choices* is *almost* where it all begins and is, therefore, what I would call book two in a five-book series. The *first* of the "series" is now in progress.

The Minimax System Defined

Minimax is a word I coined to describe a new method of cooking priorities. The first step is to minimize risks from foods and beverages that could cause potential health problems. These are commonly foods high in calories, fats, sodium, refined carbohydrates (sugars), and alcohol. Unfortunately, they are also commonly the foods that we have used for generations to provide pleasure in our favorite recipes: the chocolate in chocolate cake, the butter in your pasta's cream sauce, the fat in your turkey gravy, and so on. As you can appreciate, these pleasure-centered food ingredients cannot be reduced in our recipes without replacing them in part with something really creative.

I first introduced the term *Minimax* as a resident lecturer at the University of the Nations in Hawaii in 1978. In those days it was designed to show the relationship of consumption to health, *minimum intake for maximum energy output*. Later, in 1980 at the school of Long Range Development in Salem, Oregon, it grew into *minimum risks, maximum benefits*. In 1987, the focus became *minimum risk and maximum flavor* or *enjoyment* and remained there until the publication of this volume, where it has become *minimum risk, maximum creativity*.

The challenge is now out. The whole matter of Minimax is a call to creativity in the midst of an era of change in which we must either reverse the many destructive elements that surround us, or go under!

How Do I Make a Creative A.C.T.?

When we learn to maximize creativity in our cooking, we are using *A.C.T.*—food ingredients that are rich in fragrant aromas, vibrant colors, and varied textures. The A.C.T. foods create a sensual counterweight to balance the reduction of risk-laden foods. The recipes in your hands now are the result of many hours of experiments in my test kitchen and will give you dozens of ideas for A.C.T. items to have on hand in your cupboard. An extensive list of A.C.T. ingredients is also available to you starting on page 147.

The Power to Change

When it comes to making a change in the way we eat, the best success rates, over a five-year period, lie between 4 and 10 percent. We can dump many pounds in a few months by a variety of stern disciplines, but most of that weight is likely to return.

What is clearly needed is some means of making *creative changes that last.* When you begin to make changes, it is absolutely vital that you understand what is happening to your entire "self."

The medical profession has what is termed a "protocol" that is applied to you (or your loved one) when, for some reason, it is necessary to change.

A good physician will begin by looking at what you actually consume (diet) and then go on to see how you move around (exercise) and also what you do to manage stress (relaxation). If these self-monitoring changes have been tried, yet failed to restore health, the doctor may prescribe one or more chemicals (medication) designed to adjust body functions. If this fails, then an invasive technique that removes, bypasses, or repairs may be used (surgery).

What then follows is a period of healing that will usually be accompanied by instruction on diet, exercise, and relaxation (rehabilitation). The truth is that medical protocol is *not* a descending list of options; it's more like a continually tightening circle that keeps on repeating itself until we either change or go beyond repair.

We can choose to accept an individual approach to diet, exercise, and relaxation or, finding this too difficult, move on to a regime of chemicals that delay, to some extent, the knife. All decent physicians long to see diet, relaxation, and exercise established and maintained by their patients and regret the moment when they must intervene.

In the 1990s, we now face perhaps the most radical of all social revolutions: the lines are being drawn between prevention and remedy. At stake is not only our physical but also our economic health.

According to Aetna, the giant U.S. insurance company, the cost of health care is now neatly divided between "life-style" and "other" health issues. Counted within *life-style* are eating-, drinking-, and smoking-related diseases that are, to some measure, prevented by individual choice. In 1992, the estimated cost of repairing our life-style-abused bodies was one billion dollars every day—over $360 billion a year. The revolution before us all is how to contain and reduce this cost. We know that it must be done.

If the future holds some form of socialized medicine, and if our harmful habits are not changed, we will pay for it through ever-increasing taxation, a situation in which the majority of us will have to subsidize others' eating, drinking, and smoking habits. If medical care isn't socialized, then we will continue to pay ever-higher costs for insurance that prevent millions of the less advantaged from gaining access to health care. The big question is: Can our global economy continue to afford either?

A major part of the answer lies with each of us. Will we minimize the risks and maximize the creativity in our lives by adopting new standards?

We often choose harmful life-styles because we enjoy the immediate pleasures we receive. Food and beverage manufacturers, as well as chefs and gourmets, are always evaluating their skills. How does it smell, look, taste? What about texture? The test is first and foremost sensual. It must *please.*

Recently, as part of the revolution, nutritionists have sat in on these taste panels and proposed limits, or frames, that restrict calories, especially from fat, simple (sweet) carbohydrates, sodium, and a whole slew of suspect chemicals. Society, as a whole, is changing. We have begun to know that excessive amounts of fat, sugar, salt, and some chemicals are potentially dangerous. The problem lies in the lengthy time lapse between cause and effect, and the muddy waters of misinformation.

Faced with a large wedge of chocolate cake (that you'd die for!?) on a recent long-distance flight, I decided to take one moderate swipe at its thin end and call it quits. However, it wasn't removed quickly, and the rich coating began to fill both my mouth and my mind and eventually demanded a chaser. "Just a small slice," I reasoned. "No harm, really!"

But one bite led so easily to another, and before I knew it, the whole piece had vanished.

What happened was that I made an intelligent decision, based upon facts, not to eat chocolate cake—but I didn't set up a "frame" that restricted it . . . I just *thought* about it. And when I needed just a tiny bit of resolve, my *thoughts* weren't enough. I stepped over the line an inch, and the old phrase "a little bit of what you fancy does you good" mixed with the logic of "all things in moderation," and I was off again, leaving *thoughts* far behind.

If this sort of attitude continues, the *accumulations* of fat from very rich foods can become a problem and all the more difficult because you *think* that you've got them under control.

It has been widely suggested that we should not regard any dish as unacceptable. Once you ban anything, it becomes the subject of potential rebellion. Fair enough. I agree. However, a warning: the next step in that logic suggests we can eat *anything* and only need to compensate for the extra fat by reducing consumption over the next few meals.

Let me again use myself as an example.

I can order Fettucini Alfredo (pasta with a thick, rich, creamy, cheesy sauce)

and consume it in about twenty minutes. According to my analysis, I just swallowed about 1,700 calories with 130 grams of fat. If I wanted to wipe this excess out in one fell swoop, I would have to remove *absolutely all* fat from my diet for the next *two* days, or to adopt a *severe low-fat* diet for *four* days (about 13 percent of calories from fat).

I call this "feast-and-famine eating." What usually takes place is an attempt not to eat at all for a part of one day, but you have still overconsumed by at least 500 fat calories. Do this on a semiregular basis and it's no wonder the "all things in moderation" food plan doesn't actually work for many people.

My earnest suggestion to you is to select a standard "frame" to restrict fat consumption for *special* days to no more than double your regular days' "budget."

If your body frame calls for 2,000 calories per day and 450 of these are from fat, all you need to do is divide the 450 by 9 to get the number of fat grams. Fifty grams of fat can then be doubled as an *outer* limit in one day . . . after which you can spread the consumption over four days, perhaps at the rate of one tablespoon less per day (1 tablespoon of fat is 14 grams).

I feel this is realistic and should avoid the inevitable consequences of splurges on what is, for most folk, an unreasonably high fat risk.

I'm currently 204 pounds (6 feet, 2 inches), large-boned and roughly 5 pounds overweight. My total break-even point for calories is 2,000 per day; at this rate I neither lose nor gain. My plan is to lose the extra over a three-month period by a reduction of 22 grams of fat from my daily intake (approximately 17,000 calories over ninety-one days). Therefore, I'm looking at roughly 1,800 calories a day. Treena and I usually eat the same food and, when averaged, my dishes come out to about 24 percent calories from fat. Twenty-four percent of 1,800 calories is 432 calories; that, divided by 9 (the number of calories in a gram of fat), equals 48 grams of fat. For ease of working, I'll call it 50 grams.

I've chosen for my example a Monday-night dinner of classic Fettucini Alfredo that packs 130 grams of fat. Since I've already had breakfast and lunch, I'll add 30 grams to begin the day, a total of 160 for the day, or 110 grams more than my budget of 50. At 50 grams of fat per day, it would take me two full days of absolutely *no* fat to remedy the effects of just one dish of creamy pasta.

Let's not be so radical—let's spread it over the rest of the working week, Tuesday through Friday.

I divide 110 grams of fat by four days to get 27 grams of fat per day; I multiply that by 9 (the number of calories in a gram of fat); and get 243 calories from fat. This is just over one ounce or 13 percent of calories from fat. This is extremely low and a real difference from the 50-gram budget. In short, it means that one brief indulgence—say twenty minutes of immediate pleasure—takes four whole days of severe restriction to compensate.

The Pyramid and the Plate

Once upon a time, we had the four food groups that described the variety of foods needed to ensure good nutrition. It was an agricultural model and served a useful purpose over many years. Then, after fourteen years of intense nutritional activity, the U.S. Government gave us a better general view of good eating habits, the pyramid; however, it was still based on the old agricultural mode.

People are not farms, and few of us—even though some of us would like to be—are farmers. We are consumers who cook and measure what we do more with our subjective emotions than with objective weight scales and distribution systems. The pyramid is a good *objective* guide, but what about our *subjective* feelings?

The Four Food Groups

Fruits and Vegetables

Meat, Fish and Poultry

Dairy Products

milk

Yogurt

Grains and Cereals

Rice

Food Guide Pyramid

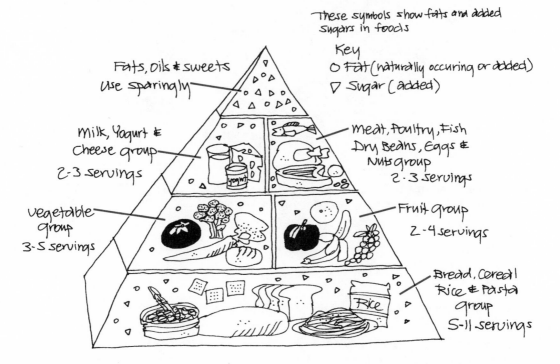

These symbols show fats and added sugars in foods

Key
O Fat (naturally occurring or added)
▽ Sugar (added)

Fats, Oils & Sweets
Use sparingly

Milk, Yogurt & Cheese group
2-3 servings

Meat, Poultry, Fish Dry Beans, Eggs & Nuts group
2-3 servings

Vegetable group
3-5 servings

Fruit group
2-4 servings

Bread, Cereal Rice & Pasta group
5-11 servings

Rice

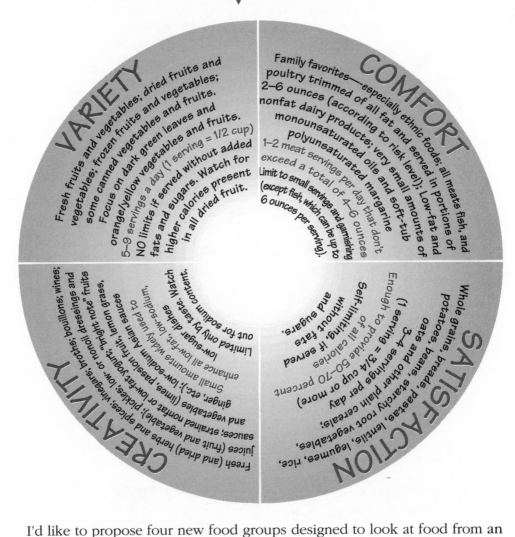

VARIETY

Fresh fruits and vegetables; dried fruits and vegetables; frozen fruits and vegetables; some canned vegetables and fruits. Focus on dark green leaves and orange/yellow vegetables and fruits. 5–9 servings a day (1 serving = 1/2 cup) NO limits if served without added fats and sugars. Watch for higher calories present in all dried fruit.

COMFORT

Family favorites—especially ethnic foods; all meats fish, and poultry trimmed of all fat and served in portions of 2–6 ounces (according to risk level); Low-fat and nonfat dairy products; very small amounts of monounsaturated oils and soft-tub polyunsaturated margarine 1–2 meat servings per day that don't exceed a total of 4–6 ounces Limit to small servings and garnishing (except fish, which can be up to 6 ounces per serving).

CREATIVITY

Fresh (and dried) herbs and spices; vinegars; bouillons; wines; broths; low- or nonfat yogurt; "bright note" fruits juices (fruit and vegetable); pickles; sauces; strained nonfat or low-fat yogurt, and vegetables (limes, passion fruit, lemon grass, ginger, etc.); low-sodium Asian sauces enhance all low-fat, low-sodium. Watch Small amounts widely used to low-sugar dishes Limited only by taste. out for sodium content.

SATISFACTION

Whole grains, potatoes, breads, pastas, rice, oats and other starchy root vegetables; beans; lentils, legumes, Self-limiting, if served without fats and sugars. Enough to provide 50–70 percent of all calories (1 serving = 3/4 cup or more) 3–4 servings per day

I'd like to propose four new food groups designed to look at food from an emotional point of view. What do you and I need to receive from food that goes beyond nutrition? My four groups are:

- Variety
- Satisfaction
- Comfort (Nostalgia)
- Creativity

The illustration above shows my four food groups and the qualities that provide for our feelings yet fall within the Minimax framework:

Variety is important because the wider we cast our net, the greater the amount of nutrients we consume. If we treat eating as a simple pit-stop exercise for refueling in convenient fast-food outlets, we can become malnourished (and over-weight) because of the very limited range of individual foods that we eat. In some reported cases, as few as eleven different foods are consumed in an average day. Here's a familiar sampling: hamburgers, french fries, ketchup, bread roll, milk shake, lettuce, tomato, candy bar, potato chips, and cookies.

Comfort (or *nostalgia*) is based mostly upon pleasant eating memories—or even images made popular by advertising and promotion. Norman Rockwell's Thanksgiving magazine cover, with its *very* healthy family clustered around Grand-pa and the turkey, is a perfect example. Our fond memories are like velvet that we love to stroke. Attempts to suggest that they are not good for us can meet with open rebellion, even anger. Let's face it, we love to feast on the familiar.

Satisfaction goes beyond comfort and relates more to a sense of being replete, of having enough to eat. It is here that we experience one of our biggest prob-lems—*the speed of eating.* Most of our mealtimes are rushed. We tend to treat the table as a trampoline as we bounce from our busy-ness to the table and onto some-thing more important. Fast eating doesn't allow the sense of satiety to catch up.

Satiety is the feeling of having eaten enough. It comes from hormones released in the bloodstream that typically take about twenty minutes to reach your mind. Twenty minutes is too long for our speedy mealtimes. By the time we've got the message, we've left the table!

The truth is that we tend to eat enough to stretch our gut, to feel filled up. However, that amount is often far more than we actually need. Were we to take the time to have some soup, salad, and bread (no butter), we would, first, be satis-fied by much smaller meat portions and tiny desserts. But no—we attack a large steak, half a chicken, or double-thick chops with heaps of french fries or baked potatoes smothered in butter, and within an hour or so, reap the resulting indiges-tion. No wonder our society consumes so many antacids every year!

Slow down, lighten up, wait for the hormone message to reach your mind, and choose the "satisfaction" foods. What a creative change this makes!

Creativity is the missing section in past and present attempts at food grouping. Nowhere, in either the basic four or the pyramid, is there reference to the hun-dreds of herbs, spices, wines, vinegars, and sauces used to create and enhance food. They're missing because the groupings we are given come from the Depart-ment of Agriculture and are designed to promote the use of major farm products.

The seasonings we use are neither consumed in sufficient bulk nor distributed fresh on a large-enough scale. They are also, to be fair, extremely hard to fit into a *product*-oriented grouping. Lift them out of the objective product groupings and set them into subjective *feelings,* and they all do just fine under *creativity*.

Cooking Above and Below . . . the Line

I have found it helpful to imagine that a line exists above which flavorings are Minimax suitable. I call them "bright notes." Foods that fall below the line are not necessarily dangerous and to be forever banished; they are simply subject to cautionary notices because of their potential risk if used to excess. I call them "velvet memories."

This isn't an exhaustive list, but it does give you an idea of how cooking above the line works. The scale in the left column gives you the intensity level, a sort of sliding scale with 10 as maximum flavors that are either a benefit (+) or a risk (-). You might like to develop your own lists with your own sliding scale—it's an important step toward knowing what works for you and why.

Bright Notes and Velvet Memories of Minimax Cooking

Intensity Level	Herbs	Liquids	Others
+10	Basil	Balsamic vinegar	Habanero pepper
+9	Cilantro	Ariel de-alcoholized wine	Garlic
+8	Oregano	Fruit vinegars	Gingerroot
+7	Mint	Lemon juice	Jalapeño
+6	Sage	Coconut essence	Lemon grass
+5	Thyme	Almond essence	Tamarind
+4	Savory	Vanilla essence	Cumin
+3	Sorrel	Clam juice	Turmeric
+2	Chervil	Tomato juice	Cloves
+1	Parsley	Worcestershire sauce	Nutmeg
	Fatty	**Salty**	**Sweet**
-1	Fish oils	Low-sodium sauces	Fruit juices
-2	Other oils	Mustards	Maple syrup
-3	Tropical oils	Canned soups	Honey
-4	Coconut milk	Ham and bacon	Cookies
-5	Lard	Processed meats	Shortbread
-6	Cheese	Potato chips	Devil's food cake
-7	Beef suet	Olives	Danish pastry
-8	Butter	Pickles	Ice creams
-9	Heavy cream	Soy sauce	Chocolate
-10	Coconut cream	Pure sodium	Pure sugar

Cooking as an Act of Kindness

In my world travels, I hear an increasingly obvious statement: "I don't have enough time." I'm sure that all of us know the feeling. *Life is taut.* Perhaps it's due to information overload, maybe the little computer that has opened us to such a big world in nanoseconds has actually extended us beyond our ability to comfortably catch up intellectually, and perhaps it's the *gap* that tires us? It may even be that our time is spent earning the money, or opportunity, to own and experience more things and we've had to make a value judgment between things and people. Were we less tired when we had time for one another? Do we feel better the morning after a pleasant evening with close friends or family than we do after four or five hours of television and snacking?

According to recent surveys, we have, in the United States, an average forty hours a week available for leisure. We spend between fifteen to twenty-five hours watching television, yet we can say with all truthfulness, "I don't have enough time [or energy?] to cook 'creatively.'

We choose to sit passively in front of television, mouths slightly open, digesting a nuked frozen entree, and consume it in nanoseconds without the slightest interest in what we've just eaten.

If this punches *any* kind of button for you (it does for me!), then here is a radical idea: Stop calling cooking . . . *cooking.* Try calling it . . . an "act of kindness." When Treena cooks for me, I *know* she's being kind; she doesn't like to cook—the very thought of it seems like an appalling waste of her time. When she feels that I am stretched and that I need to be replenished, she decides to cook . . . but what she's really doing is being "kind," and it's the creativity in that decision that touches me. I've also noticed that the kinder, the better. It really is true that she does an infinitely more creative job when, in her mind, she's being kind.

It's a rare person who doesn't want to be kind to someone else; and those that don't, I submit, have seldom received kindness . . . it simply hasn't been modeled! So next time you feel like nuking a frozen package or calling up the pizza place . . . don't do it! Do yourself and your loved ones a favor and don't think of cooking; just think of performing an act of kindness.

How to Use This Book

*I*n these pages we'll look at a variety of *basic* methods of cooking, and I'll build around each one a very simple meal for the family and close friends. You will have *my* selection of seasonings, garnishes, and accompaniments that will complete the plate, but you will also find dozens and dozens of recipes and ingredients for your own selection. Let me explain how it works.

On every main method page, you will find the outline of a plate like this . . .

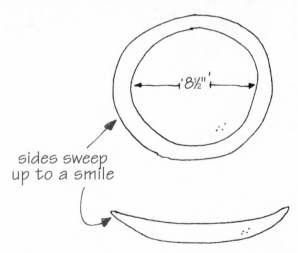

sides sweep
up to a smile

On that plain circle, I have drawn what represents a serving of the recipe that follows.

The plate represents what I call a *smiler*. It's actually a plate made by the French porcelain company Apilco that I find extremely useful for the kind of comfort food that many families enjoy. The usable diameter is 8½ inches—more than an inch less than the traditional ten. Apart from its other attributes, it makes less food look like the amount you might normally serve!

I have provided information on portion size, position, basic aroma, color, and texture (A.C.T.) for each food, and indicated the time it takes to prepare each element for the table. For example:

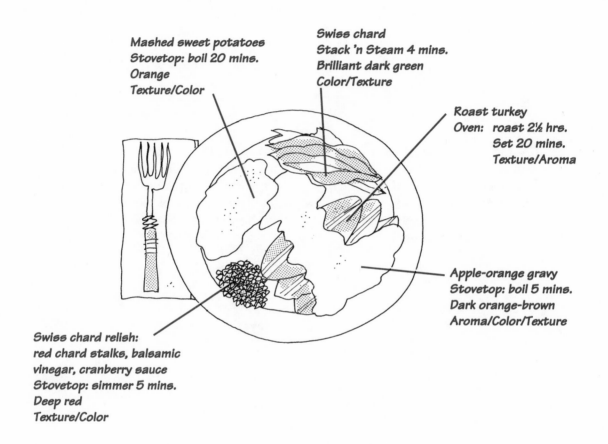

Mashed sweet potatoes
Stovetop: boil 20 mins.
Orange
Texture/Color

Swiss chard
Stack 'n Steam 4 mins.
Brilliant dark green
Color/Texture

Roast turkey
Oven: roast 2½ hrs.
Set 20 mins.
Texture/Aroma

Apple-orange gravy
Stovetop: boil 5 mins.
Dark orange-brown
Aroma/Color/Texture

Swiss chard relish:
red chard stalks, balsamic
vinegar, cranberry sauce
Stovetop: simmer 5 mins.
Deep red
Texture/Color

Timing

Throughout this book you'll notice various times are given. These times focus on three very different activities:

• Hands-on: This is the total time you actually spend opening jars, peeling vegetables, tossing and turning, testing and serving. It's been estimated conservatively, so I can pretty well guarantee that what it says is what it takes.

• Unsupervised: This is when you *do* nothing, but wait or perhaps do a hands-on project to complete another part of the meal.

• Cooking Times: These are used in the plate sketches under the call-outs. This is the time it actually takes each item on the plate to cook. Attached to each food is a numeral that indicates the order in which you cook the meal. For example:

1. Roast Turkey
   Oven: Roast 2½ hours, set 20 mins.
2. Mashed Sweet Potatoes
   Stovetop: Boil 20 mins.
3. Swiss Chard Relish
   Stovetop: Simmer 5 mins.
4. Apple-Orange Gravy
   Stovetop: Boil 5 mins.
5. Swiss Chard
   Stack 'n Steam 4 mins.

So much depends on getting everything to come together when it's at its best—not letting the peas, for example, sit around going gray for an hour while the roast is catching up!

Mixing and Matching

By mixing and matching these Minimax foods you can create many combinations uniquely capable of being enjoyed by your family and close friends.

If, for example, chard isn't available, then you only have to go to peruse the vegetable section to find an alternative in the "green" section. Or if you want to replace the carrots, you can easily find a substitute. The vegetable section has been loosely organized by color to help guide you in selecting creative alternatives.

The same goes for many of the main-dish recipes. I have used a specific meat for a given method, but in reality the method can be used for all kinds of different main ingredients. The way I roast turkey on page 66 can be used for a roast leg of lamb, roast pork, or even roast beef. The micro poached trout on page 40 can be used for halibut, salmon, sea bass, etc. The variety of methods and the accompaniments give you the potential for thousands of different plates.

And finally, there's the listing of A.C.T. foods: those foods that deliver aroma, color, and texture. By knowing something about these essential ingredients, you can further *enhance by adding* or *create by removing* one or two of my recipe items and inserting your own. There are eighty-nine of these, and so even if only one were used in each dish, its presence would change the recipes once again and provide tens of thousands of alternatives, among which will be several truly great new combinations that could make *you* famous!

Most main-course recipes that allow for maximum mixing and matching can be broken down into five elements. These are:

1. *The main ingredient:* beef, chicken, pork, etc.
2. *The basics needed for the method:* oil, onions, thickenings, etc.
3. *The seasonings:* stocks, wines, juices, herbs, etc.
4. *The vegetables:* usually served as an accompaniment, but can be included in all-in-one-pot dish
5. *The garnish and condiments:* dustings of herbs, spices, peppers, cheese, etc.

The following chart shows the almost infinite possibilities of mix 'n' match. We start with the Hearty Vegetable Stew with Beef on page 52 and begin with three variations of the main ingredient. The original recipe ingredients, usually listed in order of use, have been rearranged and classified in the five sections listed above. By mixing and matching, we come up with 961 variations.

Main Ingredient	Basic recipe: Beef	#1 Pork	#2 Chicken	#3 Venison
Basics	Oil	Oil	Oil	Oil
	Onions	Onions	Onions	Onions
	Tomato paste	Tomato paste	Tomato paste	Tomato paste
	Beef stock	Beef stock	Chicken stock	Chicken stock
	Arrowroot	Arrowroot	Arrowroot	Potato starch
Seasonings	De-alcoholized red wine	Apple juice	Tomato juice	Cranberry juice
	Carrots	Parsnips	Turnips	Turnips
	Garlic	Green onions	Green onions	Shallots
Vegetables	New potatoes	Sunchokes	Rice	Butter beans
	Mushrooms	Mushrooms	Shiitake mushrooms	Wild mushrooms
	Green beans	Green peppers	Snow peas	Lima beans
Garnish and condiments	Parsley	Chives	Coriander	Thyme
	Black pepper	White pepper	Red (cayenne) pepper	Red (cayenne) pepper
	Salt	Salt	Salt	Salt

When you attempt mix 'n' match variations, it helps to remember that you are looking for foods and liquid that deliver either one or more of the following: AROMA (sense of smell), COLOR (sense of sight), and TEXTURE (sense of touch). Let me go back to the stew as an example. The original recipe calls for red wine and garlic. The wine and garlic deliver *aroma,* and the wine and the tomato paste provide the *color.* The vegetables provide *texture* as well as *color* and *aroma* (mushrooms for *texture,* carrots and green beans for *color* and *texture*).

One Word About Nutrition

Because every recipe features a nutritional profile that fits with a typical Minimax frame of about 20 to 25 percent calories from fat, it follows that *your* job is to shuffle the ingredients to suit your taste. Keep to the suggested quantities and the basic methods, and your creation should automatically fit healthy guidelines for your family and friends.

Taking the Springboard Dive

I stress *creativity* in Minimax cooking because I want all the recipes in this book to serve as springboards for your own recipe experiments. You should use the methods you discover in these pages as springboards to dive into the sea of your own circumstances: pick and choose the spices, fruits, and vegetables that you and your family love, and substitute at will. I love to hear of your own Minimax triumphs and encourage you to write with your experiences in experimenting. (My address is at the back of the book.)

A Gourmet Carepleaser

The end result of your continued Minimax adventures will be a new definition of "gourmet." Instead of merely being a cook who pleases from the neck up, without regard to the rest of the body, you will become one of the gourmets of the future, a *carepleaser,* who cares for his or her guests' entire well-being, as well as their sense of pleasure.

Fresh Is Fantastic

There are a few important things to remember when using Minimax recipes, and one of the most basic is that all herbs and spices are the most effective A.C.T. tools 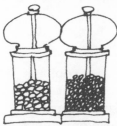 when they're fresh. This includes freshly grinding salt, pepper, and nutmeg in small mills or grating Parmesan cheese fresh for each recipe. You could substitute half of the amount of dried herbs for the fresh herbs, but the result will be a pale shadow of the full Minimax flavor possibility. I also find it works best to grate Parmesan cheese fresh for each recipe, rather than buying a pre-grated packet.

The Oil of Choice

You will see that my standard oil for cooking is extra-light olive oil with a dash of toasted sesame oil. I use olive oil because of its stable monounsaturated content. However, those unaccustomed to its taste might find the extra-virgin version too strong. If so, use a deodorized variety. I premix a light-flavored olive oil with one-sixteenth part of toasted sesame oil, because I find its light, nutty aroma wafting through the kitchen an irresistible part of the Minimax cooking process. Just make some up in advance and keep it handy for use in a lightproof sealed jar in a cool, dry place. You will note that I use very little. It is, after all, pure fat.

The Computer's Seal of Approval

The nutritional analysis of each recipe is verified by an extremely accurate computerized system. At the recommendation of the American Heart Association, I strive to keep the percentage of my *daily* calories that come from fat at or below 30 percent.

I believe this reduced percentage of calories from fat is the most important thing to remember because all the other dietary goals come naturally as a result of reducing high-fat foods. I have included other nutritional information—calories, sodium, fiber, and carbohydrates—for those of you with special health concerns such as hypertension or diabetes. Beware the descriptions of "light" or packaged foods without any nutritional figures to back the claims.

Stacking Your Steamer for Success

Your Minimax cooking will be greatly enhanced by a few basic pieces of equipment. One of the most widely used items in this book is the Stack 'n Steam pot.

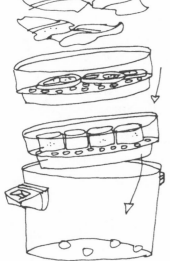

You might already be familiar with the bamboo variety, in which you can stack different vegetables on top of one another and cook everything at the same time. I have also designed a larger stainless-steel steamer that holds up a lot better than the bamboo one, and is available in kitchen stores around the country. In any case, bring the water for steaming to a vigorous boil before adding your vegetables for steaming, and you're ready for success. Steaming is a truly powerful tool for reducing fat in your diet.

Stocks Are Staples

Stocks are flavor-packed liquids for Minimax cooking. They are supremely easy to make and add so much flavor to sauces with so little fat. Yes, you can use the canned stocks, but they are usually oversalted and suffer from a tinny aftertaste. So the next time you have a free hour, one listless Saturday when you are doing chores around the house, throw a stock on the burner; then store it in the freezer for ready use whenever you're cooking. Stock recipes are on pages 141–144.

You Must Try Strained Yogurt

I estimate that this one ingredient could painlessly reduce the fat in your diet by a quarter. It's extremely easy to make, as you can see from the recipe on page 141. I use it plain, as a spread in place of butter or margarine on toast, and in infinite variations as a dairy substitute, thickener for sauces, a dessert topping—anywhere a creamy appearance is called for. Some yogurts will not strain because they contain special setting agents. Dannon plain nonfat is perfect for the job.

Wine Without Alcohol

Years (. . . and years) ago, I used a great deal of wine in my food and as a cue for commercial breaks! My personal choice to use good de-alcoholized wines is due to a desire to provide attractive alternatives to high-risk ingredients. Because some 34 million folk in North America are alcohol sensitive, I feel that my decision is warranted. I do not suggest by this that others should not drink alcohol. This is entirely a matter of individual choice.

Change Is a Joint Venture

And finally, I'm absolutely certain that all people who need to make a clear change in their life need a buddy who will make the same change with them.

Even though I'm not at such high risk as Treena, I decided to follow her new life standards. While her cholesterol has dropped about 60 points, mine has gone down 105. I have certainly benefited, but mostly by fully supporting someone I love in her creative choice.

The Recipes and Methods

Soups and Salads

♦ Leek and Potato Soup with Halibut

This recipe will work wonderfully with any good-quality white fish, such as cod, rockfish, snapper, or bass.

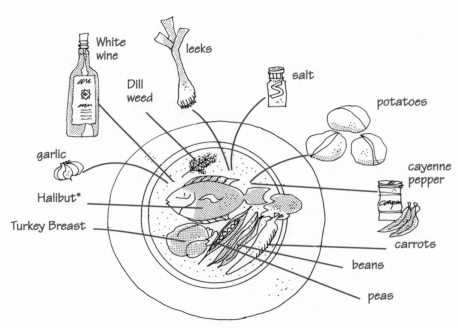

White
wine

leeks

salt

Dill
weed

potatoes

garlic

cayenne
pepper

Halibut*

Turkey Breast

carrots

beans

peas

*Just a baby so we could fit it on the plate!

Serves 6 as an appetizer, 4 as a main dish

1 teaspoon light olive oil (5 ml) with a dash of toasted sesame oil

1/2 pound leeks, root ends trimmed and discarded, sliced (225 gm)

3 cloves garlic, bashed, peeled, and chopped

1 pound potatoes, peeled and sliced to 1/2 inch thick (1.25 cm) (preferably Yellow Finn or Yukon Gold) (450 gm)

1/2 teaspoon dried dill weed (2.5 ml)

1/4 teaspoon freshly ground black pepper (1.25 ml)

6 cups water (1.4 l)

1/2 pound halibut steak (or belly) (225 gm), cut in 1/2-inch (1.5-cm) pieces

1/2 pound smoked turkey breast (225 gm), cut in 1/2-inch (1.5-cm) pieces

1 cup frozen mixed vegetables (peas, beans, and carrots), (236 ml), thawed

1 cup cooked diced potatoes (236 ml)

1 cup de-alcoholized white wine (236 ml)

Garnish

1 tablespoon fresh chopped dill weed (or parsley) (15 ml)

1/8 teaspoon cayenne pepper (.6 ml)

Heat the oil in a large soup pot or Dutch oven and sauté the leeks and garlic over medium heat for 5 minutes. Add the potatoes, dill, salt, and pepper and cook for 2 minutes. Pour in the water, bring to a boil, then simmer for 15 minutes.

Strain the soup, transferring the vegetables into a food processor and returning the liquid to the cooking pot. Puree the vegetables, then return them to the liquid in the pot.

Gently stir in the halibut and turkey and simmer until heated through for 5 minutes. Add the mixed vegetables, diced potatoes, and wine and simmer for 3 minutes.

To serve: Ladle into bowls and garnish with fresh dill or parsley and a scattering of cayenne.

Time Estimate: Hands-on, 20 minutes; unsupervised, 29 minutes

COOKING "OFF THE CUFF"
When was the last time you had close friends into your home and had a meal together? If it's been several months, may I suggest that's too long to be apart from those you love. Why not give them a call, ask them to stand in front of their open refrigerator and tell you what they have inside. Combine their list with yours and create something new on the spot. This cooking "off the cuff" can be a fun, easy way to share your table with people who mean so much to you. Why not start today—this book can be a tremendous help in getting inspired and organized!

Nutritional Profile per Serving		
	Classic	**Minimax**
Calories	344	188
Fat (gm)	25	3
Saturated fat (gm)	15	1
Calories from fat	65%	12%
Cholesterol (mg)	91	32
Sodium (mg)	374	493
Fiber (gm)	2	3
Carbohydrates (gm)	22	27
Classic compared: New England Clam Chowder		

Curried Butternut Soup

Serves 4

1 teaspoon light oil (5 ml) with a dash of toasted sesame oil
1/2 onion, peeled and coarsely chopped
1 tablespoon curry powder (15 ml)
1 apple, peeled, cored, and sliced thinly
2 cups cooked butternut squash (see page 103) (472 ml)
2 cups low-sodium chicken or vegetable broth (see pages 141, 144) (472 ml)
1/4 teaspoon salt (1.25 ml)

Heat the oil in a saucepan over medium heat and cook the onion and curry powder for 5 minutes. Add the apple and cook for 5 minutes. Add the squash, broth, and salt, bring to a boil, reduce the heat, cover, and simmer for 30 minutes.

Puree the soup in a food processor or blender and serve hot.

Nutritional Profile per Serving
Calories—78; fat (gm)—2; saturated fat (gm)—0; calories from fat—29%; cholesterol (mg)—0; sodium (mg)—163; fiber (gm)—3; carbohydrates (gm)—13.

Chinese Mustard Greens Soup

For a heartier soup, add strips of cooked skinless chicken breast and serve with rice on the side.

Serves 4

4 cups low-sodium chicken broth (see page 141, or use canned) (944 ml)
1 tablespoon finely chopped fresh gingerroot (15 ml)
4 ounces (about 6) sliced fresh mushrooms (113 gm)
1/2 pound mustard greens or bok choy, cut into fine strips (225 gm)
1 teaspoon low-sodium soy sauce (5 ml)
1/4 teaspoon toasted sesame oil (1.25 ml)

Pour the chicken broth into a large saucepan, add the ginger, and bring to a boil. Stir in the mushrooms, greens, and soy sauce; bring back to a boil, cover, and cook for 3 minutes. Just before serving, stir in the sesame oil.

Nutritional Profile per Serving:
Calories—43; fat (gm)—1; saturated fat (gm)—0; calories from fat—29%; cholesterol (mg)—0; sodium (mg)—119; fiber (gm)—2; carbohydrates (gm)—5.

- Greens should never be stored next to fruits like bananas or apples, which give off ethylene gas as they ripen. This will cause brown spots and rapid decay.
- Greens are widely available fresh all year long. Keep them crisp by washing, drying, and then layering them in clean paper or cotton towels. Place them in a plastic bag in the crisper drawer.
- In general, the darker green the leaf, the more nutritious the salad green. Romaine has up to ten times as much beta carotene as iceberg lettuce.
- Few foods give you so many nutritional benefits for so few calories as the many varieties of greens. Even if you can't find fresh produce, use frozen spinach or collard, turnip, or mustard greens—a great convenience food to have on hand.

Tomato Soup

Serves 4

1 teaspoon light oil (5 ml) with a dash of toasted sesame oil
1/2 cup chopped onions (118 ml)
1/2 teaspoon chopped garlic (2.5 ml)
1 teaspoon dried basil (5 ml)
1 teaspoon dried oregano (5 ml)
2 cups canned diced low-sodium tomatoes (472 ml)
1 ½ cups water (354 ml)
1/2 teaspoon salt (2.5 ml)

Heat the oil in a saucepan over medium heat and sauté the onions, garlic, and herbs until the onions are transparent—about 5 minutes. Add the tomatoes, water, and salt, bring to a boil, reduce the heat, and simmer for 15 minutes.

Nutritional Profile per Serving

Calories—47; fat (gm)—1; saturated fat (gm)—0; calories from fat—29%; cholesterol (mg)—0; sodium (mg)—283; fiber (gm)—2; carbohydrates (gm)—8.

APPLE SALAD

This is a very pleasant crisp salad, but do watch out for the browning that takes place when the cut apple is exposed to air. If you cut the apple in advance, toss the pieces in lemon juice.

Serves 4

Vinaigrette

1/4 cup apple-cider vinegar (59 ml)
2 tablespoons avocado oil (30 ml)
1/8 teaspoon salt (.6 ml)
1/8 teaspoon freshly ground black pepper (.6 ml)
1 teaspoon fresh chopped basil (5 ml)
1/2 teaspoon dried tarragon (2.5 ml), or 1 teaspoon (5 ml) fresh
1/2 teaspoon Dijon mustard (2.5 ml)
1 teaspoon maple syrup (5 ml)

Salad

1 medium apple, peeled, cored, and chopped
3 stalks celery, chopped
2 tablespoons fresh finely chopped basil (30 ml)
1 small head butter lettuce, torn into small pieces
1/2 cup toasted croutons (118 ml)

The vinaigrette: In a small bowl, mix the vinegar, oil, salt, pepper, basil, and tarragon and whisk to combine. Add the mustard and maple syrup and whisk again.

The salad: Just before serving, combine the freshly cut apple, celery, and fresh basil in a large bowl. Stir in the vinaigrette and mix well. Now add the lettuce leaves and croutons and toss well.

Nutritional Profile per Serving

Calories—126; fat (gm)—8; saturated fat (gm)—2; calories from fat—58%; cholesterol (mg)—0; sodium (mg)—166; fiber (gm)—2; carbohydrates (gm)—13.

> - Apples can keep for up to six weeks stored in plastic bags and refrigerated.
> - Apple juice contains no vitamin C, unless it's been added artificially. Check the label to make sure.
> - Butter lettuce is also called Boston or Bibb. It has a melting, buttery texture and a lovely mild flavor.

BEET SALAD

Serves 4

One 16-ounce or 454-gm can diced beets, drained
1/3 cup apple-cider vinegar (78 ml)
1 teaspoon fresh chives (5 ml)
1/2 cup strained yogurt (118 ml) (see page 141)
1 tablespoon fresh chopped parsley (15 ml)

In a large bowl mix the beets, vinegar, and chives and marinate for 30 minutes. Strain, discarding the marinade. Place the beets back into the bowl and stir in the yogurt and parsley.

Nutritional Profile per Serving

Calories—73; fat (gm)—28; saturated fat (gm)—0; calories from fat—3%; cholesterol (mg)—1; sodium (mg)—202; fiber (gm)—3; carbohydrates (gm)—14.

CALIFORNIA SALAD

Like bananas, papayas are usually only half ripe in the stores. Choose fruit that is at least half yellow. Fruit that is completely green has been picked too early and can never ripen. Papaya is completely ripe when it's at least three-quarters to fully yellow-orange.

Serves 4

1 papaya, halved lengthwise and seeded
1 avocado, halved and the pit removed
2 cups watermelon balls (472 ml)
4 tablespoons freshly squeezed lime juice (60 ml)
1 tablespoon fresh chopped cilantro (15 ml)

Using a melon baller, scoop the papaya and avocado into small balls and mix with the watermelon balls in a small bowl.

Stir in the lime juice and cilantro.

Nutritional Profile per Serving

Calories—127; fat (gm)—7; saturated fat (gm)—1; calories from fat—51%; cholesterol (mg)—0; sodium (mg)—12; fiber (gm)—4; carbohydrates (gm)—17.

CARROT AND ORANGE SALAD

Thin-skinned oranges are juicier than thick-skinned ones, and the smaller fruits are sweeter than larger ones. Don't worry about ripeness: oranges are always picked when they're ripe.

Serves 4

1/2 cup orange juice (118 ml)
1 tablespoon lemon juice (15 ml)
1 teaspoon honey (5 ml)
1 teaspoon cornstarch (5 ml)

1 pound carrots (450 gm), peeled and grated
1/4 cup chopped fresh mint leaves (59 ml)
1 orange, peeled and cut into small pieces

In a small saucepan, mix the orange juice, lemon juice, honey, and cornstarch. Bring to a boil and cook for 2 minutes. Remove from the heat and cool for 5 minutes.

In a large bowl, mix the grated carrots, chopped mint, and orange pieces with the cooled dressing. Place in the refrigerator to chill until serving.

Nutritional Profile per Serving

Calories—83; fat (gm)—0; saturated fat (gm)—0; calories from fat—3%; cholesterol (mg)—0; sodium (mg)—39; fiber (gm)—4; carbohydrates (gm)—20.

CHUNKY COLE SLAW

Serves 4

2 cups thinly sliced green cabbage (472 ml)
1 cup thinly sliced purple cabbage (236 ml)
1 cup thinly sliced carrots (236 ml)
2 tablespoons honey (30 ml)
2 tablespoons apple-cider vinegar (30 ml)
1/4 teaspoon salt (1.25 ml)
1/4 teaspoon freshly ground black pepper (1.25 ml)
1/2 teaspoon horseradish (2.5 ml)
1/4 cup strained yogurt (59 ml) (see page 141)

Combine the cabbages and carrots in a large bowl. In a small bowl, whisk together the remaining ingredients except the yogurt. Then fold gently into the yogurt in order not to lose the texture. Add to the vegetables and toss well.

Nutritional Profile per Serving

Calories—80; fat (gm)—trace; saturated fat (gm)—0; calories from fat—3%; cholesterol (mg)—1; sodium (mg)—181; fiber (gm)—2; carbohydrates (gm)—18.

Cucumber Raita Salad

This cooling salad is traditionally served with Indian curries, but it could easily accompany hot dishes with Thai, Creole, or Cajun origins.
Serves 4

One 1-pound or 450-gm cucumber
3 large green onions, finely chopped
2 tablespoons fresh chopped cilantro (30 ml)
1 cup strained yogurt (236 ml) (see page 141)
1 tablespoon freshly squeezed lime juice (15 ml)
1/2 teaspoon ground cumin (2.5 ml)
1/2 teaspoon ground coriander (2.5 ml)
1/4 teaspoon freshly ground white pepper (1.25 ml)
1/4 teaspoon salt (1.25 ml)

Partially peel the cucumber in long strips, leaving alternating strips of green skin and white flesh. Cut into thin slices lengthwise and then crosswise to yield tiny matchstick pieces. Transfer to a large bowl and add the onions and cilantro.

In a small bowl, stir the remaining ingredients together until smooth. Pour into the vegetables, toss well, and let marinate for 10 minutes before serving.

Nutritional Profile per Serving
Calories—91; fat (gm)—0; saturated fat (gm)—0; calories from fat—4%; cholesterol (mg)—2; sodium (mg)—235; fiber (gm)—1; carbohydrates (gm)—15.

Italian Broccoli Salad

Serves 4

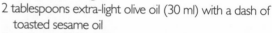

2 cups broccoli florets (475 ml)
1 cup cauliflower florets (236 ml)
1 cup low-sodium canned red kidney beans (236 ml), well rinsed and drained
4 green onions, cut in thin slices on the diagonal
2 tablespoons extra-light olive oil (30 ml) with a dash of toasted sesame oil
2 teaspoons Dijon mustard (10 ml)
2 tablespoons lemon or lime juice (30 ml)
1/8 teaspoon salt (.6 ml)
1/8 teaspoon freshly ground black pepper (.6 ml)
1 clove garlic, bashed, peeled, and finely chopped

Place the broccoli and cauliflower in a steamer tray and steam for 2½ minutes. Remove from the heat and let cool. In a large bowl, mix the steamed vegetables with the beans and onions. In a small bowl, beat the remaining ingredients together, pour over the vegetables, and toss well. Serve at room temperature.

Nutritional Profile per Serving
Calories—158; fat (gm)—7; saturated fat (gm)—1; calories from fat—42%; cholesterol (mg)—0; sodium (mg)—131; fiber (gm)—7; carbohydrates (gm)—18.

JICAMA SALAD

Jicama is a white-fleshed root vegetable from Mexico. Raw, it has the crisp texture of an apple. You can also boil or bake jicama like a potato. Choose jicama with hard, unblemished skin. It is a good source of vitamin C, and provides some potassium and calcium.

Serves 4

One 12-ounce or 340-gm jicama, peeled and cut into matchsticks
8 leaves fresh cilantro, finely chopped
2 tablespoons freshly squeezed lime juice (30 ml)
1/8 teaspoon freshly ground black peppercorns (.6 ml)

In a medium bowl, mix all ingredients together and chill until ready to serve.

Nutritional Profile per Serving

Calories—45; fat (gm)—0; saturated fat (gm)—0; calories from fat—5%; cholesterol (mg)—0; sodium (mg)—9; fiber (gm)—2; carbohydrates (gm)—10.

LETTUCE SALAD

Serves 4

Salad

5 cups of at least four varieties of different-colored greens (1.2 l) (e.g., red leaf, red-leaf romaine, radicchio, Bibb lettuce, arugula), torn into bite-size pieces
1 tablespoon fresh coarsely chopped dill (15 ml)
3 tablespoons fresh coarsely chopped parsley (45 ml)

Vinaigrette

1 clove garlic, bashed, peeled, and chopped
2 tablespoons extra-light olive oil (30 ml) with a dash of toasted sesame oil
Juice from 1 lime
5 tablespoons rice-wine vinegar (75 ml)
1/2 teaspoon ground mustard powder (2.5 ml)
2 tablespoons brown sugar (30 ml)
1/8 teaspoon cayenne pepper (.6 ml)

The salad: In a large bowl, toss the greens, dill, and parsley together until thoroughly mixed. Transfer to a salad spinner and set aside.

The vinaigrette: In a blender, whiz all the ingredients together until the garlic is dissolved—about 1 minute. Pour over the greens in the salad spinner and spin well. You will spin off all but 2 tablespoons of the dressing! Save the excess vinaigrette in the refrigerator for future use.

Nutritional Profile per Serving

Calories—38*; fat (gm)—2; saturated fat (gm)—0; calories from fat—56%*; cholesterol (mg)—0; sodium (mg)—7; fiber (gm)—1; carbohydrates (gm)—4.

*When the number of calories in a dish, especially a vegetable salad, is very low, the percentage of calories from fat gives a false impression of richness. Always note the grams of fat in a recipe; in this case, there are only 2—so it really is a low-fat recipe.

CAESAR SALAD REVISITED

I returned to this classic salad in search of the great taste without the raw egg and excessive oil. Mashing the anchovy fillets will make them much more palatable, if you've been turned off by seeing them whole on top of salads—and they are a must in this recipe.

Serves 4

2 slices whole-wheat bread
2 cloves garlic, bashed, peeled, and chopped
2 anchovy fillets
1/4 teaspoon coarsely fresh-ground black pepper (1.25 ml)
4 teaspoons freshly grated Parmesan cheese (20 ml)
1/2 cup strained yogurt (118 ml) (see page 141)

2 tablespoons de-alcoholized white wine (30 ml)
1 large head romaine lettuce, torn in 2-inch (5-cm) pieces (Save dark green top halves of outer leaves for sandwiches; set crisp inner leaves aside as garnish for another dish.)

Preheat the oven to 350°F. Make croutons by cutting the bread into 1/2-inch cubes (1.5 cm). Put on a baking sheet and bake in preheated oven for 15 minutes or until light golden brown. Set aside.

On a small cutting board, scrape the garlic and anchovy fillets together with the blade of a knife (a mortar and pestle will also work well). Sprinkle with the pepper and keep scraping until well incorporated. The coarsely ground pepper is a gritty substance that helps combine all the ingredients.

Scrape in the cheese until well combined. I've used Parmesan because this is readily available. Please feel free to use the dry cheese of your choice. Transfer to a small bowl, add the yogurt, and mix well. Pour the wine on top and scrape together.

Put the lettuce leaves in a large bowl, add the dressing, and toss until each leaf is well coated. Sprinkle with the croutons and toss again.

Nutritional Profile per Serving

Calories—98; fat (gm)—1; saturated fat (gm)—1; calories from fat—13%; cholesterol (mg)—5; sodium (mg)—234; fiber (gm)—2; carbohydrates (gm)—14.

SPINACH SALAD

The classic version of this recipe can suffer from a very high percentage of calories from fat—up to 79%—with a whopping 67 fat grams. In this conversion we have lowered the risk and introduced a new set of flavors.
Serves 4

Salad
2 medium bunches of spinach

1/2 cup canned mandarin or fresh orange sections (118 ml)
1/4 cup toasted chopped walnuts (59 ml)

Dressing
1/4 cup strained yogurt (59 ml) (see page 141)
1/4 cup orange juice (59 ml)
1 tablespoon Dijon mustard (15 ml)

Trim the stems off the spinach leaves and wash carefully, until all the dirt is removed. Spin the leaves in a salad spinner until they are perfectly dry. Tear the spinach into bite-sized pieces and put in a large salad bowl. Add the oranges and walnuts and toss.

In a small bowl mix the dressing ingredients until smooth.

To serve: Toss the salad with the dressing. If you like heavily dressed salad, use all the dressing. If you like it more lightly dressed, guess what . . . use less!

Nutritional Profile per Serving

Calories—126; fat (gm)—6*; saturated fat (gm)—1; calories from fat—40%; cholesterol (mg)—1; sodium (mg)—206; fiber (gm)—5; carbohydrates (gm)—15.

*The fat comes from the walnuts.

Szechuan Cucumber Salad

Serves 4

One 1-pound or 450-gm cucumber
3 green onions, cut into 1-inch diagonal slices
2 cloves garlic, bashed, peeled, and chopped finely
1½ tablespoons light soy sauce (22 ml)
1/2 teaspoon toasted sesame oil (2.5 ml)
1 teaspoon rice-wine vinegar (5 ml)
1/4 teaspoon granulated sugar (1.25 ml)
1/4 teaspoon ground Szechuan peppercorns (1.25 ml),
    or 1/8 teaspoon allspice (.6 ml)
1/4 teaspoon hot pepper flakes (1.25 ml)

Peel and seed the cucumbers and cut into 2-by-1/2-inch strips. Transfer to a large bowl, add the green onions and garlic, and mix well.

In a small bowl, whisk together the remaining ingredients, pour over the vegetables, and toss well. Marinate for 10 minutes before serving. Good at room temperature or chilled.

Nutritional Profile per Serving
Calories—28; fat (gm)—1; saturated fat (gm)—0; calories from fat—24%; cholesterol (mg)—0; sodium (mg)—79; fiber (gm)—1; carbohydrates (gm)—5.

Szechuan Spinach

Serves 4

4 cups fresh spinach leaves (944 ml)
8 cups water (1.9 l)
2 green onions, trimmed and sliced diagonally
1 teaspoon granulated sugar (5 ml)
1 tablespoon low-sodium soy sauce (15 ml)
1/2 teaspoon sesame oil (2.5 ml)
1 tablespoon rice-wine vinegar (15 ml)
1/8 teaspoon crushed hot chilies (optional) (.6 ml)
1/2 teaspoon finely chopped fresh gingerroot (2.5 ml)

Trim the stems from the spinach, carefully rinse off all the dirt, and set aside in a colander to drain.

Pour the water into a saucepan, bring to a boil, pour over the spinach, and let drain completely. This will wilt the spinach, but leave it a lovely bright green.

In a small bowl, mix all the remaining ingredients, making sure the sugar is completely dissolved.

Toss the spinach with the dressing, making sure it's thoroughly coated. Let it sit for at least 30 minutes before serving.

Nutritional Profile per Serving
Calories—27; fat (gm)—1; saturated fat (gm)—0; calories from fat—26%; cholesterol (mg)—0; sodium (mg)—195; fiber (gm)—2; carbohydrates (gm)—4.

String Bean Salad

Serves 4

10 ounces (283 gm) fresh string beans, topped and cut in half
1/4 large purple onion, sliced in long, thin strips
3 Italian tomatoes, sliced into small wedges
2 tablespoons balsamic vinegar (30 ml)
2 cloves garlic, bashed, peeled, and chopped
1 heaping teaspoon fresh chopped dill (15 ml)
2 tablespoons fresh chopped parsley (30 ml)
1/4 teaspoon freshly ground black pepper (1.25 ml)
1/8 teaspoon salt (.6 ml)

Place the beans in a steamer tray and steam for 6 minutes. Remove from the heat and immediately plunge into cold water to stop the cooking. Drain and transfer to a large serving bowl. Add the onion and tomatoes and mix well.

In a small bowl, whisk together the balsamic vinegar, garlic, dill, parsley, pepper, and salt. Pour over the vegetables and toss well; allow to mingle for 30 minutes.

WARM LENTIL SALAD

Serves 6

2 teaspoons light oil (10 ml) with a dash of toasted sesame oil
1 medium onion, peeled and finely chopped
1 tablespoon chopped fresh garlic (15 ml)
1 teaspoon cumin (5 ml)
2 teaspoons fresh chopped oregano (10 ml)
1 teaspoon dried basil (5 ml)
1 teaspoon dried thyme (5 ml)
1/2 cup water (118 ml)
1 cup dried lentils (236 ml)
14½ ounces canned low-sodium tomatoes, pureed (411 gm)
1/2 cup chopped fresh parsley (118 ml)
1/2 cup chopped celery (118 ml)
1/2 cup sliced green onion (118 ml)
1/4 cup lemon juice (59 ml)
2 tablespoons fresh chopped cilantro (optional) (30 ml)
1/4 teaspoon salt (1.25 ml)

Garnish
4 cups shredded fresh spinach or romaine lettuce (944 ml)
2 Italian tomatoes, chopped

Heat 1 teaspoon of the oil in a large heavy saucepan over medium heat and cook the onion, garlic, cumin, oregano, basil, and thyme until the onions are translucent—about 5 minutes. Add the water and lentils, cover, bring to a boil, reduce the heat, and simmer for 30 minutes. Add the tomatoes and simmer until the lentils are tender but not mushy. Most of the liquid will be gone.

Remove from the heat and pour into a bowl. Stir in the remaining teaspoon of oil, the parsley, celery, green onion, lemon juice, cilantro, and salt, and toss well.

Served on a bed of shredded greens sprinkled with the chopped tomatoes. This makes a side salad for six or a main-dish salad for four.

WILD RICE AND ORANGE SALAD

Serves 4

2 cups cooked wild rice (472 ml)
2 oranges, peeled and cut into chunks
4 green onions, sliced on the diagonal
1/2 cup raisins (118 ml)
1/4 cup chopped fresh spearmint (59 ml)
1 tablespoon extra-light olive oil (15 ml) with a dash of toasted sesame oil
1/4 cup orange juice (59 ml)
1/4 teaspoon salt (1.25 ml)
Freshly ground black pepper to taste

In a large bowl, mix the cooked rice, oranges, onions, raisins, and mint.

In a small bowl, whisk together the olive oil, orange juice, salt, and pepper. Pour over the salad ingredients and toss well. Let the flavors mingle for at least 1 hour before serving.

TABOULI WITH A *POP*

*A switch from bulgur to the lighter seed/grain
quinoa (see page 89) provides a wonderful
texture to this traditional Middle Eastern
salad.*

2 cups water (472 ml)
1 cup quinoa (236 ml), well rinsed
1 cup canned low-sodium garbanzo beans (236 ml), well
    rinsed and drained
1 cup chopped tomatoes (236 ml)
1/2 cup sliced green onions (118 ml)
1/2 cup fresh chopped parsley (118 ml)
2 tablespoons fresh chopped mint (30 ml)
1 tablespoon light oil (15 ml) with a dash of toasted
    sesame oil
3 tablespoons lemon juice (45 ml)
1/4 teaspoon salt (1.25 ml)

In a small saucepan,
bring the water to a boil.
Add the quinoa, bring
back to a boil, reduce the
heat, and simmer for 10
minutes. Strain and
spread out on a baking
sheet to cool rapidly.

In a large bowl, mix the cooled
quinoa, beans, tomatoes, onions, parsley, and
mint. In a small bowl, mix the oil, lemon juice,
and salt. Pour over the salad, toss well, and leave
for 30 minutes to let the flavors mingle.

Nutritional Profile per Serving
Calories—209; fat (gm)—5; saturated fat (gm)—1; calories
from fat—24%; cholesterol (mg)—0; sodium (mg)—153;
fiber (gm)—5; carbohydrates (gm)—36.

Fish and Seafood

♦ Baked Herb-Garden Salmon

I live in the Pacific Northwest, where it is possible to obtain good fresh fish, especially salmon, at a reasonable price. But what I've found surprising is that there is a shortage of information about how to bake a whole fish with its head and tail intact; even some of my favorite fish cookery references seem to avoid the issue.

Here, then, is a Minimax method for cooking a whole fish, with a special note of guidance on salmon selection. Using this technique you can cook any round-bodied whole fish: red snapper, large trout, striped bass, grouper, ocean perch, rockfish, pompano (bream), drum, mullet, or whitefish.

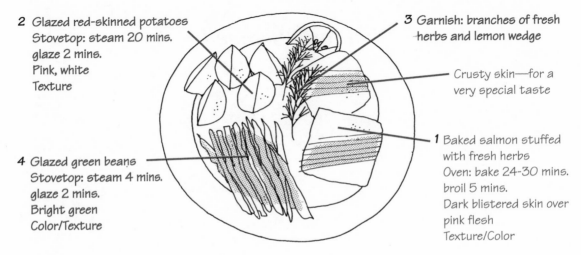

2 Glazed red-skinned potatoes
Stovetop: steam 20 mins.
glaze 2 mins.
Pink, white
Texture

3 Garnish: branches of fresh
herbs and lemon wedge

Crusty skin—for a
very special taste

4 Glazed green beans
Stovetop: steam 4 mins.
glaze 2 mins.
Bright green
Color/Texture

1 Baked salmon stuffed
with fresh herbs
Oven: bake 24-30 mins.
broil 5 mins.
Dark blistered skin over
pink flesh
Texture/Color

Serves 4, with ample leftover salmon for other uses

One whole 4–6-pound salmon (1.8–2.75 kg; the
    maximum size that fits inside the average oven)
1 teaspoon light oil (5 ml) with a dash of toasted sesame oil
1 tablespoon all-purpose flour (15 ml) mixed with 1/8
    teaspoon salt (.6 ml) and 1/8 teaspoon freshly ground
    black pepper (.6 ml)
2 cloves garlic, crushed
1/8 teaspoon salt (.6 ml)
1/8 teaspoon freshly ground black pepper (.6 ml)
1 bunch fresh tarragon or 1/2 teaspoon dried (2.5 ml)
1 bunch fresh rosemary, intact if possible
1 bunch fresh thyme
1 bunch fresh dill
1 whole lemon, cut in 1/2-inch (1.5-cm) slices

Garnish
1 lemon, cut in wedges
Rosemary branches
Thyme sprigs
Dill sprigs

Place the salmon in a sink filled with cold water. Using a small knife, brush the skin from tail to head, loosening and removing the scales. Run your hand back over the entire body, checking to make sure that all the scales are gone. Rinse under running water and place on a cutting board.

Sprinkle a little salt on a small soft piece of wet cloth; then wipe out the center of the fish so that no blood or discoloration remains.

For a delicious crispy skin, brush one side of the fish with the olive oil, making sure to work it well into the skin, and sprinkle with the flour and salt-and-pepper mixture, patting it firmly into the surface. Gently shake off any surplus, then place the fish back on the cutting board, prepared-side-up.

Using the back of a knife, mark a lengthwise center guideline on the fish body, but do not cut the skin. Using a very sharp knife or a sharp, clean razor blade, score diagonal incisions 1 inch (2.5 cm) apart from the top of the body down the center line almost to the belly. Make a final incision down the backbone so that the skin comes away easily when served.

Make a paste of the garlic, salt, and pepper, and rub into incisions. Layer the herbs inside the fish. Lay the lemon slices down the center line.

Line a shallow baking pan with heavy-duty aluminum foil, shiny-side-up. Lift the prepared fish by the head and tail and place it so that the main body of the fish (at least) is in the pan. Wrap the head and tail in oiled aluminum foil. Be sure to fan the tail out so that it holds its shape.

Preheat the oven to 450°F (230°C). Bake the prepared fish for 8 minutes per inch of thickness.

Remove from the oven and take off the foil and paper towels. Switch the oven to broil and pop the fish back in to crisp the skin for its table presentation, just until it blisters and browns— about 5 minutes.

To serve: Lift the fish out of the pan still on its aluminum-foil bed and onto a large oval serving plate, then slide the foil out from underneath. The bottom skin will usually come away with the foil. Slice by following the skin lines, serving slices from the back and belly, and garnish with pieces of the crispy skin. Save the pan drippings to drizzle over your side dishes for added taste-ooomph! The Glazed Green Beans and Glazed Potatoes (see pages 110 and 116) are clustered about the fish, and the herbs are left inside the fish.

When the top layer has been served (usually 6 portions), simply remove the head to a large side plate together with all the herbs and lemon and pry up the backbone to reveal the remaining bone-free fillet. Serve these pieces to your guests who don't want to eat the crispy skin.

Time Estimate: Hands-on, 45 minutes; unsupervised, none

Nutritional Profile per Serving		
	Classic	**Minimax**
Calories	667	378
Fat (gm)	41	11
Saturated fat (gm)	15	2
Calories from fat	55%	26%
Cholesterol (mg)	237	56
Sodium (mg)	1030	275
Fiber (gm)	1	5
Carbohydrates (gm)	13	32
Classic compared: Whole Baked Salmon with Cucumber Sauce		

◆ HALIBUT A-2-VAY

The French call this method poêle *or* poêlage *or* étuvée *(pronounced "A-2-Vay"). The idea is simply to sauté in a covered pan so that the steam and fat combine to cook the food. In this case, with very little oil, I've created a leek, mushroom, and lemon bed spiked with cayenne, mustard, and white wine. The fish is part steamed, part poached, and absolutely delicious. The vegetables blend well and make a complete dinner in just over 10 minutes cooking time.*

Garnish: chopped parsley and paprika
red, green
Color

Halibut or ling cod cooked with
bed of leek and mushrooms
(at 1) for 6 min.

Bed of fine-sliced (matchstick)
leek and quartered mushrooms
Stovetop: "A-2-Vay" (étuvée)
10 mins.
White on pale green, deep cream
Texture/Aroma

3 Steamed zucchini in dill
Stovetop: steam 4 mins.
Bright green, white
Texture/Color

2 Steamed potato
and yellow squash
Stovetop: steam
potatoes 8 mins.
steam squash 4
mins.
Yellow, white
Texture/Color

Serves 4

2 leeks, root ends trimmed and discarded
1 teaspoon light olive oil (5 ml) with a dash of toasted
    sesame oil
12 ounces white mushrooms (340 gm), quartered
2½ teaspoons fresh coarsely chopped dill (12.5ml),
    or 2 teaspoons dried dill weed (10 ml)
1/8 teaspoon cayenne pepper (.6 ml)
2 tablespoons freshly squeezed lemon juice (30 ml)
Four 6-ounce (170-gm) halibut steaks, with skin
1/8 teaspoon salt (.6 ml)
1/4 teaspoon freshly ground black pepper (1.25 ml)
2/3 cup de-alcoholized white wine (157 ml)
2 large russet potatoes, peeled and sliced in 1/4-inch
    (.75-cm) rounds
2 medium yellow summer squash, trimmed to equal
    lengths and sliced in 1/4-inch or .75-cm disks
4 medium green summer squash, trimmed to equal
    lengths, cut in half lengthwise.

1 teaspoon arrowroot (5 ml) mixed with 2 teaspoons
    de-alcoholized white wine (11 ml) (slurry)
1 tablespoon fresh finely chopped parsley (15 ml)
Paprika

Cut the leeks into two parts: the light green stem and the dark top. Slice the light green part into long, fine matchsticks (a hand-held mandolin works very well for this) and set aside. Save the dark green tops for other uses.

Heat the oil in a large skillet on medium heat and shallow-fry the leeks, mushrooms, 1 teaspoon of the dill (5 ml), and cayenne pepper for 4 minutes. Stir in the lemon juice and spread the cooked vegetables out to make a "bed."

Lay the halibut fillets on the vegetable bed and sprinkle with the salt and pepper. Pour half

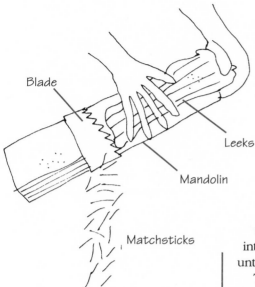

Blade

Leeks

Mandolin

Matchsticks

THE SECRET TO MATCHSTICKS
A good knife is really all anyone needs, yet when it comes to the fine matchstick (julienne) garnishes), there is nothing quite as efficient as a mandolin—no, not the musical instrument, but a board with a set of dividing and cutting blades and an adjustable chute to vary the size of the garnish. Try to find one that is strong and safe as well as sharp. It's a good investment for the kitchen drawer. Without a mandolin, add another 5 minutes to your preparation time.

For this dish, freeze the leeks for 15 minutes before slicing, to reduce the "tears." When slicing the leeks on the mandolin, cut them in half lengthwise and start them cut-side-down. You won't be able to slice the part you're still holding, so this should be finished with a knife.

of the wine around the outside edge of the pan, swirl around to mix thoroughly, cover, and cook over medium heat for 6 minutes.

Bring the water in a large Stack 'n Steam pot to a full boil. Place the potato slices in the first level of the steamer and cook for 8 minutes. After 4 minutes, place the yellow and green summer squash in a second steamer level, sprinkle with 1/2 teaspoon of the dill (2.5 ml), add to the steamer, and cook for 4 minutes. Remove from the heat.

Remove the halibut from the pan, cover to keep warm, and set aside. To the leeks and mushrooms, add the remaining wine and the rest of the dill and "deglaze" the pan, scraping the bottom of the pan to lift any pan residue flavor into the vegetables—about 1 minute. Stir in the arrowroot slurry until thickened. Remove from the heat.

To serve: Make a bed of the cooked leeks and mushrooms on one side of each dinner plate and nestle a halibut piece on top. Alternate the white, yellow, and green slices of potatoes and squash on the side. Sprinkle with sparkling green parsley and bright red paprika as a final touch.

Time Estimate: Hands-on, 39 minutes; unsupervised, 18 minutes

Nutritional Profile per Serving		
	Classic	**Minimax**
Calories	973	358
Fat (gm)	81	5
Saturated fat (gm)	11	1
Calories from fat	75%	12%
Cholesterol (mg)	120	74
Sodium (mg)	409	200
Fiber (gm)	6	12
Carbohydrates (gm)	20	49
Classic compared: Halibut Salad		

◆ POACHED TROUT WITH BABY SHRIMP

In 1974, I served as an adjunct professor (no chair!) at Cornell University's School of Hotel Management; at that time we experimented with microwave ovens, which—to be fair—were in their earliest days of development. We cooked our way through all the major classic methods and compared each with its high-tech system. Only one did better, and that was to "micro-poach" fish. It is still a wonderful idea, especially with shrimp and mushrooms. If you haven't bought into this brave new world yet, don't worry. Just use the method in the recipe for Seafood Pancakes Kareena on page 44, where simple pan poaching is used.

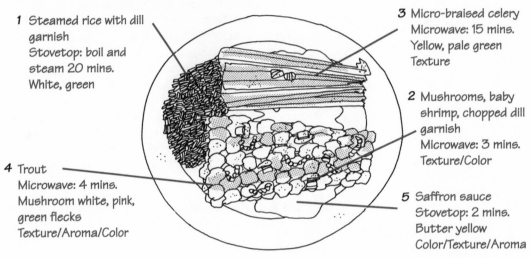

1 Steamed rice with dill garnish
Stovetop: boil and steam 20 mins.
White, green

3 Micro-braised celery
Microwave: 15 mins.
Yellow, pale green
Texture

2 Mushrooms, baby shrimp, chopped dill garnish
Microwave: 3 mins.
Texture/Color

4 Trout
Microwave: 4 mins.
Mushroom white, pink, green flecks
Texture/Aroma/Color

5 Saffron sauce
Stovetop: 2 mins.
Butter yellow
Color/Texture/Aroma

Serves 4

2 whole (12-inch or 30-cm) trout, boned and cut into 2 fillets
1/8 teaspoon salt (.6 ml)
1/8 teaspoon freshly ground black pepper (.6 ml)
3 cups water (708 ml)
4 stalks celery tops from hearts, roughly chopped
8 medium mushrooms, stems and caps trimmed and set aside
2 whole celery hearts, 6 inches or 15 cm long
4 ounces baby shrimp (113 ml)
2 teaspoons fresh chopped dill (10 ml)
1/16 teaspoon saffron powder (.3 ml) (just enough to cover the tip of a knife)
1 tablespoon arrowroot mixed with 2 tablespoons water (slurry)
Juice of 1/2 lemon
2 cups steamed rice garnished with dill

First debone the fish as described below. Lay the fillets flat, skin-side-down, on a large plate, sprinkle with the salt and pepper, and refrigerate until ready to cook.

Now make a fish stock by placing all the boning-process trimmings in a saucepan on medium-high heat with the water, celery, and mushroom stems. Cook for 25 minutes. Strain and set aside.

Cut the celery heart in two lengthwise and place in a microwavable dish. Pour in 1 cup (236 ml) of the reserved fish stock, cover, and cook on high power in the microwave for 10 minutes. Turn the celery over, rotate the dish 45°, and cook for 5 minutes. Remove the celery and set aside, reserving the liquid.

Slice the mushroom caps thinly and add

PERFECTLY BONED TROUT (AND OTHER FINE-BONED, ROUND-BODIED FISH)

Remove the head, then slice off the tail, just behind the rear dorsal fin on top of the body. Take the cut which has opened up the belly below the head and extend that down into the end where the tail was removed. Hold the fish to expose the backbone so that the open belly faces you. Gently press with your thumbs down either side of the spine in order to soften the flesh around the bones. With a small knife dig underneath the spine at the tail end until you have about an inch of bones released from the flesh. Then insert your fingers on either side of the backbone and pinch either side of the bones. Pull the backbone upward, releasing it from the main flesh. *Keep using your forefinger to detach the underlying fillets from the bone.* You will still have some exterior bones to remove. Cut the gill bones away (including the cartilage that lies beneath them). Do the same with the fins that are attached to the breast. Check for any additional large bones. Find the main dorsal fin in the middle of the back—cut it on either side and lift it out. Reserve the bones to use for the stock. Cut into 2 fillets.

to the strained fish stock, cover, and microwave on high for 3 minutes. Strain out the mushrooms; reserve the liquid. Press the mushrooms on the fish fillets; sprinkle with the shrimp and dill.

Pour the reserved fish stock into a microwavable dish, just large enough to hold the trout. Carefully lift the prepared trout into the stock; the liquid level should just reach the top of the fillets without covering them. Cover with grease-proof (waxed) paper and cook on high in the microwave for 4 to 6 minutes, depending on the size of your oven. Transfer the fish to a serving plate and keep hot.

The saffron sauce: Use the poaching liquid and enough reserved stock to make 2 cups (472 ml) of poaching stock into a small saucepan, stir in the saffron, and heat through. Make a slurry of arrowroot and water and stir this in to thicken just to the consistency of melted butter—about 1 minute. Add the lemon juice to taste.

To serve: Drizzle the tender trout with the golden saffron sauce and present to your guests with the celery heart and rice on the side.

Time Estimate: Hands-on, 1 hour; unsupervised, none

STEAMED RICE
Serves 4

2 cups water (472 ml)
1½ cups uncooked long-grained white rice (354 ml)
1/8 teaspoon salt (.6 ml)

Bring water to a boil in a medium pan. Add rice and salt; boil 15 minutes. Strain in a metal sieve; put the rice-filled sieve over a pan of boiling water and steam, covered, for 5 minutes.

Nutritional Profile per Serving		
	Classic	**Minimax**
Calories	791	473
Fat (gm)	41	10
Saturated fat (gm)	12	3
Calories from fat	47%	19%
Cholesterol (mg)	223	161
Sodium (mg)	1,767	481
Fiber (gm)	2	3
Carbohydrates (gm)	32	36

Classic compared: Trout Woolpack, stuffed with shrimp, mushrooms, and butter and bacon.

◆ SALMON CAKES WITH SWEET-CORN CILANTRO SAUCE

What we remember about the food we ate and enjoyed as children, is what I call comfort food. One of my favorite memories is the salmon fish cake made with canned salmon mixed with eggs and potatoes, breaded and shallow-fried in butter. In this recipe I've revisited past pleasure and created a present-day delight that becomes an example of fusion between the northwestern salmon and dill and the southwestern corn and cumin—comfort and creativity combined! My method uses the Stack 'n Steam. You can use a folding steamer in a large saucepan, but it won't be as tidy.

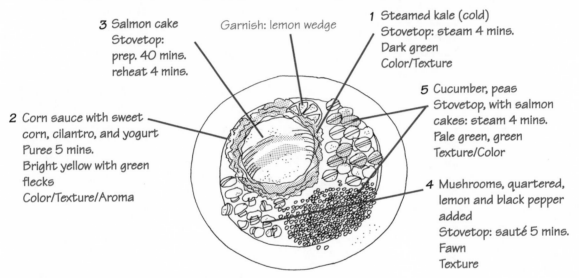

3 Salmon cake
Stovetop:
prep. 40 mins.
reheat 4 mins.

Garnish: lemon wedge

1 Steamed kale (cold)
Stovetop: steam 4 mins.
Dark green
Color/Texture

5 Cucumber, peas
Stovetop, with salmon
cakes: steam 4 mins.
Pale green, green
Texture/Color

2 Corn sauce with sweet
corn, cilantro, and yogurt
Puree 5 mins.
Bright yellow with green
flecks
Color/Texture/Aroma

4 Mushrooms, quartered,
lemon and black pepper
added
Stovetop: sauté 5 mins.
Fawn
Texture

Serves 4 as a main dish or 8 as a first course

1½ pounds russet potatoes (675 gm), peeled and cut in
2-inch or 5-cm pieces
1 pound fresh red salmon fillet (450 gm), or 12 ounces
canned salmon (340 gm)
1/4 teaspoon salt (1.25 ml)
1/4 pound smoked salmon fillet (113 gm)
1 tablespoon capers (15 ml)
1 teaspoon white pepper (5 ml)
1 large cucumber, preferably English, peeled, seeded,
and cut into 1-inch (2.5-cm) rounds
1 teaspoon dried dill weed (5 ml)
1 teaspoon ground cumin (5 ml)
4 leaves of curly kale, well washed and steamed for
4 minutes
8 ounces small white mushrooms (227 gm), quartered

Juice of 1 lemon
1/8 teaspoon black pepper (.6 ml)
8 ounces frozen green peas (227 gm), boiled for
1 minute and cooled
1 large lime, cut in wedges

Sweet-Corn Cilantro Sauce

One 11-ounce or 312-gm can corn, drained, or 2 cups
cooked frozen kernels (472 ml)
12 large leaves fresh cilantro
4 tablespoons strained yogurt (60 ml) (see page 141),
or 2 tablespoons nonfat plain yogurt (30 ml)

In a large pot, boil the potatoes for 20 minutes.
Drain, return to the pot on very low heat, and

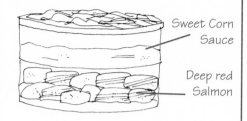

Sweet Corn Sauce

Deep red Salmon

CAN CANNED SALMON BE SUBSTITUTED?

Clearly it is possible to use a good-quality canned salmon, one without added oil. It will not be as succulent and smooth as the freshly steamed version, but it does make the dish more of a possibility for day-to-day eating.

The color of the dish will be enhanced if you buy deep red salmon. This is not normally the best or the most expensive kind, but it is pleasing for the dish to be as vivid-looking as possible.

SMOKED SALMON

It is the dark outer part of vacuum-packed "chunks" that work the best. They create a flavor "edge" that is delightful.

AS A FIRST COURSE

Fill individual soufflé dishes with the salmon mixture up to 1/2 inch (1.5 cm) from the rim and top with the corn sauce. Bake in a 350°F (180°C) oven for 20 minutes and serve with a sprig of cilantro.

cover with a cloth towel to steam out any remaining moisture for 10 minutes. Transfer to a bowl, add salt, and mash until smooth. Set aside.

Place the fresh salmon on a small plate, sprinkle on 1/4 teaspoon (.6 ml) of the salt, and steam in a Stack 'n Steam for 6 minutes. Remove from the heat, peel off the skin, take out any bones, and flake into a large bowl.

Remove the outer skin from the smoked salmon and break the meat into small flakes, removing any bones. Add to the fresh salmon with the potatoes, capers, remaining salt, and white pepper and mix well.

Shape the salmon into 4 cakes (or fill 8 small soufflé dishes if used as a first course—see the suggestions below). Put onto a steamer tray.

In a small bowl, mix the cucumber with the dill, cumin, and remaining salt and turn out onto the same steamer tray.

Place the kale leaves on the upper deck steamer and cook everything for 4 minutes.

In a large skillet on medium heat, cook the mushrooms with the lemon juice for 5 minutes, tossing to coat with the juice. Sprinkle with black pepper and set aside. Reheat just before serving with the cucumber and peas.

The sauce: Puree the corn in a food processor until smooth. Add the cilantro and yogurt and mix well.

To serve: On each dinner plate, place 1 kale leaf and spread with the corn sauce. Top with a salmon cake surrounded by the cucumber, mushrooms, and peas and garnished with a small lime wedge on the side. Sprinkle paprika over top of salmon cake.

Time Estimate: Hands-on, 70 minutes; unsupervised, none

Nutritional Profile per Serving		
	Classic	**Minimax**
Calories	565	477
Fat (gm)	32	11
Saturated fat (gm)	7	2
Calories from fat	50%	20%
Cholesterol (mg)	134	74
Sodium (mg)	757	662
Fiber (gm)	8	10
Carbohydrates (gm)	43	63
Classic compared: Salmon Croquettes		

♦ SEAFOOD PANCAKES KAREENA

When this meal is complete and on the plate, it always gets rave reviews, and the variations on the filling and sauce are endless. Try it soon for a couple of good friends. It's great fun making pancakes together, and learning to turn them—especially for novices—is a great party starter! (I named this dish after our youngest daughter, who, I trust, will now make it for her wonderful husband, Ronald.)

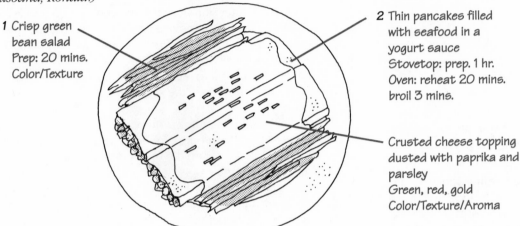

1 Crisp green
bean salad
Prep: 20 mins.
Color/Texture

2 Thin pancakes filled
with seafood in a
yogurt sauce
Stovetop: prep. 1 hr.
Oven: reheat 20 mins.
broil 3 mins.

Crusted cheese topping
dusted with paprika and
parsley
Green, red, gold
Color/Texture/Aroma

Pancakes
Yields 9 pancakes
1/2 cup all-purpose flour (118 ml)
1 egg + 1 egg yolk
1 cup nonfat milk (236 ml)
1 teaspoon light oil (5 ml) with a dash of toasted
sesame oil

Seafood Filling and Sauce
4 cups fish stock (944 ml) (see page 143)
8 ounces white button mushrooms (227 gm), cut into
quarters
1/2 pound cod fillets (227 gm), cut into 10 finger-
shaped pieces
8 ounces scallops (about 20) (227 gm)
6 tablespoons cornstarch (90 ml) mixed with 6
tablespoons water (90 ml) (slurry)
1 cup strained yogurt (236 ml) (see page 141)
1/4 cup freshly grated Parmesan cheese (59 ml)

Garnish
Paprika
Parsley

The pancakes: In a large mixing bowl, beat the flour, egg, egg yolk, and milk until smooth and set aside to rest for 20 minutes, during which time you can prepare the filling.

Heat the oil in the bottom of a nonstick 8-inch (20-cm) omelet pan, swirling it around to cover the entire bottom surface. Turn the pan upside down over the batter bowl to drain and later whisk in any surplus oil. This allows you to make all the pancakes without adding more fat.

Pour a scant 1/4 cup (59 ml) of the batter into the omelet pan over medium-high heat. Roll the pan quickly to distribute the batter over the entire bottom surface. Wait until the top turns waxy and dull, then turn the pancake and cook for 1 minute. You should have 9 pancakes, giving you 1 extra in case of mistakes.

The seafood filling: Pour the fish stock into a saucepan and heat until a rolling boil breaks the surface. Add the mushrooms and cook for 1 minute. Strain, reserving the mushrooms and

one problem with
seafood pancakes

liquid separately. Place the mushrooms in a small, covered bowl, so they'll continue cooking in their retained heat.

Return the fish stock to the saucepan and bring to a rolling boil. Add the cod and scallops, keeping the pieces separate. Cover with a piece of grease-proof or waxed paper, cut to fit, pressing it down to "seal" the surface. Watch for bubbles under the paper, lower the heat to a simmer, and cook for 4 minutes. Strain, reserving the seafood and liquid separately. Transfer the seafood to a large bowl, cover, and set aside.

Return the fish stock to the saucepan, add the cornstarch slurry, and return to a boil, stirring constantly until thickened—about 1 minute. Strain into another saucepan. Remove 1 cup (236 ml) and stir into the cooked seafood. Gently stir in half of the strained yogurt. Fold the remaining yogurt into the reserved cooking liquid to make a sauce, and set aside.

To serve: On a large ovenproof serving platter, lay a crepe brown-side-up and spoon 1/4 cup (59 ml) of the seafood filling down the center. Fold the sides over and gently turn it over so that the overlap is underneath. Repeat with the other crepes until the platter is full. Spoon the sauce on top to cover them completely. Sprinkle with the Parmesan cheese and garnish with colorful paprika stripes that follow the "ridge" of each pancake. Pop under the broiler and cook until the top is a sumptuous, speckled, golden brown—about 3 minutes. Remove from broiler and dust with parsley.

With a wide spatula lift two crepes from the platter onto a plate. The entree is complete with a serving of brightly colored String Bean Salad (see page 32).

Time Estimate: Hands-on, 1 hour, 30 minutes; unsupervised, 20 minutes

MAKE AHEAD WITH EASE
You can actually assemble the crepes completely and then refrigerate until ready to cook. Reheat at 300°F (150°C) for 20 minutes, then cover them with the sauce, broil, and serve as above.

FILLET THE COD YOURSELF
Cod has a natural muscle formation that holds the flesh in place. Before cooking, cut down either side of the central bone, and you should be able to remove this bone with one try. You'll now have two long strips of cod from which to cut your "fingers."

Nutritional Profile per Serving	Classic	Minimax
Calories	1433	376
Fat (gm)	63	8
Saturated fat (gm)	25	3
Calories from fat	39%	19%
Cholesterol (mg)	588	161
Sodium (mg)	2509	444
Fiber (gm)	7	4
Carbohydrates (gm)	93	36
Classic compared: Crêpes Fruits de Mer		

◆ SWEET LIME AND BROILED SEAFOOD SALAD

This is a genuine breakthrough dish that uses several new ideas. There are the lime vinaigrette salad dressing and the tangle of salad greens intermingled with fresh herbs. Add to these the textures of tender broiled fish with blistered, crunchy skin and stiffly whipped potatoes. But then comes a radically new glaze of lime marmalade and wine—colored with radicchio. . . .

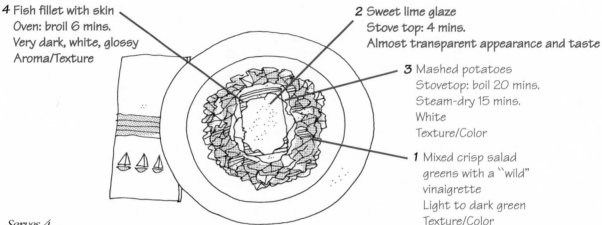

4 Fish fillet with skin
Oven: broil 6 mins.
Very dark, white, glossy
Aroma/Texture

2 Sweet lime glaze
Stove top: 4 mins.
Almost transparent appearance and taste

3 Mashed potatoes
Stovetop: boil 20 mins.
Steam-dry 15 mins.
White
Texture/Color

1 Mixed crisp salad
greens with a "wild"
vinaigrette
Light to dark green
Texture/Color

Serves 4

Mashed Potatoes

1½ pounds russet potatoes (675 gm), peeled and cut in
  2-inch (5-cm) pieces
1/2 teaspoon (2.5 ml) + 1/8 teaspoon (.6 ml) salt
1/2 to 1 cup 2%-fat milk (118 to 236 ml)
1/8 teaspoon nutmeg (.6 ml)
1/8 teaspoon white pepper (.6 ml)

Salad

1 tablespoon fresh dill (15 ml), roughly chopped, mixed
  with 3 tablespoons fresh parsley (45 ml), roughly
  chopped
5 cups of at least four varieties of lettuce (1.2 l) (for
  example, red leaf, romaine, radicchio, iceberg, or
  arugula), torn into bite-size pieces.

Vinaigrette

1 garlic clove, bashed, peeled, and chopped
2 tablespoons light olive oil (30 ml) with a dash of
  toasted sesame oil
Juice from 1 lime
5 tablespoons rice-wine vinegar (75 ml)
1/2 teaspoon ground mustard (2.5 ml)

2 tablespoons brown sugar (30 ml)
1/8 teaspoon cayenne pepper (.5 ml); use 1/4
  teaspoon (1.25 ml) if you like things hot

Fish

1 teaspoon light olive oil (5 ml) with a dash of toasted
  sesame oil
1/4 teaspoon salt (1.25 ml)
1/4 teaspoon white pepper (1.25 ml)
4 red snapper or halibut fillets, 6 ounces each (170 gm),
  with skin

Glaze

2 tablespoons lime marmalade (30 ml), preferably Rose's
1/4 cup de-alcoholized white wine
2 tablespoons very finely chopped radicchio (30 ml),
  red leaves only
1 teaspoon arrowroot (5 ml) mixed with 2 teaspoons
  de-alcoholized white wine (10 ml) (slurry)

Garnish

2 tablespoons very finely chopped radicchio (30 ml),
  red leaves only
1 teaspoon chopped parsley (5 ml)
Freshly ground black pepper

The mashed potatoes: Bring the potatoes to a boil in a large pot of water, add the 1/2 teaspoon of salt (2.5 ml), and cook for 20 minutes. Drain, return to the same pot over low heat, cover with a kitchen towel, and let steam-dry for 15 minutes. This will prevent a watery consistency in your final product. Mash together the boiled potatoes, milk, the remaining salt, and the nutmeg and white pepper until lump free.

Spoon the mashed potatoes into a large piping bag with a 1/2-inch (1.5-cm) nozzle (a star shape would look decorative). To keep the potatoes warm, place the filled piping bag into a bowl over a pot of simmering water, cover with a lid, and leave until needed.

The salad: In a large bowl toss the herbs and the torn lettuce leaves together until thoroughly mixed. Transfer to a salad spinner.

The vinaigrette: Combine all the ingredients in a blender until the garlic is dissolved—about a minute. Pour over the salad in the salad spinner, drenching the leaves thoroughly. Spin and drain off any excess vinaigrette (save for another use).

The fish: Preheat the broiler and position a broiler rack to within 4 inches (10 cm) of the heat source. Pour the oil onto a large plate, dust with salt and pepper, and wipe with the fish fillets, coating both sides. Lay the fillets on the broiler rack, skin-side-up, and broil for 6 minutes or until the skin has blistered and crisped.

The glaze: In a small saucepan on low heat, mix the lime marmalade with the wine until it forms a smooth syrup, stirring occasionally— about 3 minutes. Stir in the chopped radicchio and mix well. Remove from the heat, add the arrowroot slurry, return to the heat, and stir until clear—about 1 minute. Remove from the heat and strain to remove the radicchio, leaving a soft pink hue.

To serve: Place a quarter of the salad greens on each cold serving plate. Pipe the warm mashed potatoes on top to form a bed, and top with a fish fillet. Brush with the glaze and sprinkle with the chopped radicchio, parsley, and black pepper.

Time Estimate: Hands-on, 40 minutes; unsupervised, 6 minutes

THE RADICAL MIX FOR SUCCESS

This dish is a radical mix of sweet, sour, and bitter, but its success depends as much on its textures and temperatures as its flavors.

In order to put really hot whipped potatoes on very cold salads it helps to put them into a large piping bag and keep them hot by folding the filled bag into a double boiler, or bain marie, and covering it with a lid. When you are ready to serve, lift the lid and wrap a small terry-cloth towel around the very hot bag and you are off and running . . . If all this seems too much, then add more 2-percent milk until the potatoes resemble a *very thick* sauce that can be spooned over the greens.

Nutritional Profile per Serving		
	Classic	**Minimax**
Calories	829	356
Fat (gm)	61	6
Saturated fat (gm)	10	2
Calories from fat	66%	15%
Cholesterol (mg)	154	79
Sodium (mg)	800	497
Fiber (gm)	6	3
Carbohydrates (gm)	50	44
Classic compared: Salmon and Potato Salad		

Poultry and Meats

◆ Broiled Minimax Hamburger

A Minimax breakthrough: the combination of the bright notes of raisins, lemon juice, curry powder, and garlic with the leanest ground beef is the beginning of a beautiful hamburger for your Minimax life-style. Of course, once these Minimax Burgers are ensconced in family dining rooms across the United States, can the fast-food purveyors be far behind? I hope not!

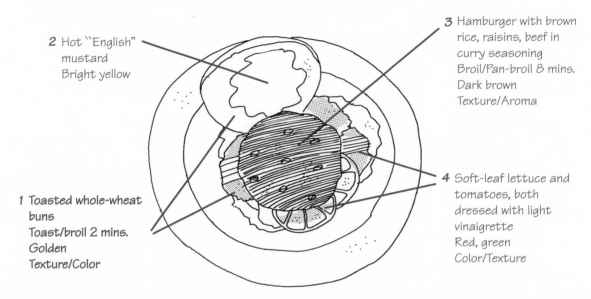

2 Hot "English" mustard
Bright yellow

3 Hamburger with brown rice, raisins, beef in curry seasoning
Broil/Pan-broil 8 mins.
Dark brown
Texture/Aroma

1 Toasted whole-wheat buns
Toast/broil 2 mins.
Golden
Texture/Color

4 Soft-leaf lettuce and tomatoes, both dressed with light vinaigrette
Red, green
Color/Texture

Serves 4

1/2 teaspoon light oil (2.5 ml) with a dash of toasted sesame oil
1½ cups chopped onion (354 ml)
2 cloves garlic, bashed, peeled, and chopped
1 tablespoon curry powder (15 ml)
1/4 cup dark raisins (59 ml)
1 tablespoon freshly squeezed lemon juice (15 ml)
2 tablespoons fresh chopped parsley (30 ml)
1 tablespoon water (15 ml)
1 cup cooked brown rice (236 ml)
8 ounces ground beef (227 gm), the leanest possible—freshly ground at home is best
1 teaspoon light olive oil (5 ml)
4 teaspoons hot English mustard (20 ml)
4 whole-wheat hamburger buns
1 large tomato
4 lettuce leaves
2 teaspoons vinaigrette salad dressing (10 ml) (see page 51)

Heat the 1/2 teaspoon oil in a large skillet on high and cook the onions until just translucent—about 5 minutes. Stir in the garlic and curry powder and cook 1 minute. Add the raisins, lemon juice, and parsley, mix well, and transfer to a large bowl. Pour the water into the hot pan, scrape up the pan residues, and add this liquid to the cooked seasonings.

Stir the cooked rice into the seasonings, then transfer it into a food processor and puree for 1 minute until well blended, but not a paste. Return the mixture to the bowl, add the freshly ground beef, and mix thoroughly.

Shape the hamburger into 4 patties and lightly brush with the 1 teaspoon oil. Heat a large nonstick skillet and, without adding any oil, cook the burgers on medium high for about 4 minutes on each side.

To serve: Spread mustard on each bun, slide in the cooked burgers, and garnish with the tomato and lettuce. Drizzle with a little vinaigrette dressing for extra zest.

Time Estimate: Hands-on, 30 minutes; unsupervised, none

TREENA'S VINAIGRETTE

In a blender, beat until well mixed 1 peeled garlic clove, 2 tablespoons canola oil (10 ml), 1/2 cup white-wine vinegar (118 ml), 1/2 teaspoon mustard powder (2.5 ml), 2 tablespoons brown sugar (30 ml), and 1/8 teaspoon cayenne pepper (.6 ml).

BEEF *BORN* WITH LESS FAT
The increasing market demand for less fat has hit meat producers hard. In their effort to keep the public happy, some ranchers have noted that certain cow breeds *are born* with less fat than others. By modifying these cows' diet, they are able to bring the fat levels of beef in some cuts down to those of turkey and chicken (figures for whole birds with fattier thighs and leaner breasts). One source for this "specialty beef" is Monson Ranch, which has been in business since 1946 in Washington State. Call them at (206) 637-9808.

Note that the amount you eat still matters. A traditional quarter-pound hamburger made from specialty beef still has 12 grams of total fat. Because of this, my recipe *halves* the normal meat content to come in at almost 9 grams of fat per serving, 22 percent calories from fat.

Nutritional Profile per Serving		
	Classic	**Minimax**
Calories	604	354
Fat (gm)	34	9
Saturated fat (gm)	10	2
Calories from fat	51%	23%
Cholesterol (mg)	86	32
Sodium (mg)	1,109	310
Fiber (gm)	3	6
Carbohydrates (gm)	45	53
Classic compared: Hamburger		

♦ HEARTY VEGETABLE STEW WITH BEEF

Is there anything more basic and comforting than a hearty meat stew? This Minimax version has switched the traditional ratio of beef to vegetables and winds up with three-quarters vegetable to one-quarter meat. Then it comforts and cares for you with familiar aromas and textures.

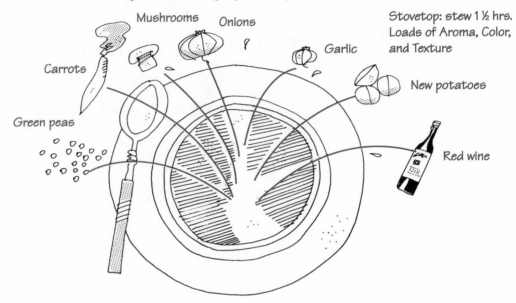

Mushrooms Onions Garlic
Carrots
Green peas
New potatoes
Red wine

Stovetop: stew 1 ½ hrs.
Loads of Aroma, Color, and Texture

Serves 4

8 ounces beef, bottom round (227 gm), all visible fat removed, cut into 1/2-inch pieces (1.5 cm)
1 ½ teaspoons light oil (7 ml) with a dash of toasted sesame oil
2 medium onions, peeled and thickly sliced
3 ounces low-sodium tomato paste (85 gm)
2 cloves garlic, bashed, peeled, and chopped
4 tablespoons de-alcoholized red wine (60 ml)
3 cups enhanced canned low-sodium beef stock (708 ml) (see page 144), reduced to 2½ cups (590 ml)
16 ounces carrots (450 gm), peeled and cut in 1-inch pieces (2.5 cm)
12 small red new potatoes, scrubbed and whole
12 medium mushrooms, cut in quarters
2 cups frozen peas (472 ml), thawed
2 tablespoons arrowroot (30 ml) mixed with 4 tablespoons de-alcoholized red wine (60 ml) (slurry)
2 tablespoons fresh chopped parsley (30 ml)
1/4 teaspoon freshly ground black pepper (1.25 ml)

Garnish
Fresh chopped parsley

Pat the meat dry with a paper towel. Heat 1 teaspoon of the oil in a large skillet over medium-high heat and brown the meat on one side—about 3 minutes. Remove and set aside.

In the same hot skillet, heat the remaining 1/2 teaspoon oil and cook the onions and tomato paste, scraping the brown meat residue into the mixture, for 5 minutes. Stir in the garlic and set aside. (This step accomplishes three important Minimax functions at one time: the onions and garlic release their aromatic volatile oils; the tomato paste caramelizes the mixture; and a flavor-filled glaze builds up on the pan—all of which adds *depth* of taste without fat.)

Transfer the browned meat into a medium saucepan. Add the tomato and onion mixture, wine, and beef stock, bring to a boil, reduce the

heat to its lowest setting, and simmer, covered, for 30 minutes. Add the carrots and potatoes, and simmer for 30 minutes. Stir in the potatoes and mushrooms and simmer for 5 minutes.

Remove from the heat, add the peas and the arrowroot slurry, return to the heat, and stir until thickened—about 1 minute. Add the parsley, pepper, and salt.

To serve: Ladle into bowls and sprinkle with a little fresh parsley.

Time Estimate: Hands-on, 20 minutes; unsupervised, 1 hour, 15 minutes

HOW BIG THE BEEF?

I've noticed that in many but not all cases the larger the piece of meat, the greater the moisture after cooking—especially when there's plenty of connective tissue to melt out in the long, slow, moist-heat method. I compared blade steak, which has a "good" ratio of fat and connective tissue, with large pieces of bottom round, which has very little melting tissue and fat (3 grams versus 8 in 2 ounces, or 57 grams): a difference of 39 calories from fat, or 24 percent for bottom round and 54 percent for blade.

I found that large pieces of the bottom round were less moist than the blade. Because of this and its clear low-fat benefits, I've opted for bottom round cut into small, 1/2-inch (1.5-cm) dice.

Nutritional Profile per Serving		
	Classic	**Minimax**
Calories	579	576
Fat (gm)	26	6
Saturated fat (gm)	10	2
Calories from fat	41%	10%
Cholesterol (mg)	125	48
Sodium (mg)	1,142	232
Fiber (gm)	8	14
Carbohydrates (gm)	37	100
Classic compared: Old-Fashioned Beef Stew		

♦ LAMB SHANKS IN A POLENTA PIE

Two very important comfort foods come together here: braised lamb and polenta—a ground yellow cornmeal made into a top and bottom "pastry crust." Both have a well-deserved reputation for being extrarich and have, by tradition, been bathed with retained or added fat. In this version, the polenta is an interesting alternative to the very fatty traditional pastry pie crust.

2 Polenta pie topping, cornmeal crust
Golden-yellow, brown
Color/Texture

3 Jicama salad, with cilantro, lime, black pepper
White, green, black
Texture/Color/Aroma

1 Braised lamb shank, slipped off bone, in red-wine and mushroom sauce
Oven: braise 2 hours.
Dark, glossy brown
Texture/Color/Aroma

5 Steamed Swiss chard
Stack 'n Steam 4 mins.
Brilliant dark green
Color/Texture

4 Mushroom sauce
Stovetop: simmer 7 mins.
Dark brown, white
Aroma/Texture/Color

Serves 4

Lamb Shanks and Mushroom Sauce

1 teaspoon light oil (5 ml) with a dash of toasted sesame oil
1 large onion, peeled and cut into thick slices
3 large stalks celery, sliced across into 1-inch pieces
1 large carrot cut into "turncut" pieces, cut on the diagonal and partly turned after each cut
2 cloves garlic, bashed, peeled, and chopped
One 3-ounce (85-gm) can low-sodium tomato paste
4 (about 1/2 pound or 225 gm each) lamb shanks
2 cups de-alcoholized red wine (472 ml)
One 4-inch (10-cm) sprig rosemary
12 medium-sized mushrooms, sliced into thirds
2 tablespoons arrowroot (30 ml) mixed with 1/4 cup de-alcoholized red wine (59 ml) (slurry)
1 pound Swiss chard (450 gm), steamed until just wilted
1 tablespoon freshly grated Parmesan cheese

Polenta

3 cups cold water (708 ml)
1 cup fine-grain yellow cornmeal (236 ml)
1/4 teaspoon salt (1.25 ml)
1/4 teaspoon freshly ground black pepper (1.25 ml)
2 tablespoons freshly squeezed lemon juice (30 ml)

The lamb shanks: Preheat the oven to 350°F (180°C). Heat the oil in a large stockpot on medium heat and sauté the onions, celery, and carrots for 3 minutes. Stir in the garlic and tomato paste and cook until the mixture becomes deep brown—about 3 minutes. Add the lamb shanks and wine, making sure to scrape up any pan residues, and mix them in well. Add water until the liquid is level with the top of the lamb shanks. Gently nestle in the rosemary, until it is completely buried, cover, and bake for 2 hours, or until the meat slips easily off the bone.

The polenta: In a large saucepan, bring the water to a rapid boil and stir in the cornmeal in a slow, steady stream. Do not allow the water to stop boiling. When all the cornmeal has been added, sprinkle in the salt and pepper. Stir constantly, scraping the sides and bottom of the saucepan, until the polenta becomes a thick porridgelike texture that pulls cleanly from the sides of the pan and a spoon will stand up in it. This takes about 25 minutes for the large-grain cornmeal and 5 minutes for the fine-grain variety.

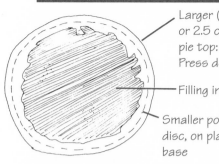

Larger (by 1 inch, or 2.5 cm) polenta pie top:
Press down to seal

Filling in the middle

Smaller polenta disc, on plate as base

JICAMA SALAD

Stir together in a bowl and set aside in fridge until ready to serve: one 12-ounce jicama (340 gm), peeled and sliced into large matchsticks; 8 cilantro leaves, finely chopped; 2 tablespoons freshly squeezed lime juice (30 ml); and 1/8 teaspoon freshly ground black pepper (.6 ml).

POLENTA

There are two grades of cornmeal: fine and coarse. For some textural reasons, the coarse is often used for traditional polenta dishes. Unfortunately it takes roughly five times longer to cook. The fine grade comes with *slightly* less lusciousness and quite a bit less color: a somewhat faded yellow compared to the brilliance of the larger-grained type. I've settled for the finer grain with some regret, largely because in our brave new world there are few who want to do aerobic cooking—15 minutes of steady stirring over a hot stove.

Lower the heat if the mixture starts to stick. Add the lemon juice and mix well.

Brush light oil over two dinner plates. Pour on the polenta, smoothing out to make two circles, one 1 inch (2.5 cm) smaller than the other. Leave to cool until set—1 hour at room temperature or 30 minutes in the refrigerator.

Transfer the cooked lamb from the pot onto a large plate and trim off any fat. Gently pry the meat off the bone so that you end up with pieces mostly still in their original muscle shapes and set aside.

Strain the remaining liquid into a fat separator, discarding the vegetables. You should have 2½ cups (590 ml) of liquid. Add wine or stock to come up to this level if you don't have enough. To make the mushroom sauce, pour the liquid from the fat separator into a medium saucepan, leaving the surface fat at the bottom of the separator. Add the mushrooms and gently warm through on medium heat for 5 minutes.

Just before serving, pour the slurry into the sauce and stir over medium heat to thicken for 2 minutes.

To serve: Slip the smaller polenta circle from the plate onto a large oval platter. Pile the meat in the center and cover with the Swiss chard, and sprinkle with the Parmesan cheese. Top with the remaining polenta circle to make a "sandwich." If you are not going to eat the dish immediately, cover with aluminum foil and keep in the refrigerator. When ready to serve, bake at 300°F (150°C) for 30 minutes. The top can be browned slightly by brushing with a teaspoon of oil and slipping under the broiler for about 5 minutes. The sandwich cuts neatly into four wedges and looks terrific with the mushroom sauce and a jicama salad (see recipe at left) served on the side.

Time Estimate: Hands-on, 1 hour, 30 minutes; unsupervised, 2 hours, 30 minutes

Nutritional Profile per Serving		
	Classic	**Minimax**
Calories	954	706
Fat (gm)	48	23
Saturated fat (gm)	14	8
Calories from fat	46%	30%
Cholesterol (mg)	312	209
Sodium (mg)	1,094	503
Fiber (gm)	2	7
Carbohydrates (gm)	12	50
Classic compared: Lamb Shanks		

♦ PORK AND POTATO PIE

Ask anyone who has put in serious ethnic eating time in the British Isles about pork pies, and you'll see the gleam in their eyes. Although cursed along with many cultural food favorites by mass production, the original homemade recipe is terrific and, of course, supersaturated with fat! I've taken a wide swing at this and created a potato topping to replace the traditional hot-water-and-lard pastry and then gone wild with the textures and colors. The result bears no resemblance whatsoever to the original, but once you try it, you'll notice that same gleam in the eye!

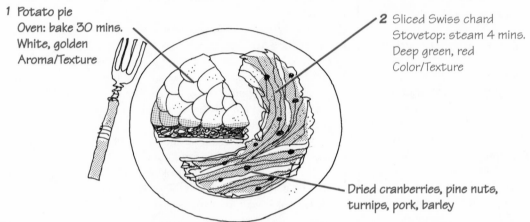

1 Potato pie
Oven: bake 30 mins.
White, golden
Aroma/Texture

2 Sliced Swiss chard
Stovetop: steam 4 mins.
Deep green, red
Color/Texture

Dried cranberries, pine nuts,
turnips, pork, barley

Serves 6

1 pound boneless pork loin chops (450 gm), all visible fat removed

4 medium-sized russet potatoes, peeled and cut in 1/2-inch slices (1.5 cm)

1/2 teaspoon salt (2.5 ml)

1/4 teaspoon freshly ground black pepper (1.25 ml)

1 pound collard greens (450 gm), heavy stalks removed

2 teaspoons light oil (10 ml) with a dash of toasted sesame oil

2 onions, peeled and coarsely chopped

2/3 cup whole pot barley (157 ml) (unpolished)

1 tablespoon mild curry powder (15 ml)

1 (4-inch or 10-cm) sprig rosemary

2 cups ham hock broth (472 ml) (see page 143)

1/4 cup water (59 ml)

3 medium-sized turnips, peeled and cut in 1/4-inch round slices (.75 cm), then halved

1/2 cup (118 ml) + 4 tablespoons (60 ml) dried cranberries (or currants)

2 tablespoons pine nuts (30 ml)

Slice the pork into 1-inch cubes (2.5 cm), place in a food processor, and whiz to a smooth paste.

Lay the potato slices in a steamer tray, sprinkle with the salt and pepper, and steam for 15 minutes. Remove from the heat and set aside.

Trim the white stalks from the collard greens. Roll the green leaves tightly, lay them on a board, and slice into 1/4-inch strips (.75 cm). Set aside.

Preheat the oven to 350°F (180°C). Heat 1 teaspoon of the oil (5 ml) in a medium saucepan over medium-high heat and shallow-fry the onions until translucent—about 5 minutes. Add the barley, curry powder, rosemary, and ham hock broth, bring to a boil, reduce the heat, cover, and simmer for 30 minutes.

Heat the remaining oil in a large skillet over medium high and brown the ground pork well (the meat actually turns a whitish color). Stir well, breaking the meat into the texture of a fine crumb.

Remove the rosemary sprig before turning the cooked onion/barley mixture onto the pork. Deglaze the bottom of the vegetable skillet with the water and add this to the stewing mixture of pork and vegetables. Stir in the turnips, 1/2 cup of the dried cranberries (118 ml) and the pine nuts, and mix well. Lay the cooked potato slices on top in overlapping circles. Press the potatoes gently, letting the juices well up through the gaps. Bake, uncovered, for 30 minutes. Just before serving, switch on the broiler and give the top a quick browning.

While the pie is cooking, spread the collard greens in a steamer tray, sprinkle with the 4 tablespoons cranberries, and cook for 4 minutes. Remove from the heat and set aside.

To serve: Mound the cooked greens on top of the pie, letting the browned potatoes show through as a border, and present at the table with a flourish.

Time Estimate: Hands-on, 1 hour; unsupervised, 45 minutes

FRESH-GROUND MEAT

Huge quantities of meat are ground up every day as an obvious convenience to all of us who want to make "hamburger"-styled recipes. There are three major drawbacks to offset the convenience: First, meat varies as to its fat content and its flavor—cut by cut. Even though an estimate of fat is made, you can never be sure of fat or flavor. Second, the moment that meat is cut or ground, its surface is exposed to the air and the meat begins to oxidize (darken in color). This is the work of free radicals that exist in the air. We take antioxidants such as vitamins A and E to prevent those free radicals from damaging our own cells, yet we consume large quantities of premixed oxidized meats that bear the very risk we try to avoid. Third, there is the remote threat of an *E. coli* combination in meats ground "in bulk." By grinding one's own, that risk is virtually removed.

Nutritional Profile per Serving		
	Classic	**Minimax**
Calories	426	467
Fat (gm)	23	12
Saturated fat (gm)	11	3
Calories from fat	48%	23%
Cholesterol (mg)	143	49
Sodium (mg)	662	384
Fiber (gm)	6	10
Carbohydrates (gm)	22	72
Classic compared: Fillet of Pork with Turnips		

♦ PORK MEDALLIONS

Here's another dish that works well during a busy week. It is also an unusual combination of elegance and comfort—the two don't often overlap. The tenderloin medallions (named for their shape) are truly elegant in the balsamic, ginger, and garlic marinade, but it's the rough, mashed blend of fresh roots and steamed kale that pulls in the comfort. There's lots of flavor and satisfaction here at just under 400 calories.

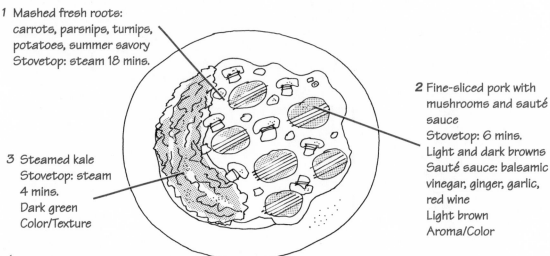

1 Mashed fresh roots: carrots, parsnips, turnips, potatoes, summer savory
Stovetop: steam 18 mins.

2 Fine-sliced pork with mushrooms and sauté sauce
Stovetop: 6 mins.
Light and dark browns
Sauté sauce: balsamic vinegar, ginger, garlic, red wine
Light brown
Aroma/Color

3 Steamed kale
Stovetop: steam 4 mins.
Dark green
Color/Texture

Serves 4

Marinade
1 clove garlic, bashed, peeled, and slivered
1 teaspoon freshly grated gingerroot (5 ml)
2 tablespoons balsamic vinegar (30 ml)
1 tablespoon fresh thyme leaves (15 ml), bruised
1 bay leaf

Pork Medallions
8 ounces pork tenderloin (225 gm), cut into medallion slices (10–12 pieces)
2 teaspoons light olive oil (10 ml) with a dash of toasted sesame oil
8 ounces mushrooms (227 gm), sliced
1 teaspoon freshly squeezed lemon juice (5 ml)
1 teaspoon dried summer savory (5 ml)
1/4 teaspoon salt (1.25 ml)
1/4 teaspoon freshly ground black pepper (1.25 ml)
1/4 cup de-alcoholized red wine (59 ml)
1 teaspoon arrowroot (5 ml)

Vegetables
3 cups water (708 ml)
1/2 pound carrots (225 gm), peeled and roughly chopped
1/2 pound parsnips (225 gm), peeled and roughly chopped
1/2 pound turnips (225 gm), peeled and roughly chopped
1/2 pound potatoes (225 gm), peeled and roughly chopped
1¼ teaspoons dried summer savory (6.25 ml)
1 pound kale (450 gm), stalks removed
1 tablespoon freshly squeezed lemon juice (15 ml)
1/4 teaspoon freshly grated nutmeg (1.25 ml)
1/4 teaspoon freshly ground black pepper (1.25 ml)

Garnish
Cayenne pepper

The marinade: Mix all the ingredients in a large bowl, immerse the meat, and marinate in the refrigerator for at least 1 hour.

Put the carrots, parsnips, turnips, and potatoes over vigorously boiling water in a Stack 'n Steam pot, sprinkle with 1 teaspoon of the summer savory (5 ml) and steam for 12 minutes. Remove all the vegetables except the parsnips and set aside. Replace the lid and continue steaming the parsnips for 6 minutes.

While the vegetables are cooking, heat half of the oil in a large skillet on medium high. Remove the pork medallions from the marinade, shake off the excess liquid, and add to the pan, one piece at a time, searing to form a slight crust on the underside—about 5 minutes. Turn the pieces over, reduce the heat to medium, and cook for 2 minutes. Reserve the marinade to make a sauce.

Heat the remaining oil in another skillet on medium heat, add the mushrooms, lemon juice, summer savory, salt, and pepper and cook for 3 minutes. Add to the cooked pork, cover, and set aside.

Pour the wine into the remaining marinade. Pour through a strainer into the arrowroot, stir well, and pour into the meat and mushrooms. Return to the heat, bring to a boil, and stir until it glistens—about 1 minute.

Remove the parsnips from the heat and add to the other cooked vegetables. Place the kale in the steamer, cook for 4 minutes, and set aside. To the other cooked vegetables, add the lemon juice, nutmeg, remaining summer savory, and pepper and mash well.

To serve: Mound the mashed vegetables into a bed on one side of each plate. Top with the glistening pieces of pork, mushrooms, and sauce. Sprinkle with a dusting of cayenne pepper and serve with the kale on the side.

Time Estimate: Hands-on, 49 minutes; unsupervised, 91 minutes

BOILING MARINADES
I suggest that you bring the arrowroot marinade slurry to the boil. Arrowroot, unlike cornstarch, doesn't *have* to be boiled to remove the raw starch taste but boiling kills off any bacteria from the raw meat.

VACUUM MARINADE
See the discussion on page 61.

Nutritional Profile per Serving		
	Classic	**Minimax**
Calories	865	268
Fat (gm)	46	6
Saturated fat (gm)	19	1
Calories from fat	48%	19%
Cholesterol (mg)	163	53
Sodium (mg)	2,414	247
Fiber (gm)	11	8
Carbohydrates (gm)	63	36
Classic compared: Smoked Pork with Split Pea–Potato Puree		

♦ PORK TENDERLOIN STIR-FRY

This recipe is a great illustration not only of the stir-fry method but also of the technique of using a marinade as a flavor enhancer. Whenever fat is significantly reduced in a dish, there is a corresponding loss of flavor. A classic way of boosting flavor is by the use of a marinade. I've combined East and West here by using a red wine, soy, and juniper berry combination that gives the dish a dark, glossy appearance enhanced by the spicy aroma of juniper (see page 167).

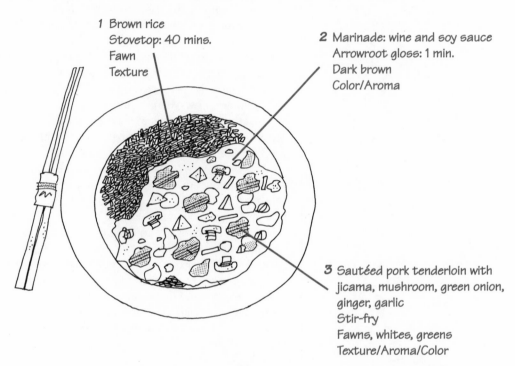

1 Brown rice
Stovetop: 40 mins.
Fawn
Texture

2 Marinade: wine and soy sauce
Arrowroot gloss: 1 min.
Dark brown
Color/Aroma

3 Sautéed pork tenderloin with jicama, mushroom, green onion, ginger, garlic
Stir-fry
Fawns, whites, greens
Texture/Aroma/Color

Serves 4

Marinade

1/4 cup de-alcoholized red wine (59 ml)
1 tablespoon low-sodium soy sauce (15 ml)
1 teaspoon chopped fresh rosemary (5 ml)
1 teaspoon garlic (5 ml), bashed, peeled, and chopped
6 juniper berries, crushed
1 tablespoon chopped onions (15 ml)

Stir-Fry

8 ounces pork tenderloin (227 gm), thinly sliced
2 cloves garlic, bashed, peeled, and finely chopped
5 quarter-sized slices of fresh gingerroot, finely chopped

4 ounces green onions (113 gm), sliced diagonally into 1-inch pieces (2.5 cm), green and white pieces separated
1 teaspoon light oil (5 ml) with a dash of toasted sesame oil
1/4 teaspoon toasted sesame oil (1.25 ml)
12 ounces mushrooms (340 gm), trimmed and sliced
6 ounces jicama (170 gm), peeled and sliced
2 tablespoons low-sodium soy sauce (30 ml)
1/2 cup de-alcoholized red wine (118 ml)
1 tablespoon arrowroot (15 ml) mixed with 2 tablespoons de-alcoholized red wine (30 ml) (slurry)
1 recipe brown rice (472 ml), cooked (see page 87)

FLAVOR IS ONLY SKIN-DEEP— OR IS IT?

I've always been a fan of the marinade. However, I've noticed that its major contribution is to the sauce rather than the meat. This is because the seasoned liquid penetrates the flesh by only less than a sixteenth of an inch (.1 cm)! All this changed recently with the introduction of the vacuum marinade concept, in which the natural moisture of meat (about 70%) is drawn out under vacuum, allowing the marinade partially to take its place. I was skeptical at first, but after several tests I became convinced that it *works*.

A word of caution: The vacuum machine is bulky for a small kitchen and relatively expensive *if you do not use it often*. With the need to boost vegetable use and enhance smaller meat portions, however, it can be a very important tool in the Minimax kitchen. Please note that the classic marinade/soak still works and can still be used. It just takes longer and is less effective.

PEELING JICAMA

The easiest way to peel jicama is first to cut it into eighths, then cut those wedges in half, then slice them into 1 ½-inch (4-cm) "chips." After this, the outer rind comes off in "one fell swoop."

The marinade: Mix all the ingredients in a large bowl. Add the meat, stir well, and marinate for at least 2 hours.

In a small bowl, combine the garlic, ginger, and the chopped white parts of the green onions. Heat the oils in a wok on high heat, add the garlic, ginger, and the white part of the chopped green onions, cook, and stir-toss for 1 minute. Remove from the wok with a slotted spoon, and set aside.

Strain the meat, reserving the marinade. In the same wok on medium high, cook the meat until browned on all sides—about 10 minutes. Add the mushrooms, jicama, and cooked onions and cook for 2 minutes. Add the green part of the chopped green onions, reserved marinade, soy sauce, and red wine and bring to a boil. Remove from the heat, stir in the arrowroot slurry, return to the heat, and stir until thickened, glossy, and clear—about 1 minute.

To serve: Spoon onto plates with steaming brown rice on the side.

Time Estimate: Hands-on, 30 minutes; unsupervised, 2 hours

Nutritional Profile per Serving		
	Classic	**Minimax**
Calories	521	430
Fat (gm)	17	7
Saturated fat (gm)	3	2
Calories from fat	29%	14%
Cholesterol (mg)	53	53
Sodium (mg)	1,243	639
Fiber (gm)	7	7
Carbohydrates (gm)	64	67
Classic compared: Pork Chow Mein		

◆ SCOTTISH-IRISH STEW

If such a thing as a classic Irish stew exists (for every home there's a variation), then surely it would have potatoes in the pot, right? In fact, it's true to say that the Scots have an almost identical favorite made with pot barley. In the continued interest of fusion (a combination of cultures), I've taken a leaf from each book and used both potato and barley. It really is delicious, especially with the completely new wilted-spinach garnish.

1 Scottish-Irish stew, with lamb, carrots,
potatoes, onions, pot barley
Stovetop: boil gently 2 ½ hrs.
Pale yellow with orange and brown relief
Texture/Aroma

2 Large raw spinach leaves
Color/Texture

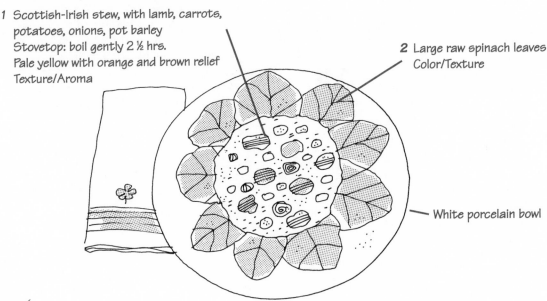

White porcelain bowl

Serves 4

Broth

Two 14-ounce (397-gm) cans low-sodium chicken
broth (or fresh, see page 141)
One 14-ounce (397 gm) can beef broth (or fresh, see
page 142)
1 bouquet garni: 1 bay leaf, 2 sprigs thyme (1/2
teaspoon or 2.5 ml dried), 6 peppercorns, 2 cloves,
4 sprigs parsley
1 medium potato, unpeeled, cut into thin slices
1 cup water (236 ml)

Stew Base

1 teaspoon light oil (5 ml) with a dash of toasted
sesame oil
4 ounces yellow onion (113 gm), peeled and roughly
chopped (1 small onion)

1 ½ cups enhanced chicken and beef broth (354 ml)
(see page 144)
1 ¼ pounds lamb necks (565 gm)
1/4 cup pot barley (59 ml), well rinsed
3/4 cup boiling water (177 ml)

Stew

16 ounces carrots (454 gm), peeled and cut into 1/2-
inch chunks (1.5 cm) (2 medium carrots)
16 ounces yellow potatoes (454 gm), peeled and cut
into 1/2-inch chunks (1.5 cm) (3 medium potatoes)
16 boiling onions, 1 ½ inches (4 cm) in diameter, peeled
1/8 teaspoon freshly ground black pepper (.6 ml)
1 (3-inch or 8-cm) sprig fresh rosemary
16 whole mushrooms, medium, to match onions
1 pound fresh spinach leaves (450 gm), well rinsed

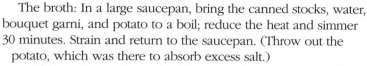

The broth: In a large saucepan, bring the canned stocks, water, bouquet garni, and potato to a boil; reduce the heat and simmer 30 minutes. Strain and return to the saucepan. (Throw out the potato, which was there to absorb excess salt.)

The stew base: Heat the oil in a large saucepan over medium heat and cook the onions, without browning, until slightly limp—about 5 minutes. Add the broth and lamb necks, bring to a boil, reduce the heat, and simmer for 2½ hours, or until the meat falls off the bone.

While the lamb necks are cooking, in a separate small saucepan mix the barley with the boiling water, stir once, cover, and return to a boil. Reduce the heat and simmer for 30 minutes. Drain and retain.

When the lamb is cooked, remove it from the broth, strip off the meat, and set aside. Strain the broth into a fat separator cup.

The stew: Return the defatted broth to the large saucepan and add the carrots, potatoes, boiling onions, and pepper; bring to a boil; reduce the heat so that it just bubbles; add the rosemary and lamb; and simmer for 10 minutes. Then stir in the cooked barley and simmer for 10 minutes. Finally, add the mushrooms and cook for 5 minutes.

To serve: Line four large soup bowls with several of the spinach leaves. Ladle the hot stew on top and serve with the uncooked spinach leaves sticking up around the side of the bowl like a garland.

Time Estimate: Hands-on, 45 minutes; unsupervised, 3 hours, 30 minutes

POT BARLEY

Untreated, or pot, barley is much like a whole-wheat berry or brown rice: it's complete with its overcoat of bran. The familiar pearl barley, which has the outer husk removed, is only marginally lower in nutritional value; it's the taste that improves.

PEELING ONIONS

Small, 1–1½ inch (3–4 cm) boiling onions are a pain to peel, *except* using the following method: Bring 4 cups of water (944 ml) to the boil, take the pan from the stove, drop in the onions, cover, and let them stand for 10 minutes. Then take the pot to the sink and run cold water over them. You will be able to twist off the skin in "one fell swoop"— whatever that means . . . It's quick!

Nutritional Profile per Serving		
	Classic	**Minimax**
Calories	700	328
Fat (gm)	33	5
Saturated fat (gm)	14	1
Calories from fat	42%	15%
Cholesterol (mg)	327	28
Sodium (mg)	974	154
Fiber (gm)	5	10
Carbohydrates (gm)	31	56
Classic compared: Blanquette of Lamb à l'Ancienne		

♦ Slow Beef Curry

The curries of Thailand richly deserve to be as famous as the regional delicacies of India. This adaptation is a remarkable example of how the "above-the-line" bright notes (see page 10) work to stimulate the senses and cover up the changes made in both meat and fat content. Even if all the meat is removed, the vegetables remain utterly delicious.

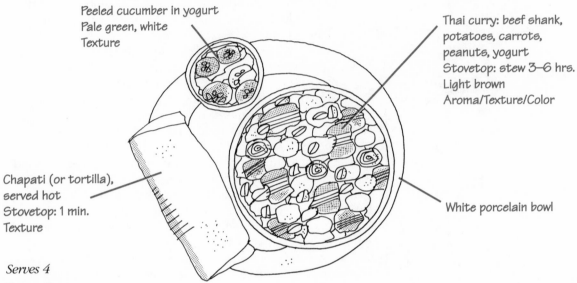

Peeled cucumber in yogurt
Pale green, white
Texture

Thai curry: beef shank, potatoes, carrots, peanuts, yogurt
Stovetop: stew 3–6 hrs.
Light brown
Aroma/Texture/Color

Chapati (or tortilla), served hot
Stovetop: 1 min.
Texture

White porcelain bowl

Serves 4

Curry Paste

5 small dried red chilies with seeds
3 whole cloves
1 (1/2-inch or 1.5-cm) piece of cinnamon stick
1/2 teaspoon black cardamom seed (2.5 ml)
1 teaspoon light oil (5 ml) with a dash of toasted sesame oil
7 garlic cloves, bashed, peeled, and chopped
7 shallots, peeled and sliced very fine
1/2 teaspoon ground ginger (2.5 ml)
1/2 teaspoon freshly grated nutmeg (2.5 ml)
1 tablespoon zest of lime (15 ml), cut in fine matchsticks (see page 172)
2 tablespoons water (30 ml)
1/2 teaspoon coconut extract (2.5 ml)
3 tablespoons Thai fish sauce (45 ml)

Stew

1 pound meaty beef shanks (450 gm) or 8 ounces (227 gm) of another *very* lean stew meat, trimmed of all visible fat and cut into 1-inch pieces (2.5 cm)

1 1/2 pounds new potatoes (675 gm), scoured and cut into 1-inch pieces (2.5 cm)
1 pound carrots (450 gm), peeled and cut into 1-inch pieces (2.5 cm)
1/2 cup water (118 ml)
2 tablespoons cornstarch (30 ml) mixed with 4 tablespoons water (60 ml) (slurry)
1 cup strained yogurt (118 ml) (see page 141)
1/2 cup unsalted dry-roasted peanuts (118 ml)

The Curry Paste: Place the chilies, cloves, cinnamon stick, and cardamom into a small coffee grinder and whiz for 30 seconds. As a precaution, press the mixture through a very fine sieve to remove any large, gritty particles.

Heat the oil in a large skillet over medium heat and cook the garlic and shallots until they are brown—about 5 minutes. Transfer to a small food processor, add the rest of the curry paste

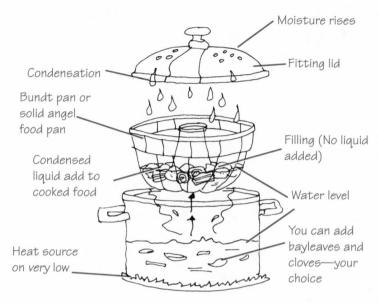

Moisture rises

Condensation

Fitting lid

Bundt pan or solid angel food pan

Filling (No liquid added)

Condensed liquid add to cooked food

Water level

Heat source on very low

You can add bayleaves and cloves—your choice

ingredients, and puree until the mixture is well blended and forms a fairly smooth paste—about 30 seconds.

In a large bowl, mix the beef, potatoes, and carrots with the curry paste, covering all the surfaces with the spices. Transfer to a Bundt or Kugelhopf pan and set it inside a large saucepan containing boiling water, so that the water comes halfway up the side of the Bundt pan. Cover and simmer over very low heat until the meat is tender—at least 3 hours and up to 6 hours.

Strain the cooking liquids from the meat and vegetables into a medium saucepan. (The cooking liquid is the result of steam's condensing on the lid and dropping back into the pan.) Rinse the Bundt pan with 1/2 cup water (118 ml) and add this to the strained liquid in the saucepan. Bring the liquid to a boil, add the cornstarch slurry, and stir until thickened—about 1 minute. Remove from the heat and gently whisk in the yogurt. Return the meat and potatoes to the saucepan and cook until just heated through. The dish should not boil, otherwise the yogurt will "break" into hundreds of tiny flecks.

To serve: Ladle into bowls and sprinkle with the peanuts. I like to serve this dish with chapati bread (see page 86). If you can't find chapati, use whole-wheat tortillas. A refreshing side dish of peeled cucumber in yogurt goes very well with this curry (see page 29).

Time Estimate: Hands-on, 35 minutes; unsupervised, 3 hours

COCONUT MILK AND CREAM
The coconut creams traditionally used in both Thai and southern Indian curries are truly delicious. But tropical oils are loaded with fat—higher in saturated fat than any other source. To keep the flavor, there's a very small amount of coconut essence in the curry paste, the strained yogurt added at the end provides the lightened appearance and some of the *mouthfeel* that coconut creams provide—with none of the risks.

Nutritional Profile per Serving		
	Classic	**Minimax**
Calories	1237	440
Fat (gm)	80	13
Saturated fat (gm)	47	2
Calories from fat	59%	26%
Cholesterol (mg)	151	31
Sodium (mg)	1,239	918
Fiber (gm)	2	7
Carbohydrates (gm)	72	60
Classic compared: Thai Beef Curry		

♦ ROAST TURKEY WITH APPLE-ORANGE GRAVY, SWISS CHARD, AND SWEET POTATOES

A revolutionary roast turkey: bread-and-sausage-based stuffing is replaced by aromatic spices and fruits that infuse flavor into the turkey meat. The traditional pan-drippings gravy becomes a turkey-meat broth spiked with citrus. And the pièce-de-résistance? A cranberry relish studded with crisp red chard and the deep tang of balsamic vinegar. I hope you'll celebrate this recipe with me: a feast fit for kings and queens and one of the healthiest meals you'll ever celebrate.

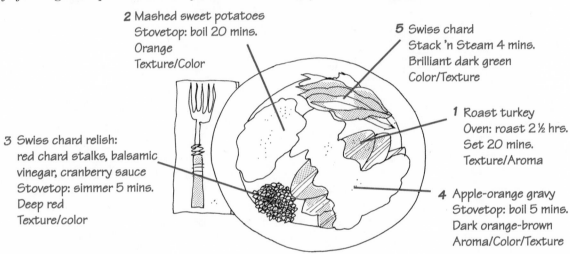

2 Mashed sweet potatoes
Stovetop: boil 20 mins.
Orange
Texture/Color

5 Swiss chard
Stack 'n Steam 4 mins.
Brilliant dark green
Color/Texture

1 Roast turkey
Oven: roast 2½ hrs.
Set 20 mins.
Texture/Aroma

3 Swiss chard relish:
red chard stalks, balsamic
vinegar, cranberry sauce
Stovetop: simmer 5 mins.
Deep red
Texture/color

4 Apple-orange gravy
Stovetop: boil 5 mins.
Dark orange-brown
Aroma/Color/Texture

Serves 6 with ample leftover turkey

Swiss Chard and Sweet Potatoes
3 pounds Swiss chard (1.4 kg)
3 tablespoons balsamic vinegar (45 ml)
1/2 cup jellied cranberry sauce (118 ml)
6 medium deep-orange sweet potatoes

Turkey
1 teaspoon light oil (5 ml) with a dash of toasted sesame oil
1/2 cup coarsely chopped onion (118 ml)
One 10-pound or 4.5-kg turkey (usually a hen if under 10–15 pounds, or 4.5–6.8 kg), with wings and liver removed, and neck, gizzard, and heart reserved
2 cups unsweetened apple juice (472 ml), preferably canned
2 cups unsweetened orange juice (472 ml)
1 tablespoon all-purpose flour (15 mg)
1 onion, peeled and stuck with 6 whole cloves
1 orange, slashed with a small knife several times

1/2 cup fresh thyme leaves (118 ml)
1/2 cup fresh sage leaves (118 ml)
1/2 cup water (118 ml)
2 tablespoons arrowroot (30 mg) mixed with 2 tablespoons water (30 ml) (slurry)

Cut the red stems off the chard leaves. Finely chop the stems, mix them in a small bowl with the vinegar, and marinate for 2 hours. Reserve the leaves separately.

To make a turkey stock for the gravy: Heat the oil in a large skillet on low heat and fry the chopped onion until soft—about 10 minutes. Add the turkey wings, neck, gizzard, and heart and the apple and orange juice, bring to a boil, reduce the heat, and simmer, uncovered, for 1 hour. This should yield 2 cups stock (472 ml). Strain and set aside.

Preheat the oven to 325°F (165°C). Rinse the turkey and its cavity thoroughly. Dust the top of the bird with flour. Stuff the cavity with the clove-studded onion, orange, and fresh herbs. Tuck the drumsticks back into the metal clip (often provided with the bird), or tie the legs together with string. Put on a rack in a roasting pan, add the water, and roast for 2½ hours, or until the internal temperature of the thigh is 175°F (77°C). Check every half hour, and if the pan is dry, add another 1/2 cup (118 ml) of water. Remove from the oven and let stand about 20 minutes before carving.

After the turkey has been cooking for 1½ hours, place the sweet potatoes in the oven with the turkey and bake for 40 minutes. Remove and peel off the skin. Mash them in a small bowl and keep warm until ready to serve, or simply cut in half.

Pour the chopped chard stalks and vinegar marinade into a small pan. Over low heat, stir in the cranberry jelly until completely incorporated and just heat through—about 5 minutes. Don't cook the jelly until it becomes syrupy. Remove from the heat and transfer to a small serving bowl.

To complete the gravy: Put the roasting pan full of turkey cooking juices on a stovetop burner on medium heat. Pour in the turkey-apple-orange stock, scraping the pan until you have stirred in all the flavor-filled pan residue. Strain in a fat-separator cup, allowing the fat to rise to the top—about 5 minutes.

Pour the separated turkey juice from the strainer cup into a medium saucepan, making sure not to include any of the separated fat, and heat through to the boil. Remove from the heat, stir in the arrowroot slurry, return to the heat, and stir until thickened over low heat—about 30 seconds. Remove from the heat and set aside.

Place the reserved chard leaves in a steamer, cover, and cook for 4 minutes. Remove from the heat and set aside.

To serve: Carve the turkey into thin slices, put 3 on each dinner plate, and ladle with the gravy. Spoon a mound of sweet potatoes and chard on the side and garnish with the Swiss chard relish.

Time Estimate: Hands-on, 1 hour; unsupervised, 2 hours

Nutritional Profile per Serving		
	Classic	**Minimax**
Calories	1173	600
Fat (gm)	55	12
Saturated fat (gm)	20	3
Calories from fat	42%	18%
Cholesterol (mg)	336	141
Sodium (mg)	1594	496
Fiber (gm)	9	8
Carbohydrates (gm)	91	68
Classic compared: Roast Turkey with Pan Gravy and Candied Yams		

Nonmeat Entrees

◆ GRILLED VEGETABLE QUESADILLAS WITH SALSA

There is nothing quite as luscious as a roasted (actually broiled or grilled is more accurate) sweet bell pepper—regardless of its color. But when you combine the bright, slightly hot taste of a roasted Anaheim pepper with the sweetness of Italian (plum) tomatoes and the pungency of sliced red onions, you've got the makings of a truly great appetizer! I took these vegetables and wrapped them in an avocado, yogurt, and cilantro-filled tortilla—what a wonderful experience. This one you've got to try . . . please!

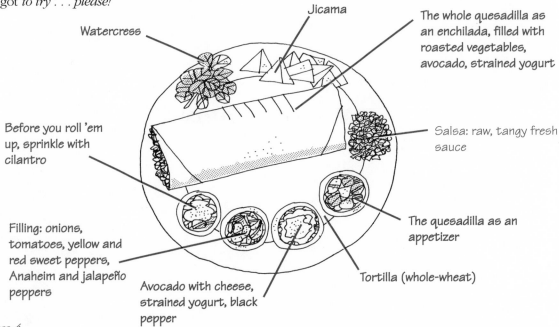

Jicama

Watercress

The whole quesadilla as an enchilada, filled with roasted vegetables, avocado, strained yogurt

Before you roll 'em up, sprinkle with cilantro

Salsa: raw, tangy fresh sauce

Filling: onions, tomatoes, yellow and red sweet peppers, Anaheim and jalapeño peppers

Avocado with cheese, strained yogurt, black pepper

The quesadilla as an appetizer

Tortilla (whole-wheat)

Serves 4

6 large Italian tomatoes, halved and seeded
2 red bell peppers, top and bottom sliced off and reserved, seeded and quartered lengthwise
1 green bell pepper, top and bottom sliced off and reserved, seeded and quartered lengthwise
2 yellow bell peppers, top and bottom sliced off and reserved, seeded and quartered lengthwise
2 Anaheim chili peppers, seeded
1 red onion, peeled and sliced in 1/4-inch rings (.75 cm)
1 large avocado, peeled and mashed
3 tablespoons strained yogurt (45 ml) (see page 141)
1 tablespoon freshly grated Parmesan cheese (15 ml)
1/8 teaspoon freshly ground black pepper (.6 ml)
4 whole-wheat tortillas
3 tablespoons fresh chopped cilantro (45 ml)

Place the tomatoes, peppers, and onion directly on an oven rack, skin-side-up, within 2 inches (5 cm) of the heating element. After about 5 minutes, remove the tomatoes, turn the onions, and broil 5 minutes. The pepper skins will be blistered and black. Set the onions aside with the tomatoes. Transfer the charred peppers directly into a paper bag, seal, and let cool for 20 minutes. Peel or rinse the charred black pepper skins off (I prefer to peel them—to retain the flavor).

Mix the mashed avocado with the strained yogurt, Parmesan cheese, and black pepper and spread evenly over the tortillas.

Preheat the oven to 400°F (205°C). Cover two-

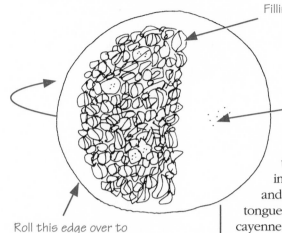

Filling placed on 2/3 of tortilla

Leave uncovered or slightly dampened with avocado.

Roll this edge over to cover filling tightly, until it is enclosed and the fold is underneath.

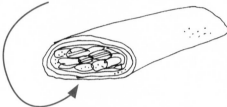

The quesadilla can then be cut into bite-sized hors d'oeuvres.

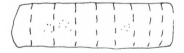

THE CLASSIC QUESADILLA is literally 2 tortillas held together with cheese and some "shreds" of garnish. When I downsized the cheese and upgraded the garnish, guess what? . . . it didn't hold together! So we decided to roll it in the enchilada style and then cut it into bite-sized discs as an appetizer.

thirds of each tortilla with layers of the roasted vegetables in the following order: onions, tomatoes, yellow, red, green, and Anaheim peppers. (If you have the same asbestos-lined tongue as my wife, and "like it hot," then at this stage a little cayenne pepper or finely chopped jalapeño pepper will light your fire.) Sprinkle with the cilantro and roll the quesadillas from the filled side to the empty flap. Transfer the quesadillas to a shallow baking pan, cover with foil, and bake for 10 minutes.

To serve: For an appetizer, cut each quesadilla into 1-inch pieces (2.5 cm) and present with a bowl of salsa on the side. You can garnish the platter with watercress, cilantro, and finely cut discs of jicama . . . or just "set 'em out 'n' watch 'em go."

Time Estimate: Hands-on, 30 minutes; unsupervised, 30 minutes

Nutritional Profile per Serving		
	Classic	**Minimax**
Calories	1,058	323
Fat (gm)	79	10
Saturated fat (gm)	42	2
Calories from fat	67%	28%
Cholesterol (mg)	204	2
Sodium (mg)	1,787	372
Fiber (gm)	6	11
Carbohydrates (gm)	45	54
Classic compared: Well-Filled Quesadillas		

♦ Salsa De Quesadilla

Serves 4

In a food processor, chop the following:
1/2 large jicama and 1 large tomato, both
chopped into 1/4-inch pieces (.75 cm);
reserved tops and bottoms of the bell
peppers from the Quesadilla recipe,
chopped into 1/4-inch pieces (.75 cm); 2
tablespoons green onions (30 ml),
chopped into 1/4-inch pieces (.75 cm); 1/4
cup fresh chopped cilantro leaves (59 ml);
1 or more jalapeño peppers, chopped fine;
and the juice of 1 lime.

Nutritional Profile per Serving
Calories—52; fat (gm)—0; saturated fat (gm)—.04;
calories from fat—7%; cholesterol (mg)—0; sodium
(mg)—15; fiber (gm)—2; carbohydrates (gm)—12.

♦ Mango and Black Bean Salsa

*This salsa is a great accompaniment
for fish.*

Serves 4

1 medium ripe mango (gives slightly to the
   touch)
15 ounces (425 gm) canned low-sodium cooked
   black beans, drained and well rinsed
2 green onions, coarsely chopped
1/4 teaspoon crushed red pepper (1.25 ml)
1 garlic clove, bashed, peeled, and chopped
1/4 teaspoon salt (1.25 ml)

Prepare the mango: Slice off the stem end
and cut away the skin. Trim the flesh away
from the large seed and dice as evenly and
neatly as possible, about the same size as
the black beans.

Add the rest of the ingredients to the
mango, mix well, and let the flavors
marinate for 30 minutes before serving.

Nutritional Profile per Serving
Calories—188; fat (gm)—1; saturated fat (gm)—0;
calories from fat—4%; cholesterol (mg)—0; sodium
(mg)—137; fiber (gm)—9; carbohydrates (gm)—38.

HOW TO CUT PEPPERS

It really does help to cut off the top and bottom, and then de-seed and slice the outer "walls" of the peppers into *flat* pieces. In this way, they don't have to be turned and they get to blister *evenly*.

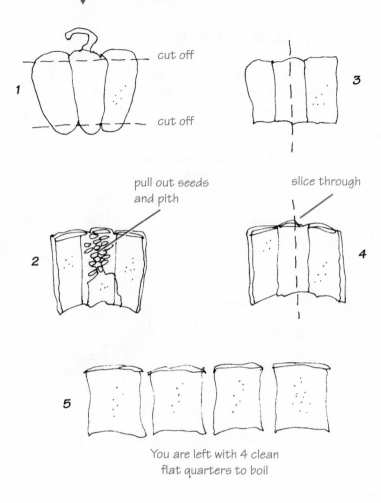

cut off

cut off

1

3

pull out seeds and pith

slice through

2

4

5

You are left with 4 clean flat quarters to boil

◆ Light and Creamy Fruit Curry

Many years ago—in 1963, to be precise—I included a recipe for a mild but fruity curry in my first book. The recipe was, not surprisingly, complete with clarified butter and dairy and coconut cream—loads of saturated fat. For Minimax, I developed an entirely new and truly delicious curry that can be used as a basic method for other light curries, including chicken, seafood, and various vegetables. After you master this recipe, it's open season on your own creativity—just do it!

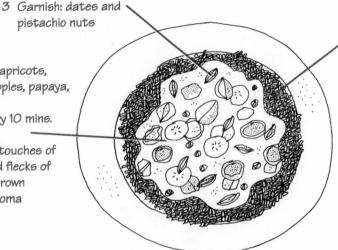

3 Garnish: dates and pistachio nuts

2 Turban of rice
Stovetop: boil 10 mins.
steam 5 mins.
White with brown and green flecks
Texture/Color

1 Fruit curry, with apricots, raisins, pears, apples, papaya, bananas
Stovetop: stir-fry 10 mins.
simmer 18 mins.
Pale golden with touches of warm orange and flecks of green and dark brown
Texture/Color/Aroma

Serves 4

1/2 teaspoon light oil (2.5 ml) with a dash of toasted sesame oil
1/4 pound shallots (113 gm), finely chopped (about 4 shallots)
1 tablespoon finely grated fresh gingerroot (15 ml)
1 tablespoon curry powder (15 ml)
2 cups de-alcoholized white wine (472 ml), preferably Ariél Blanc
1/4 pound dried apricots (113 gm)
6 tablespoons dark raisins (90 ml)
2 pears, peeled, cored, and cut into eighths
1 Granny Smith apple, peeled, cored, and cut into eighths
1 papaya, peeled, seeded, and cut into 1-inch chunks (2.5 cm)
2 medium-sized firm bananas, peeled and cut into 1-inch chunks (2.5 cm)
1 tablespoon cornstarch (15 ml) mixed with 1 teaspoon de-alcoholized white wine (15 ml) (slurry)

1/4 teaspoon essence of real coconut (1.25 ml)
1/8 teaspoon salt (.6 ml)
6 tablespoons strained yogurt (90 ml) (see page 141)
2 cups cooked long-grain rice, basmati or texmati (472 ml)
8 dates, sliced into fine matchsticks
4 tablespoons shelled green pistachio nuts or sliced almonds (60 ml)

Heat the oil in a medium saucepan over medium-high heat and sauté the shallots until they just begin to turn brown—about 5 minutes. Stir in the gingerroot, curry powder, wine, apricots, and raisins and simmer for 5 minutes. Add the pears, apple, and papaya and simmer for 18 minutes. Stir in the bananas, remove from the heat, and strain. Transfer the fruit to a bowl and cover to retain the heat. Return the liquid to the pan (this will be about 1 cup, or 236 ml).

To make the curry sauce, stir the cornstarch

COCONUT FAT

White fat can be extracted by heating grated coconut flesh, then squeezing and finally cooling—to let the fats set hard on the surface. Coconut fat is highly saturated and, as a result, bad news for those who need to watch the cholesterol and fat content of their daily foods.

As with any food, however, it is possible to make a commercial extract of the *flavor* and avoid the fat. In this recipe I've used just such an extract to give a hint of coconut. Depending upon the process used, between ¼ and ½ teaspoon (1.25 and 2.5 ml) is quite enough. Also, as you will see from the ingredients, I've used cornstarch and yogurt to provide the creamy finish also associated with coconut.

KEEP COCONUT EXTRACT PURE

If an "extract" is created from chemical compounds, it must then be labeled artificial. I prefer to use natural, pure extracts or essences from the *real* food.

slurry into the juices, return to the heat, and gently stir until thickened—about 1 minute. Remove from the heat and stir in the coconut essence and salt. Transfer to a medium bowl and whisk in the yogurt. Transfer to a large casserole, stir in the cooked fruit, and heat to your desired serving temperature, but do not boil (if you do, the yogurt will separate).

To serve: Spoon onto plates with the rice and sprinkle with the dates and pistachio nuts—if you really want to show off. *Mmmmmmmmmmmm!!* You can also chill the fruit in its completed sauce and serve as a cool and refreshing summer salad over salad greens.

Time Estimate: Hands-on, 40 minutes; unsupervised, 20 minutes

Nutritional Profile per Serving		
	Classic	**Minimax**
Calories	414	397
Fat (gm)	22	4
Saturated fat (gm)	16	0
Calories from fat	49%	9%
Cholesterol (mg)	42	1
Sodium (mg)	431	115
Fiber (gm)	6	8
Carbohydrates (gm)	53	86
Classic compared: Fruit Curry		

♦ PICADILLO WITH TEXTURED VEGETABLE PROTEIN

In Mexico, picadillo is a simple day-to-day meat sauce that is cooked almost dry and used as a stuffing for chili peppers or to pour over tortillas—a robust reflection of British mince on toast?

I wanted to see if Textured Vegetable Protein could take the place of meat in picadillo. For the uninitiated, TVP is the residue left behind after soybeans are crushed to remove their oil. It is most readily available at health-food stores or food co-ops. I think you'll be pleasantly surprised by the final dish: a fiesta of red, green, and black colors that packs a warm, fiery taste from the cumin and red peppers and has a remarkably satisfying texture.

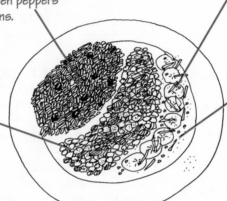

1 Golden rice: brown rice with turmeric and green peppers
Stovetop: 40 mins.
Bright yellow
Texture/Color

2 Picadillo: Textured Vegetable Protein, onion, garlic, sweet peppers, tomatoes, raisins, capers, black beans (and hot peppers if you like 'em!)
Stovetop: boil-simmer 13 mins.

4 Sautéed banana with cloves, cinnamon
Pale golden
Texture/Color/Aroma

3 Garnish: fine-diced tomato, green onion slivers
Red, green
Color

Serves 4

7/8 cup hot water (207 ml)
2 tablespoons balsamic vinegar (30 ml)
1 (2-inch or 5-cm) piece of cinnamon stick
6 whole cloves
1 cup Textured Vegetable Protein (TVP) (236 ml)
1 teaspoon light olive oil (5 ml) with a dash of toasted sesame oil
1 medium onion, peeled and finely chopped
2 cloves garlic, bashed, peeled, and chopped
1 green bell pepper, seeded and finely chopped
One 16-ounce (450-gm) can pureed tomatoes, or 8 fresh Italian tomatoes
1/4 cup dark raisins (59 gm)
1 tablespoon capers (15 gm)
1 teaspoon red pepper flakes (5 ml); for those who might have a tender tongue, use only 1/2 teaspoon (2.5 ml)
1/2 teaspoon ground cumin (2.5 ml)

15 ounces (425 gm) canned low-sodium black beans, well rinsed
1/8 teaspoon freshly ground black pepper (.6 ml)
1/8 teaspoon salt (.6 ml)

Garnish
Chopped tomato
Green onions, finely sliced lengthwise

In a small bowl mix the water with the balsamic vinegar. Put the cinnamon stick and cloves into a small coffee grinder and whiz until a powder is formed—about 1 minute. Push half of the spice powder through a fine mesh sieve into the water. (Reserve the other half for the Sautéed Bananas; see below.) In a small bowl, mix the spice-infused water with the TVP and let sit until all the liquid has been absorbed—about 3 minutes.

I have heard many comments to the effect that "you can't disguise the flavor of the dried soybean," the main ingredient of TVP. In my work, I always seek synergy, not disguises—that is, I attempt to marry one flavor to another so that the sum of the two is greater than the originals.

I discovered that this happens when you pair cumin with the soy in TVP. I sense that the best ratio is ¼–½ teaspoon (1.25–2.5 ml) powdered cumin, preferably freshly powdered from seeds, to each cup (236 ml) of TVP.

Now it's over to you to agree or go on to make additional marriages. Let me know when you do, *please!*

Heat the oil in a medium skillet over medium heat, add the onion, garlic, and green pepper and cook until soft and lightly browned—about 5 minutes. Raise the heat to medium high, add the marinated TVP, and cook for 5 minutes. Push the mixture to one side of the pan; pour in the pureed tomatoes, raisins, capers, red pepper flakes, and cumin; raise the heat to high; and bring to a boil. Mix the TVP mixture with the tomato sauce and cook for 3 minutes. Return the heat to low, stir in the black beans, cover, and warm through. Sprinkle with the pepper and salt.

To serve: Spoon a quarter of the picadillo in a mound in the center of each serving plate and encircle with a wreath of Yellow Rice (see page 89). Arrange a crescent of Sautéed Bananas on the side and garnish with a sprinkling of the bright red chopped tomato and a spray of green onion.

Time Estimate: Hands-on, 35 minutes; unsupervised, none

Nutritional Profile per Serving

	Classic	Minimax
Calories	797	360
Fat (gm)	45	3
Saturated fat (gm)	12	0
Calories from fat	51%	6%
Cholesterol (mg)	161	0
Sodium (mg)	1,234	614
Fiber (gm)	7	14
Carbohydrates (gm)	55	66
Classic compared: Picadillo		

♦ SAUTÉED BANANAS

Serves 4

One 1-inch (2.5-cm) piece of cinnamon stick
3 whole cloves
1 teaspoon light oil with a dash of toasted sesame oil (5 ml)
2 firm bananas, sliced on a thick diagonal

Put the cinnamon and cloves in a small coffee-bean grinder and puree to a powder—about 30 seconds. Push through a fine sieve to remove any large pieces.

Heat the oil in a small skillet over medium heat, add the bananas, sprinkle with the spice powder, and cook until well browned—about 2 ½ minutes on each side.

Nutritional Profile per Serving

Calories—65; fat (gm)—2; saturated fat (gm)—0; calories from fat—22%; cholesterol (mg)—0; sodium (mg)—1; fiber (gm)—1; carbohydrates (gm)—14.

VEGETABLE PAPOOSE

Part of the pleasure to be found in a Minimax change is the avalanche of fresh vegetables. This recipe suggests a novel method of presentation: the papoose. Here a colorful mix of root vegetables is well seasoned with a touch of Canadian bacon and horseradish, wrapped in Swiss chard leaves, and dusted with cheese. It's a terrific low-fat and low-calorie meal with tons of aromas, colors, and textures.

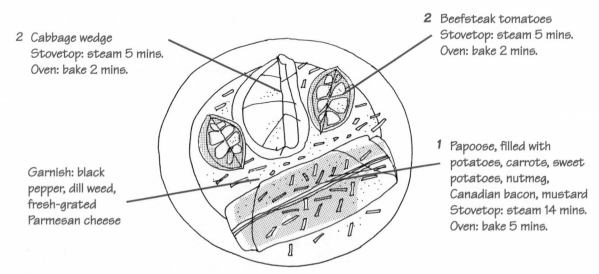

2 Cabbage wedge
Stovetop: steam 5 mins.
Oven: bake 2 mins.

2 Beefsteak tomatoes
Stovetop: steam 5 mins.
Oven: bake 2 mins.

Garnish: black pepper, dill weed, fresh-grated Parmesan cheese

1 Papoose, filled with potatoes, carrots, sweet potatoes, nutmeg, Canadian bacon, mustard
Stovetop: steam 14 mins.
Oven: bake 5 mins.

Serves 4

8 large red chard leaves, heavy bottom stalks removed
4 medium baking potatoes, preferably Yukon Gold, cut in 1/2-inch dice (1.5 cm)
4 medium carrots, peeled and cut in 1/2-inch discs (1.5 cm)
2 large sweet potatoes, peeled and cut into 1/2-inch dice (1.5 cm)
1/4 teaspoon nutmeg (1.25 ml)
1/8 teaspoon salt (.6 ml)
1/4 teaspoon freshly ground black pepper (1.25 ml)
3½ ounces Canadian bacon (100 gm), coarsely chopped
1/4 cup freshly grated Parmesan cheese (59 ml)
4 teaspoons hearty mustard (20 ml), preferably Grey Poupon
4 teaspoons prepared horseradish (20 ml)
1/2 medium head of cabbage, cut into 4 wedges
4 very large beefsteak tomatoes, cut in half
2 tablespoons fresh chopped dill (30 ml)

Steam the chard leaves until just tender—about 3 minutes. Remove from the heat and, as soon as you can touch them, transfer the leaves to a cold plate to stop further cooking. Cut the bright red veins out of the leaves, chop the veins finely, and set aside.

Start steaming the diced potatoes and cook for 2 minutes. Add the carrots and cook for 2 minutes. Add the sweet potatoes, nutmeg, salt, and pepper; toss well; and continue steaming for 10 minutes until just tender. Immediately transfer the steamed vegetables to a large bowl and toss with the Canadian bacon, half of the cheese, the mustard, horseradish, and reserved chopped chard veins.

Place the cabbage wedges and tomatoes on a steamer rack. Sprinkle lightly with salt, pepper, and 1 tablespoon of the dill. Cover, and cook for 5 minutes.

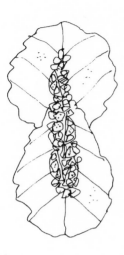

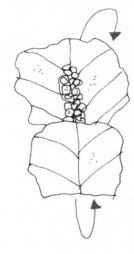

Preheat the oven to 350°F (180°C). On individual ovenproof dinner dishes, place two of the cooked chard leaves. Cover with 1/4 of the seasoned vegetables in a long line down the middle of the leaf. Turn the edges of the chard leaves over the top and gently roll them over, tucking the edges under to form a neat cylinder (papoose). Repeat the process to form 3 more papooses. Gently push the chard papoose to one side of the plate. On the other side, place the cabbage wedge and flank it with the tomato halves. Dust both lightly with freshly ground black pepper and salt. Place in the oven and reheat for 5 minutes.

To serve: Sprinkle the entire plate with black pepper, to taste, and the remaining Parmesan cheese and dill.

*Time Estimate: Hands-on, 58 minutes;
unsupervised, 27 minutes*

STEAMING
I've used my own Stack 'n Steam device to prepare the vegetables. I designed a stainless-steel two-tier unit to fit in a 10-inch-diameter saucepan (25 cm) or skillet, and it works brilliantly—allowing for all kinds of creative steamed dishes. It's a sturdy and hygienic alternative to the bamboo steamers that can become a bit "woofy" with age and only sporadic use. I mention it here as a helpful hint because steaming is, in my judgment, an essential part of Minimax cooking.

Nutritional Profile per Serving

	Classic	Minimax
Calories	1,360	374
Fat (gm)	86	4
Saturated fat (gm)	29	2
Calories from fat	57%	11%
Cholesterol (mg)	360	16
Sodium (mg)	4,254	776
Fiber (gm)	15	12
Carbohydrates (gm)	118	72
Classic compared: Corned Beef and Cabbage		

♦ GEORGETOWN FLAKEY

Literally hundreds of tons of Textured Vegetable Protein (TVP) is given away to food banks each year. Unfortunately there are few recipes to guide people in its preparation. I worked with the local Georgetown Food Bank in south Seattle and its clients to develop a tasty, simple recipe, and Georgetown Flakey is the inexpensive and hearty result. It's something like a vegetarian ragout with a chili flavor. Here's a wonderful idea: Why not serve it once in a while and donate the money you save from preparing a regular meal to a local food bank?

Serves 1   This recipe was designed specifically for a single serving.

1½ cups spicy tomato juice (354 ml), such as V-8

1/2 teaspoon dried garlic flakes (2.5 ml)

2 teaspoons dried chopped onion flakes (10 ml)

1/4 teaspoon ground cumin (1.25 ml)

3/4 cup Textured Vegetable Protein (TVP) granules (177 ml)

6 dried banana chips (or one-half fresh banana, sliced)

1/4 teaspoon dried parsley (1.25 ml)

Chili pepper flakes to taste (optional)

Pour the vegetable juice into a medium saucepan and bring it to a boil. Stir in the garlic, onion, cumin, the TVP, and banana chips. (If you're using fresh banana, add it when all the liquid has been absorbed.) Remove from the heat and let sit for 3 minutes.

To serve: Spoon into a bowl and garnish with the parsley, and the pepper flakes, if desired.

Time Estimate: Hands-on, 10 minutes; unsupervised, none

FOUR PARTS TO TASTE . . . OR IS IT FIVE?

For years now we've all been told that our taste buds respond to only four elements: salt, sweet, sour, and bitter. Some brave folk have suggested that it be stretched to five and include "piquant" or "spicy/hot" as in pepper, for example.

The truth is, pepper causes our sense of *touch* to react, not *taste*; and yet, it's so much a part of the dining experience.

Try it out with this recipe. Here we get salt, sweet, sour, bitter, and spice/hot. It's a royal flush to the sense of taste . . . and touch!

Nutritional Profile per Serving		
	Classic	**Minimax**
Calories	494	415
Fat (gm)	26	2
Saturated fat (gm)	8	0
Calories from fat	47%	4%
Cholesterol (mg)	118	0
Sodium (mg)	1,418	1,741
Fiber (gm)	3	14
Carbohydrates (gm)	17	13
Classic compared: Hell's Kitchen Chili		

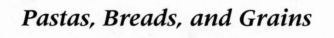

Pastas, Breads, and Grains

SMOOTH PASTA SAUCES

Frankly, I'm fascinated by the almost universal popularity of smooth-sauced pastas. For instance, I've seen Alfredo sauce flowing as freely as creamy lava over dozens of restaurant offerings. I fully appreciate the delight that comes from the "smooooooth mouthfeel" and set out to capture some of the texture while removing almost all the fat. Here are two quite different sauces that are made by the same method. By the way, they also make quite appetizing first-course soups.

♦ GREEN PEA SAUCE

Orange Butternut Sauce

Oven: bake 50 mins.
Stovetop: 23 mins.
Orange, yellow
Color/Aroma/Texture

Green Pea Sauce

Stovetop: 11 mins.
Pale green
Texture/Color/Aroma

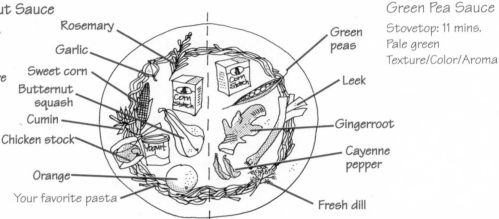

Rosemary · Garlic · Sweet corn · Butternut squash · Cumin · Chicken stock · Orange · Your favorite pasta · Green peas · Leek · Gingerroot · Cayenne pepper · Fresh dill

Serves 4

1 teaspoon light oil (5 ml) with a dash of toasted sesame oil

1 tablespoon very finely chopped fresh gingerroot (15 ml)

1 leek, thinly sliced

3 cups vegetable stock (708 ml) (see page 144)

1/2 cup loosely packed fresh dill (118 ml)

3 cups frozen peas (708 ml)

2 tablespoons cornstarch (30 ml) mixed with 4 tablespoons water (60 ml) (slurry)

1/4 teaspoon salt (1.25 ml)

1/8 teaspoon cayenne pepper (.6 ml)

Pour the oil into a medium preheated saucepan over medium-high heat and cook the ginger for 2 minutes. Add the leek and cook for 3 minutes, or until wilted. Stir in the stock and dill and bring to a boil. Add the peas and bring back to a boil.

Remove from the heat. Pour into a blender and puree until smooth—about 5 minutes. Add the cornstarch slurry, return to the heat, and stir until thickened—about 1 minute.

To serve: Add salt and cayenne, and toss with your pasta-of-choice and enjoy.

Time Estimate: Hands-on, 20 minutes; unsupervised, none

Nutritional Profile per Serving		
	Classic	**Minimax**
Calories	259	129
Fat (gm)	13	2
Saturated fat (gm)	1	0
Calories from fat	44%	15%
Cholesterol (mg)	31	0
Sodium (mg)	873	261
Fiber (gm)	9	6
Carbohydrates (gm)	27	21
Classic compared: Sweet Pea Soup		

♦ Orange Butternut Sauce

Serves 7–8

1/4 teaspoon light oil (1.25 ml) with a dash of toasted sesame oil

2 garlic cloves, bashed, peeled, and chopped

3 cups chicken stock (708 ml) (see page 141); use a vegetable stock if you prefer to make the dish completely vegetarian

One 2-pound or 900-gm butternut squash, baked for 50 minutes at 350°F (180°C) to yield 3 cups of pulp (708 ml)

1 (6-inch or 15-cm) piece rosemary

1 cup frozen corn (236 ml)

1/4 teaspoon freshly ground black pepper (1.25 ml)

1/8 teaspoon salt (.6 ml)

1/4 teaspoon cumin (1.25 ml)

2 tablespoons cornstarch (30 ml) mixed with 1/4 cup unsweetened orange juice (59 ml) (slurry)

1/4 cup strained yogurt (59 ml) (see page 141)

Heat the oil in a large saucepan over medium heat and fry the garlic for 3 minutes. Stir in the stock, cooked butternut squash, and rosemary and simmer for 15 minutes. Remove the rosemary and discard.

Stir in the corn, pepper, salt, cumin, and cornstarch slurry and cook for 3 minutes. Pour into a blender and puree until very smooth—about 5 minutes.

To serve: Just before serving, whisk in the yogurt for a sense of added richness. Present immediately, tossed with your favorite pasta (see list on page 192), or refrigerate before adding the yogurt and reheat later.

Time Estimate: Hands-on, 20 minutes; unsupervised, 15 minutes

BAKING BUTTERNUT SQUASH

There are two reasons for baking the squash: First, removing its armored coating (skin) is a tough job. When it's baked, all you do is spoon it out as if it were an orange-colored avocado. Second, if it's boiled, it absorbs liquid like a sponge and the sauce with be thin and watery. The baking method actually serves to reduce the moisture content in the squash and therefore concentrates its flavor.

FABULOUS FRESH GINGER

Fresh gingerroot is such a fabulous, inexpensive addition to your flavoring pantry. Just buy a small piece and store it in a paper bag in the refrigerator. If it's young, the skin will be *very* thin, in which case it doesn't need to be peeled before use.

WHEN CORNSTARCH IS BEST

I use cornstarch rather than arrowroot as a thickener in these sauces because of their robust texture. I save the arrowroot for finely textured, clear, glossy sauces.

Nutritional Profile per Serving		
	Classic	**Minimax**
Calories	104	78
Fat (gm)	6	1
Saturated fat (gm)	3	0
Calories from fat	52%	13%
Cholesterol (mg)	82	0
Sodium (mg)	759	63
Fiber (gm)	1	3
Carbohydrates (gm)	8	16
Classic compared: Pumpkin Soup		

♦ SPAGHETTI SALMONARA

Treena and I have toured Italy from Naples to Venice, and we lived in that country briefly in the early seventies. We eat frequently at Italian restaurants, all over the world. To these I must now add Babbo Ganza in Santa Fe, where the pasta was cooked better than at any other restaurant in my lifetime of experience. Congratulations to owner/chef Giovanni Scorzo on his commitment to excellence, and my thanks to him for letting me springboard off several of the key ideas he uses to make his seafood pastas.

3 Spaghettini (thin spaghetti)
Stovetop: boil 5 mins.
(last-minute cooking)
Creamy white
Texture

1 Marinara sauce: tomatoes,
carrots, celery, oregano
Stovetop: 15 mins.
Deep red, orange
Aroma/Color/Texture

2 Salmon sauce
Stovetop: 13 mins.
Pink, red
Texture/Color/Aroma

4 Garnish: fresh-grated
Parmesan cheese, parsley,
black pepper, lemon wedges

Serves 6 This recipe allows for an extra cup of Marinara to be saved for another dish.

Marinara Sauce
1 teaspoon light oil (5 ml) with a dash of toasted sesame oil
1/3 cup diced onion (78 ml)
1/3 cup diced carrots (78 ml)
1/3 cup diced celery (78 ml)
2 pounds Italian tomatoes (900 gm)
1/4 teaspoon salt (1.25 ml)
1/4 teaspoon freshly ground black pepper (1.25 ml)
Three (3-inch or 8-cm) sprigs fresh oregano (see page 165)

Salmon Sauce
1/2 teaspoon light oil with a dash of toasted sesame oil (2.5 ml)
2 ounces shallots (57 gm), peeled and chopped (about 2)
2 cups fish stock (472 ml) (see page 143)
Two 6-ounce or 170-gm salmon steaks
4 large beefsteak tomatoes, quartered and seeded, seeds and pulp reserved

1/4 teaspoon salt (1.25 ml)
2 tablespoons arrowroot (10 ml) plus 2 tablespoons water (10 ml) (slurry)
2 tablespoons fresh oregano leaves (30 ml)

1 pound spaghettini, or thin spaghetti (450 gm)

1/2 cup freshly grated Parmesan cheese (118 ml)
1/4 cup fresh chopped parsley (59 ml)
1/4 teaspoon freshly ground black pepper (1.25 ml)

Garnish
1 lemon, cut in wedge

The marinara sauce: Heat the oil in a medium saucepan over medium-high heat. Fry the diced vegetables for 15 minutes.

Put the tomatoes, skins still on, into a plastic bag and press down gently until they are somewhat squashed; do not mash completely. Transfer them to the saucepan and stir in the salt, pepper, and oregano; cover and cook for 15 minutes. Remove from the heat and strain, to yield 2 cups of sauce (472 ml).

The salmon sauce: Heat the oil in a large skillet over medium-high heat and shallow-fry the shallots until just translucent—about 5 minutes. Add the fish stock, bring to a boil, then reduce the heat until just simmering. Add the salmon, cover, and cook for 8 minutes, or until the salmon flakes easily.

Leaving the stock simmering, transfer the salmon to a plate and carefully remove the skin and bones. Add the skin and bones with the reserved tomato seeds and pulp to the simmering stock to reinforce its flavor. Break the salmon meat into bite-sized pieces and set aside.

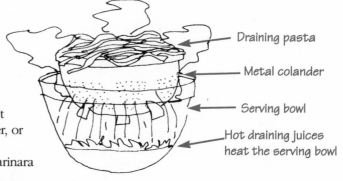

Remove the stock from the heat and strain to yield 1½ cups (354 ml). If you don't have 1½ cups (354 ml), add fish stock, water, or wine to come to that level. Return to the saucepan and add 1 cup (236 ml) of the marinara sauce, the quartered tomatoes, salt, and the arrowroot slurry. Return to the heat and stir until thickened—about 1 minute. Gently stir in the oregano and salmon meat and keep warm until ready to serve.

Cook the pasta in a large pot of boiling water until just tender—about 5 minutes, depending on the pasta. Strain in a metal colander, letting the cooking water pour into a serving bowl. Pour out the water when the bowl is heated through.

To serve: Pour 2 cups (472 ml) of the salmon sauce into the hot serving bowl. Add the hot, drained pasta, Parmesan cheese, parsley, and black pepper, toss well, and bring to the table to serve. Offer lemon wedges on the side.

Time Estimate: Hands-on, 45 minutes; unsupervised, 30 minutes

FRESH, BEST, AND
LAST-MINUTE COOKING
Commitment to excellence in the Minimax kitchen begins with buying the *freshest and best in season*. A great learning place is a local farmers' market. Cut and slice everything just prior to cooking.

ROBUST AND RED
For the salmon sauce choose beefsteak tomatoes that are a deep red (as opposed to orange-toned ones). These will produce a sauce with richer color and flavor.

Nutritional Profile per Serving		
	Classic	**Minimax**
Calories	958	497
Fat (gm)	64	10
Saturated fat (gm)	25	3
Calories from fat	60%	18%
Cholesterol (mg)	273	39
Sodium (mg)	548	375
Fiber (gm)	43	6
Carbohydrates (gm)	43	75
Classic compared: King Salmon with Pesto		

CHAPATIS

Some fun food works best on a solid ceramic-topped burner like the one I have at home. But a griddle pan will work just as well. This flat bread is a classic accompaniment to Indian dishes of all sorts.

Yields 8

1½ cups finely ground whole-wheat flour (354 ml)
1/2 cup water (118 ml)

In a large bowl, mix 1 cup of the flour (236 ml) with the water, adding a little at a time until it clumps together in an easy-to-handle dough. You probably won't need all the water. Turn the dough out onto a flat surface and knead for 8 minutes by hand or 1½ minutes with a dough hook on a mixer. Cover the dough with a damp cloth and allow to rest for at least 30 minutes and up to 3 hours.

Just before cooking, knead the dough a dozen times. Divide it into 8 balls and cover with a damp cloth. Preheat a large skillet over medium heat until it's quite hot. Heat another burner to just medium heat.

Dip the dough balls in flour until well coated. Scatter the remaining 1/2 cup flour (118 ml) on a rolling surface to keep from sticking. Roll each ball out flat to form a thin 5-inch circle (13 cm).

Cook the chapatis one at a time in the hot pan. When the dough starts to bubble, flip it over with a pair of tongs and finish cooking. Both sides of the bread should have brown spots on them. Now lay the cooked chapati directly on the hot burner—it should start to puff up immediately. Turn it over on the other side for a few seconds. If the burner is too hot, the bread will burn; if it's not hot enough, it won't puff! You'll have to experiment a little with your particular stove.

Nutritional Profile per Serving (2 chapatis)
Calories—153; fat (gm)—1; saturated fat (gm)—0; calories from fat—5%; cholesterol (mg)—0; sodium (mg)—2; fiber (gm)—5; carbohydrates (gm)—33.

WILD RICE

Wild rice is really a grass seed, not a grain. It has about twice the protein of other rices, as well as more B vitamins. It can be mixed with equal parts brown or white rice for a very attractive presentation. See page 195 for more on wild rice.

Serves 4

4 cups water (944 ml)
1 cup raw rice (236 ml)

Rinse the rice in a strainer until the water runs clear. Transfer to a saucepan, add the water and bring to a boil, and boil for 30 minutes. The rice will still be chewy. Drain and serve.

Nutritional Profile per Serving
Calories—160; fat (gm)—1; saturated fat (gm)—0; calories from fat—3%; cholesterol (mg)—0; sodium (mg)—5; fiber (gm)—1; carbohydrates (gm)—34.

BROWN RICE

Brown rice has had only its outer husk removed. It is the only form of rice that contains vitamin E; it also has more fiber, iron, and other minerals. I think it has a deeper flavor and chewier texture.

Serves 4

1½ cups raw brown rice (354 ml)
1/4 teaspoon salt (1.25 ml)
3 cups water (708 ml)

Rinse the rice in a strainer until the water runs clear. Transfer to a saucepan, add the water and salt, and bring to a boil. Reduce the heat, cover, and simmer for 30 minutes or until water is all absorbed.

Nutritional Profile per Serving
Calories—258; fat (gm)—2; saturated fat (gm)—0; calories from fat—7%; cholesterol (mg)—0; sodium (mg)—145; fiber (gm)—4; carbohydrates (gm)—53.

BROWN RICE IN THE PRESSURE COOKER

Serves 4

2¼ cups water (531 ml)
1 cup raw brown rice (236 ml)
1/2 teaspoon salt (2.5 ml)
1/4 teaspoon freshly ground pepper (1.25 ml)

Pour the water into a pressure cooker and bring to a boil. Add the rice and seasonings, stir, close the cooker, and bring to full pressure on high heat. Reduce the heat and cook for 12 minutes.

Remove from the heat. Reduce pressure by pressing on the release valve. Transfer the rice to a colander to drain, if necessary.

Nutritional Profile per Serving
Calories—172; fat (gm)—1; saturated fat (gm)—0; calories from fat—7%; cholesterol (mg)—0; sodium (mg)—274; fiber (gm)—3; carbohydrates (gm)—36.

COUSCOUS

Couscous is actually a pasta whose individual pieces are tinier than grains of rice. It's a neutral food that can be served with any favorite meats, vegetables, spices— even at breakfast time with fruit.

Serves 4

1½ cups stock of your choice (354 ml) (see pages 143–146) or water
1 cup precooked "instant" couscous (236 ml)

Pour the stock into a medium saucepan and bring to a boil. Add the couscous, reduce the heat to its lowest setting, and cook for 5 minutes. Remove from the heat and fluff with a fork.

Nutritional Profile per Serving
Calories—183; fat (gm)—1; saturated fat (gm)—0; calories from fat—3%; cholesterol (mg)—0; sodium (mg)—159; fiber (gm)—2; carbohydrates (gm)—36.

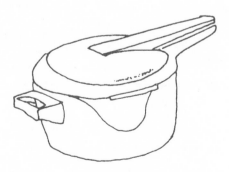

POLENTA

Polenta is a porridge made from cornmeal. Normally it has fat added, and it is often made into cakes that are sliced, oiled, and broiled. Cornmeal is the only widely used grain that has vitamin A; the brighter the color of the cornmeal, the more A there is. To get the classic polenta texture, avoid the stone-ground cornmeal.

Serves 4

7 cups cold water (1.7 l)
2 cups yellow cornmeal (472 ml)
1/2 teaspoon salt (2.5 ml)
1/4 teaspoon freshly ground black pepper (1.25 ml)

In a large saucepan, bring the water to a rapid boil. Slowly sprinkle in all the cornmeal, stirring constantly. Do not let the water stop boiling. When all the cornmeal has been added, sprinkle in the salt and pepper. Adjust the heat to maintain the boil, stirring and scraping the sides and bottom of the saucepan. Lower the heat if the mixture starts to stick. When done, the polenta will be a thick porridge that pulls cleanly from the sides of the saucepan, and a spoon will stand up in it. This takes about 25 minutes. To shorten the time and labor, use fine-ground cornmeal. It cooks in half the time, but beware that it loses color and some of the texture of regular cornmeal.

Nutritional Profile per Serving

Calories—253; fat (gm)—1; saturated fat (gm)—0; calories from fat—4%; cholesterol (mg)—0; sodium (mg)—269; fiber (gm)—4; carbohydrates (gm)—54.

POT BARLEY A-2-VAY

I believe pot barley has better texture and more taste than its "pearly" cousin. This simple side dish cooks in its own steam— hence the term étuvée *(diabolically presented in an easily pronounced form in the name of the recipe), which implies cooking, covered, in natural juices.*

Serves 4

1 teaspoon light oil (5 ml) with a dash of toasted sesame oil
1/8 teaspoon toasted sesame oil (.6 ml)
2 leeks, dark green tops only
2 cloves garlic, bashed, peeled, and chopped
1 cup uncooked long-grain brown rice (236 ml)
1/2 cup pot barley (118 ml)
3 cups water (708 ml)
1/2 teaspoon salt (2.5 ml)

Heat the oils in a small saucepan over medium heat and sauté the diced leek tops and garlic for 2 minutes. Stir in the rice, barley, water, and salt. Cover and cook over medium-low heat for 45 minutes.

Nutritional Profile per Serving

Calories—331; fat (gm)—3; saturated fat (gm)—1; calories from fat—9%; cholesterol (mg)—0; sodium (mg)—147; fiber (gm)—8; carbohydrates (gm)—64.

QUINOA

Not a true grain, quinoa (pronounced kee-NO-ah) is related to leafy green vegetables such as Swiss chard. Its almost neutral flavor allows it to be substituted for almost any grain, and nutritionally it has no equal: more iron than any other grain, high levels of potassium and many other minerals, and of riboflavin. It is also an excellent source of plant protein.

Serves 4

2 cups water (472 ml)
1 cup quinoa (236 ml) (see page 193)
1/4 teaspoon salt (1.25 ml)

In a medium saucepan, bring the water to a boil and add the quinoa and salt. Bring back to a boil, reduce the heat, and simmer for 10 minutes. Remove from the heat and set aside until ready to serve.

Nutritional Profile per Serving
Calories—93; fat (gm)—1; saturated fat (gm)—0; calories from fat—7%; cholesterol (mg)—0; sodium (mg)—142; fiber (gm)—2; carbohydrates (gm)—20.

RICE PILAF

Serves 4

3 cups beef stock (708 ml) (see page 142)
1/2 cup uncooked long-grain rice (118 ml)
1/4 cup uncooked wild rice (59 ml)
1/4 cup uncooked pearl barley (59 ml)
1 bay leaf
2 sprigs tarragon
2 sprays parsley
2 tablespoons Dijon mustard (30 ml)
2 teaspoons fresh chopped tarragon (10 ml)

Preheat the oven to 375°F (190°C). Pour the stock into a medium ovenproof saucepan and add the long-grain rice, wild rice, and pearl barley. Lay the bay leaf, tarragon, and parsley on top and bake for 45 minutes. When done, remove the herbs. Add the Dijon mustard and tarragon and stir thoroughly.

Nutritional Profile per Serving
Calories—200; fat (gm)—1; saturated fat (gm)—0; calories from fat—7%; cholesterol (mg)—0; sodium (mg)—140; fiber (gm)—2; carbohydrates (gm)—40.

YELLOW RICE

Serves 4

3 cups water (708 ml)
1/4 teaspoon turmeric (1.25 ml)
1½ cups uncooked long-grain white rice (354 ml)
1/8 teaspoon salt (.6 ml)
1/4 cup raisins

Pour the water into a medium saucepan, stir in the turmeric, and bring to a boil. Add the rice and salt and boil for 15 minutes. Strain through a metal sieve, then place the rice-filled sieve over a pan of boiling water and steam, covered, for 5 minutes. Stir in raisins and serve.

Nutritional Profile per Serving
Calories—306; fat (gm)—2; saturated fat (gm)—0; calories from fat—6%; cholesterol (mg)—0; sodium (mg)—83; fiber (gm)—4; carbohydrates (gm)—66.

BEAUTIFUL RED SAUCE

Serves 4

1 teaspoon extra-light olive oil (5 ml) with a dash of
   toasted sesame oil
1/2 onion, peeled and coarsely chopped
2 cloves garlic, bashed, peeled, and chopped
1 teaspoon dried basil (5 ml)
1 teaspoon dried oregano (5 ml)
1/2 cup chopped green bell pepper (118 ml)
1 cup button mushrooms (236 ml), cut in
   quarters
One 28-ounce or 790-gm can crushed tomatoes
2 teaspoons arrowroot (10 ml) mixed with
   1 tablespoon water (15 ml) (slurry)

Heat the oil in a saucepan over medium heat and
sauté the onion, garlic, basil, and oregano until
the onion starts to turn transparent—about 5
minutes. Add the green pepper and
mushrooms, cover, and cook for 5 minutes.

Pour in the tomatoes and their
juice, bring to a boil, reduce the
heat, and simmer for 5 minutes.
Stir in the arrowroot slurry and
stir until the sauce is shiny.

Serve immediately over your
choice of pasta.

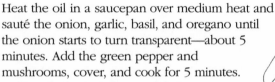

Nutritional Profile per Serving
Calories—81; fat (gm)—2; saturated fat
(gm)—0; calories from fat—23%; cholesterol
(mg)—0; sodium (mg)—325; fiber (gm)—4;
carbohydrates (gm)—15.

Vegetables

Most people call them "accompaniments"; just as a hat, handbag, or briefcase is to the suit, so vegetables are to the main dish. In our case, I want to switch roles and make the accessory important . . . no . . . *crucial!*

When meats and poultry—complete with cholesterol, animal fats, and dense calories—are substantially scaled back, the satisfaction we crave is going to have to come from the accompaniments. This means that each vegetable or sauce must be very well cooked and not boiled to indifferent death while the meat is being coaxed to perfection. In this section, I have attempted to gather the dishes by major colors, rather than food types. In this way, you can flick through the pages en route to a colorful collection that *you* like. Your natural taste and color preferences may now lead you to an extraordinary combination that could make you as famous as the Caesar who tossed his fatty salad into the Hall of Fame.

But don't stop there, please! On page 145 begins the A.C.T. (Aroma, Color, Texture) section, in which all manner of seasonings are grouped together under their sensual contribution. This is where you can find an herb, spice, or liquid that can enhance the very simple accompaniments in this section.

To accompany the Lamb Shanks (page 54), you may decide to make mashed potatoes instead of the Polenta Pie. Or you might wonder if Canadian bacon and hot English mustard, instead of chives, would flavor a simple potato dish. It's stuff like this, often wild experiments, that pushes back the boundaries of traditional tastes to include maximum creativity!

Welcome to the Brave New World!

One piece of equipment to help you prepare Minimax accompaniments is the Stack 'n Steam unit for your favorite Dutch oven. Just take the lid for this piece and measure it from the outer rim insert to the other side . . .

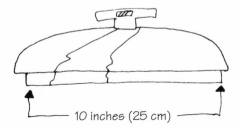

10 inches (25 cm)

If you have that measurement (which is standard, by the way) or a large skillet that is

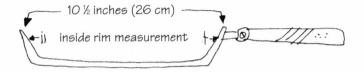

10 ½ inches (26 cm)

inside rim measurement

then you can purchase a Stack 'n Steam unit to fit in between what you now have.

I'm convinced that Stacking 'n Steaming will become *the* most popular method of cooking as we approach the year 2000. It's clean, quick, healthy, and inexpensive, and steaming allows for creativity and great taste. What else is needed?

Percentage of Calories from Fat

If you have heard the American Heart Association say *anything,* you must have heard about "30 percent of calories from fat." This guideline is for healthy people who want to stay well. However, if some elements of risk are present, then according to the severity and number of those risks, you or your loved ones may need to go lower. When you *know* your percentage, then you will be able to work out how much fat to have in any one day.

My limit is 50 grams, although sometimes I might exceed that by another 50. If I do, I set about reducing my fat intake by one tablespoon a day (14 grams) for five days. I *never* exceed 100 grams a day, because the rich indulgence just isn't worth the lower fat remedy (please see page 5 for a detailed explanation). This means that individual meat recipes can be assembled; and even though their individual percentage may exceed 30 percent, when they are matched to lower fat

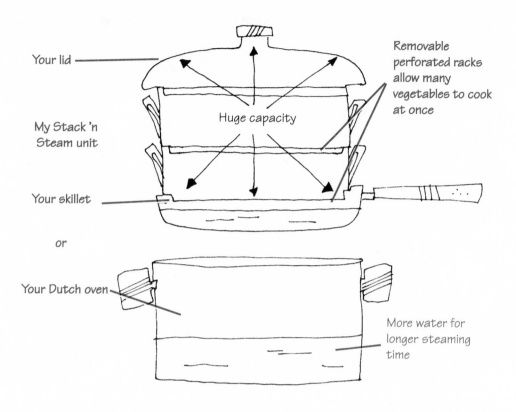

Your lid

My Stack 'n Steam unit

Your skillet

Huge capacity

Removable perforated racks allow many vegetables to cook at once

or

Your Dutch oven

More water for longer steaming time

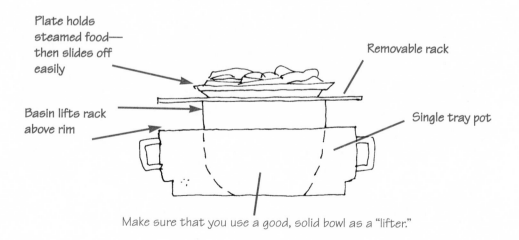

Plate holds steamed food— then slides off easily

Basin lifts rack above rim

Removable rack

Single tray pot

Make sure that you use a good, solid bowl as a "lifter."

accompaniments, the total can be right down around 20 percent. Remember, *please,* it's the total calories and the total fat in any one day that *really* matter. Throughout the vegetable and A.C.T. sections, where the calories are low, no matter how low the fat, it looks high as a percentage. It's important to note *fat grams* and remember them, then the selections you'll make will be based upon knowledge as well as desire.

MAKING MORE OUT OF LESS

If meat has been your focus—whatever kind of meat or poultry that may be—then let it take second billing to the vegetables. Let meat properly, healthily, and reasonably become an accompaniment to the vegetables. If a 12-ounce (340-gm) strip steak or prime rib is your pioneer portion, then you could start out by sharing half of it with someone else.

If you accumulate body weight (especially around the middle), or if you have a cholesterol count over 200 milligrams per liter or elevated LDL (low-density lipoprotein), if you have a family history of heart disease or have been (or are) a smoker, then you will need to halve that steak portion once again.

"No!" I can hear you yell. "That's impossible!"

OK! I know how tough it sounds, but I'm not asking you to cut it out completely. What I'm asking you to do, however, is to add food to your plate; not just one item to replace the beef, but many; not one color, but many; not one aroma, but many; not one texture, but many. It's not what you lose, it's what you gain. You'll gain a better night's sleep, better digestion, and a better feeling of being in control. As you inevitably lose weight without being hungry, you'll have more energy, you'll lose inches, and you'll look better! It's not the amount of meat that you lose, it's all the benefits you gain that make this kind of change possible.

Stewed Tomatoes

Serves 4

1 teaspoon light oil (5 ml) with a dash of toasted
   sesame oil
1/2 cup chopped onion (118 ml)
1 clove garlic, bashed, peeled, and chopped
1 teaspoon fresh, finely chopped basil (5 ml)
1 teaspoon fresh, finely chopped oregano (5 ml)
1/4 teaspoon salt (1.25 ml)
1/4 teaspoon freshly ground pepper (1.25 ml)
4 cups chopped fresh Italian tomatoes (944 ml)
1/2 cup bread crumbs (118 ml) mixed with 2
   tablespoons freshly grated Parmesan cheese (30 ml)

Preheat the oven to 350˚ (180˚C). Heat the oil in a
medium saucepan over medium heat and sauté
the onion, garlic, basil, oregano, salt, and pepper
until the onions are transparent—about 5
minutes. Add the tomatoes and mix well. Cover
and cook for 10 minutes.

Divide the tomato mixture among four small
ovenproof dishes. Sprinkle with the bread crumbs
and cheese and bake for 15 minutes.

Nutritional Profile per Serving

Calories—126; fat (gm)—3; saturated fat (gm)—1; calories
from fat—23%; cholesterol (mg)—3; sodium (mg)—290;
fiber (gm)—4; carbohydrates (gm)—22.

Braised Fennel in Spicy Tomato Juice

*Fennel is known also as finocchio, Florence
fennel, and sweet fennel. Eat it cooked or
raw—a mildly licorice-tasting alternative for
weight watchers who are tired of celery.
When buying fennel, make sure that the
stalks are straight, the bulb firm without
cracks or blemishes, and the leaves a fresh
green. If the stalks have little flowers on them,
it means that the plant was picked when it
was too old. Because fennel dries out quickly,
store bulbs and stalks separately in plastic
bags. In your refrigerator crisper, it should
stay fresh for from three to four days.*

Serves 4

2 medium fennel bulbs, 3½ inches (9 cm) in diameter
1 teaspoon fennel seeds (5 ml)
1 cup spicy tomato juice (236 ml), such as V-8
1/4 teaspoon arrowroot (1.25 ml) mixed with
   1 teaspoon water (5 ml) (slurry)

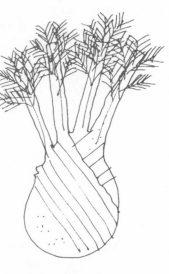

Preheat the oven to 350˚
(180˚C). Trim the stems
off of the fennel bulbs,
saving the feathery
leaves for garnish. Cut
into quarters.

Lay the fennel
quarters in a casserole
dish large enough to hold
them without stacking.
Sprinkle with fennel seeds.
Pour in the tomato juice,
cover, and bake for 15
minutes. Remove from the
oven and spoon the juice
over the fennel. Return to
the oven and bake for 15
minutes. Baste again and cook for 15 minutes.

Place the fennel pieces in a serving dish and
pour the sauce into a little pan. Bring to a boil,
then add the arrowroot slurry. It will thicken very
quickly.

Pour over the fennel bulbs and garnish with
the chopped fennel leaves.

Nutritional Profile per Serving

Calories—17; fat (gm)—0; saturated fat (gm)—0; calories
from fat—10%; cholesterol (mg)—0; sodium (mg)—238;
fiber (gm)—1; carbohydrates (gm)—4.

BROILED TOMATOES

Serves 4

4 large tomatoes
8 teaspoons fresh chopped dill (40 ml)
8 teaspoons bread crumbs (40 ml)
1/8 teaspoons salt (.6 ml)
1/8 teaspoon freshly ground black pepper (.6 ml)

Cut the tomatoes in half, place on a baking sheet, and sprinkle with dill, bread crumbs, salt, and pepper. Pop under the broiler for 5 minutes. Serve immediately.

Nutritional Profile per Serving
Calories—62; fat (gm)—1; saturated fat (gm)—0; calories from fat—13%; cholesterol (mg)—0; sodium (mg)—117; fiber (gm)—3; carbohydrates (gm)—13.

BOK CHOY STIR-FRY

This can be used as a side dish or a colorful nest for a fish fillet or chicken breast broiled with Oriental seasonings.

Bok choy is higher in calcium and vitamin A than other types of cabbage. An uncut head can keep up to 2 weeks in the refrigerator. After cutting, wrap the head tightly in plastic and finish using it in a couple of days to derive the maximum vitamin C benefit. Avoid buying precut cabbages: as soon as the leaves are cut, they begin to lose vitamin C.

Serves 4

1½ pounds bok choy (675 gm)
1 teaspoon light oil (5 ml) with a dash of toasted sesame oil

1 tablespoon sesame seeds (15 ml)
1/4 yellow onion, peeled and cut into long strips
1 large carrot, peeled and cut into matchsticks
1/2 red bell pepper, seeded and cut into 1-inch strips (2.5 cm)
1 tablespoon oyster sauce (15 ml)
1/2 teaspoon cornstarch (2.5 ml) mixed with 1/4 cup chicken broth (59 ml) (slurry)

Cut the bottom inch (2.5 cm) off the bok choy. Separate the stalks and wash carefully. Cut across the stalks diagonally in pieces about 1/2 inch thick (1.5 cm).

Heat a large wok over medium heat. When hot, add the oil and sesame seeds and cook until the seeds start turning brown—about 3 minutes. Add the onion, carrot, and pepper and cook until the onion just begins to wilt—about 3 minutes. Add the bok choy and cook until it's just slightly wilted—about 3 minutes. Stir in the oyster sauce and the cornstarch-and-chicken-broth slurry, and mix well. Heat to a boil and cook just until the sauce clears. Serve immediately.

Nutritional Profile per Serving
Calories—66; fat (gm)—3; saturated fat (gm)—0; calories from fat—40%; cholesterol (mg)—0; sodium (mg)—244; fiber (gm)—4; carbohydrates (gm)—8.

SPINACH-STUFFED RED PEPPERS

Serves 4

2 large red bell peppers, seeded and cut in half lengthwise
10 ounces spinach leaves (284 gm), washed
1/8 teaspoon salt (.6 ml)
1/8 teaspoon freshly ground black pepper (.6 ml)
1/4 teaspoon nutmeg (1.25 ml)

Place the red peppers in a steamer tray, cook for 3 minutes, and set aside.

Place the spinach in a steamer tray and cook for 3 minutes. Remove and chop the spinach coarsely, seasoning with the salt, pepper, and nutmeg.

Fill each pepper half with the chopped spinach, place in a steamer tray, and cook for 2 minutes. Remove, cut each pepper half in two, and serve.

Nutritional Profile per Serving

Calories—28; fat (gm)—0; saturated fat (gm)—0; calories from fat—8%; cholesterol (mg)—0; sodium (mg)—108; fiber (gm)—2; carbohydrates (gm)—6.

RED BEANS AND MUSHROOMS

Serves 4

2 cups canned low-sodium red kidney beans (472 ml)
1 teaspoon light oil (5 ml) with a dash of toasted sesame oil
1/2 cup sliced onion (118 ml)
2 garlic cloves, bashed, peeled, and chopped
1 cup chopped green bell pepper (236 ml)
12 medium white mushrooms, cut into quarters
1 tablespoon mild chili powder (15 ml)
1 teaspoon powdered cumin (5 ml)
1 teaspoon red wine vinegar (5 ml)
1/2 teaspoon arrowroot (2.5 ml) mixed with 1/4 cup bean liquid (59 ml) (slurry)

Drain the beans, reserving the liquid.

Heat the oil in a large skillet on medium and cook the onions until they just begin to wilt—about 5 minutes. Add the garlic, green pepper, mushrooms, chili powder, and cumin; cover and cook for 5 minutes. Add the beans, vinegar, and 1/4 cup of the reserved bean liquid; cover and just heat through. Add the arrowroot slurry and stir over the heat until the sauce clears.

Nutritional Profile per Serving

Calories—157; fat (gm)—2; saturated fat (gm)—0; calories from fat—11%; cholesterol (mg)—0; sodium (mg)—4; fiber (gm)—9; carbohydrates (gm)—28.

STEAMED BEETS AND GREENS

Beets have the highest sugar content of any vegetable but are still quite low in calories. Their sweet flavor seems quite unaffected by the canning process.

Choose small, young beets, about 1½ inches (4 cm) in diameter for the finest texture. Very large beets, over 2½ inches (6.5 cm) in diameter, can be tough with woody cores. Clip off the greens from beets before storing, leaving about 1 inch (2.5 cm) of stem. If you put the unwashed vegetables in a plastic bag in the refrigerator, they should last up to 3 weeks.

Serves 4

4 medium beets with greens, trimmed to leave 2 inches (5 cm) of root and 2 inches (5 cm) of green stem, greens reserved
1/2 cup orange juice (118 ml)
1/4 teaspoon salt (1.25 ml)

Place the beets in a steamer tray and steam for 25 minutes. Plunge into cold water and peel when cool enough to handle. Cut into quarters and set aside.

While the beets are steaming, trim the stems off the greens and wash well. Drain completely in a colander and then cut into thin strips.

Heat the orange juice in a large skillet on medium high, add the greens, cover, and cook for 4 minutes. Add the steamed beets and cook until the greens are tender and most of the liquid is gone—about 5 minutes. Season with salt.

Nutritional Profile per Serving

Calories—34; fat (gm)—0; saturated fat (gm)—0; calories from fat—3%; cholesterol (mg)—0; sodium (mg)—218; fiber (gm)—2; carbohydrates (gm)—8.

RED CABBAGE AND CHESTNUTS

Serves 4

8 cups shredded red cabbage (1.9 l)
3/4 cup beef stock (117 ml) (see page 142)
1 tablespoon apple-cider vinegar (15 ml)
1/4 teaspoon salt (1.25 ml)
1 tablespoon horseradish (15 ml)
1 teaspoon green peppercorns (5 ml)
3/4 cup chopped chestnuts (117 ml)

In a large saucepan, combine the cabbage, stock, vinegar, salt, horseradish, and peppercorns; bring to a boil, cover, reduce the heat, and simmer for 20 minutes.

Stir in the chestnuts and cook, uncovered, for 5 minutes—until the liquid disappears. The cabbage should have a crisp texture.

Nutritional Profile per Serving
Calories—67; fat (gm)—1; saturated fat (gm)—0; calories from fat—12%; cholesterol (mg)—0; sodium (mg)—176; fiber (gm)—5; carbohydrates (gm)—14.

MARINATED VEGETABLES

Easier to prepare than onions, milder than scallions, leeks also supply more vitamins and minerals than equal portions of either of their more popular cousins.

Leek bulbs should be a maximum of 1½ inches (4 cm) in diameter—larger than that, and the flesh could be tough. If stored in the refrigerator, they could last for up to a week. Wrapping them in plastic bags will help keep them moist and prevent their odor from spreading to other foods.

Serves 4

2 leeks, light green parts only, cut into matchsticks
1/2 red bell pepper, seeded and cut lengthwise into thin slices
1/2 green bell pepper, seeded and sliced lengthwise into thin slices
1/8 large red onion, thinly sliced
4 sprigs Italian (flat-leaf) parsley
1/4 cup rice-wine vinegar (59 ml)
1/4 teaspoon toasted sesame oil (1.25 ml)

In a large bowl, combine the leeks, peppers, onion, and parsley. Stir in the vinegar and sesame oil and let rest for 15 minutes. If you have a Vacuum Marinade Unit (see page 61), it takes 4 minutes.

Nutritional Profile per Serving
Calories—26; fat (gm)—0; saturated fat (gm)—0; calories from fat—15%; cholesterol (mg)—0; sodium (mg)—8; fiber (gm)—2; carbohydrates (gm)—6.

ROASTED SWEET PEPPERS

Serves 4

2 red bell peppers
2 yellow bell peppers
In fact, any combination of colors of peppers that are available will work well.

Cut the tops and bottoms off each pepper and reserve for later use. De-seed and slice lengthwise in quarters. This method of preparation allows the peppers to be roasted without turning and to "blister" evenly.

Arrange a cooking rack 2 inches (5 cm) from the broiling heat source. Place the peppers on a baking tray, skin-side-up, and broil until blistered and black—about 10 minutes. Remove from the oven and immediately transfer to a paper bag. Seal well and let the peppers "steam" for 20 minutes.

Remove the skins either by peeling or rinsing under cold running water (I prefer to peel them, because more of the flavor is retained that way.)

Nutritional Profile per Serving

Calories—20; fat (gm)—0; saturated fat (gm)—0; calories from fat—6%; cholesterol (mg)—0; sodium (mg)—1; fiber (gm)—1; carbohydrates (gm)—5.

FARMERS' MARKET SAUTÉ

Serves 6

2 medium eggplants
1 teaspoon light oil (5 ml) with a dash of toasted sesame oil
1 shallot, peeled and finely chopped
2 garlic cloves, bashed, peeled, and finely chopped
1/2 green bell pepper, seeded and finely chopped
1/2 red bell pepper, seeded and finely chopped
6 mushrooms, finely chopped
2 cups fresh tomatoes (472 ml), seeded and finely chopped (about 6)
2 tablespoons fresh chopped basil (30 ml)
1 teaspoon fresh chopped thyme (5 ml)
1 teaspoon fresh chopped oregano (5 ml)
1/4 cup chopped fresh parsley (59 ml)
2 tablespoons freshly squeezed lemon juice (30 ml)
1/4 teaspoon crushed hot chilies (1.25 ml)
1/8 teaspoon salt (.6 ml)
1/8 teaspoon freshly ground black pepper (.6 ml)

Preheat the oven to 350°F (180°C). Cut the eggplants in half, place on a baking tray skin-side-up, and bake for 35 minutes. When cool enough to handle, peel and cut into small cubes.

Heat the oil in a large skillet over medium-high heat and sauté the shallots and garlic until they just begin to turn golden. Add the peppers, mushrooms, and tomatoes and simmer for 10 minutes. Add the cooked eggplant and simmer for 15 minutes. Stir in basil, thyme, oregano, parsley, lemon juice, chilies, salt, and pepper and just heat through. Serve as a side dish or on thinly sliced toasted bread as an hors d'oeuvre.

Nutritional Profile per Serving

Calories—147; fat (gm)—5; saturated fat (gm)—1; calories from fat—29%; cholesterol (mg)—0; sodium (mg)—89; fiber (gm)—7; carbohydrates (gm)—27.

POACHED COBBLE CORN

Serves 4

1¾ cups fresh or canned vegetable broth (413 ml) (see page 144)
1/6 teaspoon saffron (.3 ml) (or less . . . be careful here, please)
4 ears fresh or frozen corn, husked (if using frozen, thaw first)
1½ teaspoons arrowroot (7.5 ml) mixed with 2 tablespoons vegetable broth (30 ml) (slurry)

In a saucepan just big enough to hold the ears of corn flat, pour the broth, bring to a boil, and reduce by half—about 10 minutes. Stir in the saffron and lay in the corn, cover, and cook for 2 minutes. Turn each ear over and cook for 2 minutes. Transfer the corn to a serving platter.

Stir the arrowroot slurry into the pan liquid. Bring to a boil and stir until it clears—less than 1 minute. Pour the sauce over the corn and serve.

Nutritional Profile per Serving

Calories—98; fat (gm)—1; saturated fat (gm)—0; calories from fat—13%; cholesterol (mg)—0; sodium (mg)—39; fiber (gm)—2; carbohydrates (gm)—21.

CORNY SUNCHOKES

Sunchokes, also called Jerusalem artichokes, are the roots of sunflowers. They are sweet, nutty, and crisp, and you can eat them raw or cooked in a wide variety of dishes. They are a great source of iron, almost as much as many meats, but with none of the fat.

Choose sunchokes that are clean and unblemished. They store well sealed in plastic bags for two weeks in the crisper.

Serves 4

1 pound sunchokes (450 gm), well scrubbed and cut into 1/4-inch-thick slices (.75 cm)
1 cup corn kernels (236 ml)
1/4 cup chopped red bell pepper (59 ml)
1 teaspoon cumin (5 ml)
1 tablespoon chopped fresh dill (15 ml)
1/2 cup vegetable stock (118 ml) (see page 144)

Garnish
1 tablespoon chopped fresh dill (15 ml)

Preheat the oven to 350°F (180°C). Combine all but the garnish ingredients in a 2-quart (1.9-l) casserole, cover, and bake for 30 minutes. Garnish with the tablespoon (15 ml) of dill.

Nutritional Profile per Serving
Calories—117; fat (gm)—0; saturated fat (gm)—0; calories from fat—3%; cholesterol (mg)—0; sodium (mg)—15; fiber (gm)—3; carbohydrates (gm)—27.

STEAMED SUMMER SQUASH

Serves 4

2 medium yellow summer squash, trimmed to equal lengths and cut in half lengthwise

4 medium green summer squash, trimmed to equal lengths and cut in half lengthwise
1/8 teaspoon freshly ground black pepper (.6 ml)
1/8 teaspoon salt (.6 ml)
1 teaspoon fresh chopped dill (5 ml) or 1/2 teaspoon dried dill (2.5 ml)

Place the yellow and green squash in a steamer tray, sprinkle with the seasonings, and steam for 4 minutes.

Nutritional Profile per Serving
Calories—42; fat (gm)—0; saturated fat (gm)—0; calories from fat—9%; cholesterol (mg)—0; sodium (mg)—76; fiber (gm)—4; carbohydrates (gm)—9.

GOLDEN PUREE

Serves 4

2 parsnips, peeled and coarsely chopped
2 carrots, peeled and coarsely chopped
2 turnips, peeled and coarsely chopped
1/4 teaspoon nutmeg (1.25 ml)
3 tablespoons fresh chopped parsley (45 ml)
1/4 teaspoon salt (1.25 ml)
1/4 teaspoon freshly ground black pepper (1.25 ml)

Place the parsnips in a steamer tray and steam for 6 minutes.

Add the carrots and turnips to the steamer tray and steam until soft—about 18 minutes. Transfer to a food processor or blender, add the nutmeg and parsley, and puree until combined, but not smooth like a sauce. Spoon into a bowl and keep warm until ready to serve.

Season with salt and pepper.

Nutritional Profile per Serving
Calories—69; fat (gm)—0; saturated fat (gm)—0; calories from fat—4%; cholesterol (mg)—0; sodium (mg)—191; fiber (gm)—4; carbohydrates (gm)—17.

WINTER VEGETABLE PUREE

Tired of bran cereal with bananas? Parsnips contain enough insoluble fiber to rival bran flakes and like bananas are powerfully packed with potassium (although the thought of eating parsnips at breakfast might seem a big daunting). Unlike carrots, parsnips contain no beta carotene; but they are a good source of vitamin C.

Serves 4

1/2 pound carrots (225 gm), peeled and coarsely chopped
1/2 pound parsnips (225 gm), peeled and coarsely chopped
1/2 pound turnips (225 gm), peeled and coarsely chopped
1/2 pound potatoes (225 gm), peeled and coarsely chopped
1/4 teaspoon dried summer savory (1.25 ml)
1 tablespoon freshly squeezed lemon juice (15 ml)
1/4 teaspoon nutmeg (1.25 ml)
1/4 teaspoon freshly ground black pepper (1.25 ml)

Place the carrots, parsnips, turnips, and potatoes in a Stack 'n Steam pot, scatter with the summer savory, and cook for 12 minutes. Remove all the vegetables except the parsnips and set aside. Replace the lid and continue steaming the parsnips for 6 minutes.

Transfer all the cooked vegetables to a large bowl, add the remaining ingredients, and mash vigorously.

Nutritional Profile per Serving
Calories—116; fat (gm)—0; saturated fat (gm)—0; calories from fat—3%; cholesterol (mg)—0; sodium (mg)—61; fiber (gm)—5; carbohydrates (gm)—28.

MASHED BUTTERNUT SQUASH WITH TARRAGON

Butternut squash is buttery brown and shaped like a long bell. Choose one with a hard rind that feels heavy for its size. The rind should also be dull-looking; a shiny skin indicates that the squash was picked early and hasn't attained its full, ripe sweetness.

Butternut squash is the anticancer orange bullet: an outstanding source of vitamin C, fiber, and beta carotene, it actually gives you more than a day's recommended allowance in a single serving. Extra value: Stored squash actually has more beta carotene and vitamin-A value than when it is freshly picked!

Serves 4

1 butternut squash
2 teaspoons dried tarragon (10 ml) or 4 teaspoons fresh (20 ml)
1/4 teaspoon salt (1.25 ml)
1/2 teaspoon freshly ground black pepper (2.5 ml)

Preheat the oven to 350°F (180°C). Cover a large baking sheet with aluminum foil. Cut the squash in half, remove the seeds, and place cut-side-down on the prepared baking sheet. Bake until it's very soft—about 1 hour. Let cool for 30 minutes before handling.

Spoon the pulp out into a bowl and mash well. Stir in the seasonings and transfer to a serving dish. Reheat before serving.

Nutritional Profile per Serving
Calories—69; fat (gm)—1; saturated fat (gm)—0; calories from fat—15%; cholesterol (mg)—0; sodium (mg)—135; fiber (gm)—5; carbohydrates (gm)—15.

SPAGHETTI SQUASH

Good news: *It's easy to choose a great spaghetti squash. There's no such thing as overmature or too big. The longer a spaghetti squash grows, the sweeter it'll be—just pick the size that suits your appetite. Then look for a smooth, clean rind that's not shiny. A glossy skin could mean it was picked too early and hasn't achieved its full sweetness.*

Serves 6

One 3½-pound or 1.5-kg spaghetti squash
1 tablespoon light oil (15 ml) with a dash of toasted sesame oil
3/4 cup finely chopped onion (177 ml)
1 teaspoon finely chopped garlic (5 ml)
1/2 large green bell pepper, finely chopped
1/2 large red bell pepper, finely chopped
1 teaspoon fresh chopped oregano (5 ml)
1/2 teaspoon dried basil (2.5 ml)
1/2 teaspoon dried summer savory (2.5 ml)
1/8 teaspoon salt (.6 ml)
1/4 teaspoon freshly ground black pepper (1.25 ml)
3 tablespoons freshly grated Parmesan cheese (45 ml)

Preheat the oven to 350°F (180°C). Pierce the skin of the squash with a fork in 3 or 4 places. Place on a baking sheet, bake for 35 minutes, then turn over and bake 35 minutes more. Cool on a rack. As soon as you can handle it, cut it in half lengthwise and let the inside cool. Remove the seeds and strands and discard the seeds.

While the squash is baking, heat the oil in a large skillet and sauté the vegetables and herbs together until they are tender—about 10 minutes. Transfer to a casserole dish. Add the reserved spaghetti squash strands, salt, pepper, and toss well. Sprinkle with the Parmesan cheese and bake for 15 minutes.

Nutritional Profile per Serving
Calories—142; fat (gm)—5; saturated fat (gm)—1; calories from fat—30%; cholesterol (mg)—2; sodium (mg)—95; fiber (gm)—7; carbohydrates (gm)—25.

BAKED SWEET POTATOES

Serves 4

4 medium sweet potatoes, well scrubbed
1/2 teaspoon freshly ground black pepper (2.5 ml)
2 tablespoons chopped fresh parsley (30 ml)
1 lemon

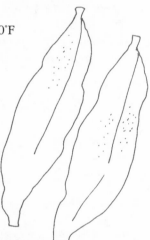

Preheat the oven to 350°F (180°C). Put the sweet potatoes on a baking sheet and bake for 40 minutes or until a fork easily punctures the skin. I like to split them lengthwise and dust with a little black pepper and parsley, and a squeeze of lemon juice.

Nutritional Profile per Serving
Calories—117; fat (gm)—0; saturated fat (gm)—0; calories from fat—1%; cholesterol (mg)—0; sodium (mg)—11; fiber (gm)—3; carbohydrates (gm)—28.

MASHED SWEET POTATOES

Serves 4

1½ pounds sweet potatoes (675 gm), perfectly dark orange
1½ pounds russet potatoes (675 gm)
1/4 cup finely chopped green onions (59 ml), white bulb only
1 orange, peeled and chopped
1/8 teaspoon ground cloves (.6 ml)
1/8 teaspoon freshly ground black pepper (.6 ml)

Preheat the oven to 350°F (180°C). Wash the sweet potatoes and russets well and prick several times with a fork. Bake in the preheated oven for 1 hour. Remove and let cool.

Peel off the skins and discard. In a large bowl, mash the sweet potato and russet potato meat, then stir in the green onions, orange, cloves, and pepper.

Just before serving, transfer the mashed potatoes to a small saucepan over low heat and heat through.

Nutritional Profile per Serving
Calories—223; fat (gm)—0; saturated fat (gm)—0; calories from fat—1%; cholesterol (mg)—0; sodium (mg)—17; fiber (gm)—5; carbohydrates (gm)—52.

STEAMED SWEET POTATOES AND THYME

Among the most nutritious members of the vegetable kingdom, sweet potatoes have an enzyme that converts most of its starches to sugars as it ripens—a sweetness that increases during storage and cooking.

Avoid sweet potatoes with spots that are shriveled, sunken, or black; even if you cut the blemishes away, they might have already given the entire potato a bitter flavor.

Keep sweet potatoes in a cool, dry place but never the refrigerator—which can give them an "off" taste. At room temperature, they should be used within a week of buying.

Serves 4

4 large sweet potatoes, peeled and cut into 1/2-inch slices
1 teaspoon fresh chopped thyme (5 ml)
1/4 teaspoon freshly ground black pepper (1.25 ml)

Put the sweet potatoes on a steamer tray, sprinkle with half of the thyme and half of the pepper, and steam for 22 minutes. Arrange the cooked potatoes on a serving dish and sprinkle with the remaining thyme and pepper.

Nutritional Profile per Serving
Calories—66; fat (gm)—0; saturated fat (gm)—0; calories from fat—3%; cholesterol (mg)—0; sodium (mg)—24; fiber (gm)—1; carbohydrates (gm)—16.

STEAMED CARROTS AND GREEN BEANS

Green beans are distinct from other edible beans by the stage of ripening at which we eat them. Green beans are picked when the seeds have just started to form. Nutritionally, they have more beta carotene and vitamin C than dried seeds, which are high in carbohydrates and protein.

Serves 4

2½ cups carrots (590 ml), cut into matchsticks
2½ cups fresh green beans (590 ml), trimmed and coarsely chopped
1/4 teaspoon salt (1.25 ml)
1/2 teaspoon chopped fresh dill (2.5 ml),

Place the carrots in a steamer tray and steam for 4 minutes. Add the green beans, salt, and dill. Steam 6 minutes longer.

Nutritional Profile per Serving
Calories—61; fat (gm)—0; saturated fat (gm)—0; calories from fat—4%; cholesterol (mg)—0; sodium (mg)—206; fiber (gm)—5; carbohydrates (gm)—14.

STEAMED CARROTS WITH SNOW PEAS

Serves 6

1/2 pound snow peas (225 gm)
1 pound peeled baby carrots (450 gm)
1 teaspoon finely chopped fresh gingerroot (5 ml)
1 teaspoon arrowroot (5 ml) mixed with 1/2 cup
    orange juice (118 ml) (slurry)

Pull the strings off the snow peas and cut any large ones in half.

Place the carrots and gingerroot in a steamer tray and steam for 10 minutes. Add the snow peas and steam for 1 minute. Remove from the heat and transfer to a serving dish.

In a small saucepan, bring the arrowroot slurry to a boil. Pour over the steamed vegetables and toss well.

Nutritional Profile per Serving
Calories—85; fat (gm)—0; saturated fat (gm)—0; calories from fat—3%; cholesterol (mg)—0; sodium (mg)—71; fiber (gm)—4; carbohydrates (gm)—19.

STEAMED ASPARAGUS

Keep fresh asparagus cold, with the stalk bottoms in a wet paper towel, in the refrigerator crisper. Asparagus is best used the day you buy it: it will lose almost half of its vitamin-C content within two days if kept at room temperature rather than refrigerated. It will also lose some of its sugars, and the stalks will become tougher and stringier.

Serves 4

1 pound asparagus (450 gm), preferably fine, thin stalks
1/8 teaspoon salt (.6 ml)

Soak the asparagus in water to remove any accumulated grit. Break off the tough, stringy ends, place in a steamer tray, sprinkle with the salt, cover, and steam for 5 minutes.

Nutritional Profile per Serving
Calories—13; fat (gm)—0; saturated fat (gm)—0; calories from fat—14%; cholesterol (mg)—0; sodium (mg)—69; fiber (gm)—1; carbohydrates (gm)—2.

GLOSS BROTH

I find this broth especially suited to asparagus. It's a fine way to add that butter/oil sheen, but without fat, to your favorite vegetable.

Serves 4

1/2 cup vegetable broth (118 ml) (see page 144)
1 teaspoon balsamic vinegar (5 ml)
1/8 teaspoon turmeric (.6 ml)
1 teaspoon arrowroot (5 ml) mixed with 1 tablespoon
    vegetable broth (15 ml) (slurry)

In a small saucepan, heat the broth, vinegar, and turmeric until boiling. Add the arrowroot slurry and stir until thickened—less than 1 minute.

Nutritional Profile per Serving
Calories—6; fat (gm)—0; saturated fat (gm)—0; calories from fat—19%; cholesterol (mg)—0; sodium (mg)—8; fiber (gm)—0; carbohydrates (gm)—1.

GINGERED BROCCIFLOWER

This is not gene splicing. It's good old-fashioned cross-cultivation, in which cauliflower is crossed with broccoli. I simply wish that they had found a more lasting name for this Star Trek vegetable!

Serves 4

1/2 cup vegetable or chicken broth (118 ml) (see pages 144, 141)
1 tablespoon low-sodium soy sauce (15 ml)
1 teaspoon honey (5 ml)
1 tablespoon grated fresh ginger (15 ml)
1/2 teaspoon toasted sesame oil (2.5 ml)
1 head brocciflower or cauliflower, stems trimmed and cut into florets
1 carrot, peeled and cut thinly on the diagonal
1 teaspoon arrowroot (5 ml) mixed with 1/4 cup broth (59 ml) (slurry)

In a small bowl, mix the broth, soy sauce, honey and ginger.

Heat a large wok or skillet over medium heat. When it's hot, add the oil, brocciflower, and carrot and stir-fry for 2 minutes. Add the liquid mixture, cover, and cook for 3 minutes, or until just crisp-tender. Add the arrowroot slurry and stir until the liquid thickens and clears—less than 1 minute. Serve immediately.

Nutritional Profile per Serving
Calories—50; fat (gm)—1; saturated fat (gm)—0; calories from fat—17%; cholesterol (mg)—0; sodium (mg)—193; fiber (gm)—2; carbohydrates (gm)—9.

STEAMED BROCCOLI

Serves 4

1 bunch (1½ pounds or 675 gm) broccoli
1/8 teaspoon salt (.6 ml)
1 teaspoon lemon juice (5 ml)

Cut off 2 inches (5 cm) of the thick broccoli stalks. Peel the stalks up to the florets. Cut off the peeled stalks 1 inch (2.5 cm) below where the florets begin to branch out. Cut the stalks into 1/4-inch (.75-cm) diagonal slices. Break apart the florets, leaving some stem on each.

Place the sliced stalks and florets in a steamer tray, sprinkle with salt and lemon juice, and steam for 2½ minutes.

Nutritional Profile per Serving
Calories—28; fat (gm)—0; saturated fat (gm)—0; calories from fat—4%; cholesterol (mg)—0; sodium (mg)—93; fiber (gm)—3; carbohydrates (gm)—5.

Microwave Method
Prepare the same as for Steamed Broccoli but put the sliced stalks and florets into a microwave-proof pie plate with the salt. Cover with wax paper and microwave on high for 2 minutes. Stir; test for tenderness. Then, if necessary, cook one more minute. Sprinkle with lemon juice and serve immediately.

Nutritional Profile per Serving
Calories—28; fat (gm)—1; saturated fat (gm)—0; calories from fat—4%; cholesterol (mg)—0; sodium (mg)—93; fiber (gm)—3; carbohydrates (gm)—5.

SAUCE FOR BROCCOLI OR CAULIFLOWER

For one 1½-pound bunch of broccoli (675 gm) or one 1½-pound head of cauliflower (565 gm).

Serves 4

1/4 cup fat-free cream cheese (59 ml)
1 tablespoon chopped fresh parsley (15 ml), with stalks
1 tablespoon chopped fresh chives or green onion tops (15 ml)
1/2 teaspoon maple syrup (2.5 ml)
1/8 teaspoon freshly ground black pepper (.6 ml)
1 tablespoon lemon juice (15 ml)
1/2 cup strained yogurt (118 ml) (see page 141)

Put all the ingredients except the yogurt into a blender and process until the parsley and chives are little green specks—about 2 minutes. Stir in the yogurt by hand gently in order to preserve the "mouthfeel." Spoon over crisp, tender steamed broccoli or cauliflower.

Nutritional Profile per Serving

Calories—75; fat (gm)—0; saturated fat (gm)—0; calories from fat—6%; cholesterol (mg)—2; sodium (mg)—306; fiber (gm)—1; carbohydrates (gm)—10.

STEAMED BRUSSELS SPROUTS

Serves 4

1 pound Brussels sprouts (450 gm)
1/4 teaspoon salt (1.25 ml)
1/4 teaspoon freshly ground black pepper (1.25 ml)

Cut the bottom 1/8 inch (.5 cm) off the Brussels sprouts and remove any tough or discolored outside leaves. Cut the stalks with a deep X. In a

steamer tray, cook until just tender—about 10 minutes. Season with salt and pepper.

Nutritional Profile per Serving

Calories—41; fat (gm)—0; saturated fat (gm)—0; calories from fat—8%; cholesterol (mg)—0; sodium (mg)—156; fiber (gm)—5; carbohydrates (gm)—8.

STEAMED CABBAGE WEDGES

Serves 4

1/2 medium head cabbage, quartered
1/4 teaspoon fresh chopped dill (1.25 ml)
1 tablespoon freshly grated Parmesan cheese (15 ml)

Place the cabbage wedges on a steamer tray, sprinkle with the dill, cover, and steam for 5 minutes.

Remove from the heat, dust with the Parmesan cheese, and serve.

Nutritional Profile per Serving

Calories—29; fat (gm)—1; saturated fat (gm)—0; calories from fat—20%; cholesterol (mg)—1; sodium (mg)—44; fiber (gm)—2; carbohydrates (gm)—5.

APPLEY BRUSSELS SPROUTS

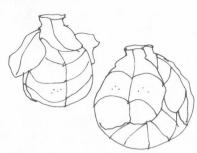

Serves 4

1 pound Brussels sprouts (450 gm)
1 cup unsweetened apple juice (236 ml)
1½ teaspoons arrowroot (7.5 ml) mixed with 1 tablespoon water (15 ml) (slurry)

Cut the bottom 1/8 inch (.5 cm) off the Brussels sprouts and remove any tough or discolored outside leaves. Cut the stalks with a deep X. In a small saucepan, bring the sprouts and apple juice to a boil, cover, turn the heat to medium, and cook for 10 minutes. Use a slotted spoon to transfer the cooked sprouts to a serving dish.

Remove the cooking liquid from the heat, stir in the arrowroot slurry, return to the heat, and stir until it clears—about 1 minute. Pour over the cooked sprouts and serve.

Nutritional Profile per Serving

Calories—74; fat (gm)—0; saturated fat (gm)—0; calories from fat—5%; cholesterol (mg)—0; sodium (mg)—24; fiber (gm)—5; carbohydrates (gm)—16.

STIR-STEAMED CABBAGE

Serves 4

1/4 cup chicken stock (59 ml) (see page 143)
2 cups finely sliced Chinese cabbage (472 ml)
2 cups finely sliced red cabbage (472 ml)
1⅔ cups enokitake mushrooms (393 ml)

Heat the chicken stock in a large skillet on high. Add the cabbages and the mushrooms and heat through, about 2–4 minutes. Serve immediately to preserve the crunchy texture.

Nutritional Profile per Serving

Calories—30; fat (gm)—1; saturated fat (gm)—0; calories from fat—15%; cholesterol (mg)—0; sodium (mg)—23; fiber (gm)—3; carbohydrates (gm)—6.

BRAISED CELERY HEARTS

I'm not a microwave expert, and I'm old enough to be worried that I've got a poor attitude to the device. But I'm trying it out,

slowly, on special foods that seem to respond well. Celery is one of them, so here goes.

Serves 4

2 celery hearts
2 cups stock (472 ml) (fish, chicken, beef, or vegetable; see pages 141–144)

Cut the celery hearts in two lengthwise. Place these pieces in a microwave-proof pan, add the stock, cover, and cook on high in the microwave for 10 minutes. Turn the celery over, rotate 45 degrees, and cook for another 5 minutes.

Nutritional Profile per Serving

Calories—15; fat (gm)—0; saturated fat (gm)—0; calories from fat—28%; cholesterol (mg)—0; sodium (mg)—45; fiber (gm)—1; carbohydrates (gm)—1.

STEAMED COLLARD GREENS

Serves 4

One 1-pound (450-gm) bunch of collard greens, heavy stalks trimmed
4 tablespoons dried cranberries (60 ml)
1/8 teaspoon salt (.6 ml)
1/8 teaspoon freshly ground black pepper (.6 ml)

Roll the collard green leaves into tight cylinders and slice into 1/4-inch (.75-cm) strips. Transfer to a steamer tray, and sprinkle with the cranberries, salt, and pepper. Steam for exactly 4 minutes.

Nutritional Profile per Serving

Calories—73; fat (gm)—0; saturated fat (gm)—0; calories from fat—3%; cholesterol (mg)—0; sodium (mg)—87; fiber (gm)—2; carbohydrates (gm)—18.

MIXED GREENS

Serves 4

3 cups collard greens (708 ml), washed, thick stems removed
2 cups kale (472 ml), washed, thick stems removed
2 cups loosely packed mustard greens (472 ml), washed, thick stems removed
1/4 teaspoon salt (1.25 ml)
1/4 teaspoon freshly ground black pepper (1.25 ml)
1 tablespoon mild vinegar (15 ml)

Place the greens in a steamer tray, sprinkle with salt and pepper, and steam, covered, for 4 minutes. Sprinkle vinegar over the top before serving.

Nutritional Profile per Serving

Calories—24; fat (gm)—0; saturated fat (gm)—0; calories from fat—7%; cholesterol (mg)—0; sodium (mg)—19; fiber (gm)—2; carbohydrates (gm)—5.

MIXED GREENS, SOUTHERN STYLE

Sometimes, when the fresh leafy greens are not so fresh, it's better to dig out the frozen packs. I keep a full range of frozen greens on hand so that this special vegetable combination is possible at the drop of a snow shovel . . . so to speak.

Serves 6

1 teaspoon light oil (5 ml) with a dash of toasted sesame oil
1 onion, peeled and sliced
2 ounces Canadian bacon (57 gm), finely diced
One 10-ounce or 284-gm box frozen chopped collard greens

One 10-ounce or 284-gm box frozen chopped mustard greens
One 10-ounce or 284-gm box frozen chopped turnip greens
2 small dried chili peppers (optional)
1 cup ham hock stock (236 ml) (see page 143)

Heat the oil in a large heavy-bottomed saucepan and sauté the onion over medium heat until it just begins to wilt—about 3 minutes. Add the bacon and continue cooking until the onions are translucent—about 3 minutes. Add the frozen greens and chili peppers (if you like things zingy) and ham stock, cover, and cook for 10 minutes. Stir, making sure to break up any icy chunks of greens, cover, and cook for 10 minutes. Stir again and cook for 10 minutes.

Nutritional Profile per Serving

Calories—90; fat (gm)—3; saturated fat (gm)—1; calories from fat—30%; cholesterol (mg)—7; sodium (mg)—239; fiber (gm)—5; carbohydrates (gm)—12.

GLAZED GREEN BEANS

Serves 4

2 cups stock (472 ml) (choose your favorite, see pages 141–144)
4 sprigs fresh dill
1 pound fresh green beans (450 gm), topped and tailed
1/8 teaspoon nutmeg (.6 ml)
1/8 teaspoon salt (.6 ml)
1/8 teaspoon freshly ground black pepper (.6 ml)
1 teaspoon arrowroot (5 ml) mixed with
   1 tablespoon cold stock or water (15 ml) (slurry)
1 teaspoon fresh finely chopped dill (5 ml)

Pour the stock into a large skillet, add the dill, bring to a boil, and reduce to 1/2 cup (118 ml) liquid—about 10 minutes. Remove the dill sprigs and discard.

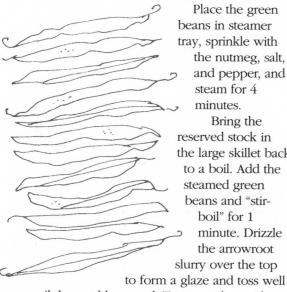

Place the green beans in steamer tray, sprinkle with the nutmeg, salt, and pepper, and steam for 4 minutes.

Bring the reserved stock in the large skillet back to a boil. Add the steamed green beans and "stir-boil" for 1 minute. Drizzle the arrowroot slurry over the top to form a glaze and toss well until thoroughly coated. To serve, dust with chopped dill.

Nutritional Profile per Serving

Calories—39; fat (gm)—1; saturated fat (gm)—0; calories from fat—15%; cholesterol (mg)—0; sodium (mg)—108; fiber (gm)—3; carbohydrates (gm)—7.

STEAMED KALE

Kale is too often cooked until it's pale, a kind of muddy army-fatigue green. I literally dump it in a vigorous steam for only 4 minutes. When properly prepared, with its radiant color and crispness respected, kale is one of my all-time favorites.

Serves 4

One 1-pound (450-gm) bunch of kale
1/8 teaspoon salt (.6 ml)
1/8 teaspoon freshly ground black pepper (.6 ml)

Trim the stalks from the kale, wash carefully, and cut into thin strips. Place the kale in a steamer tray, cover, and steam for 4 minutes. Season with salt and pepper.

Nutritional Profile per Serving

Calories—21; fat (gm)—0; saturated fat (gm)—0; calories from fat—6%; cholesterol (mg)—0; sodium (mg)—79; fiber (gm)—2; carbohydrates (gm)—5.

STEAMED LEEKS

Serves 4

4 large leeks, about 6 inches (15 cm) of white stalk
1 teaspoon light oil (5 ml) with a dash of toasted sesame oil
One 2-inch (5-cm) piece of fresh gingerroot, bruised and finely sliced
4 cups water (944 ml)

Cut each leek into two 3-inch (8-cm) pieces, separating the white bulbs.

Put the oil into the steamer base and heat. Add gingerroot and sauté for 2 minutes to heighten flavor. Add water to a depth of 2 inches (5 cm). Boil. Fit the steamer rack, add the 8 pieces of leek, cover, and steam for 12 minutes. Put the white leek halves in a steamer platform, cover, and steam for 12 minutes.

Nutritional Profile per Serving

Calories—32; fat (gm)—0; saturated fat (gm)—0; calories from fat—5%; cholesterol (mg)—0; sodium (mg)—5; fiber (gm)—3; carbohydrates (gm)—7.

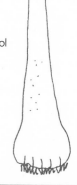

MUSHROOMS AND LEEKS

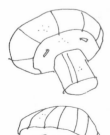

Invaluable for their meaty texture without meat's high fat content, mushrooms also boast a good deal of protein, B vitamins, copper, and other minerals. Cooked fresh mushrooms have almost three times the niacin and potassium, twice the iron, and fifteen times the riboflavin of canned mushrooms. Canned mushrooms can also contain up to fifteen times more sodium!

Serves 4

2 leeks, root ends trimmed and
    discarded
1 teaspoon light oil (5 ml) with a
    dash of toasted sesame oil
12 ounces white mushrooms (340 gm), quartered
1 teaspoon fresh, coarsely chopped dill (5 ml), or 1/2
    teaspoon dried dill weed (2.5 ml)
1/8 teaspoon cayenne pepper (.6 ml)
2 tablespoons freshly squeezed lemon juice (30 ml)

Divide the leeks into two parts: the light green stem and the dark top. Slice the light green pieces into long, fine matchsticks (a hand-held mandolin works very well for this task) and set aside. Save the dark green tops for other uses.

Heat the oil in a large skillet over medium heat; add the leeks, mushrooms, dill, and cayenne pepper; and cook for 4 minutes. Stir in the lemon juice and mix well.

Nutritional Profile per Serving
Calories—45; fat (gm)—2; saturated fat (gm)—0; calories from fat—33%; cholesterol (mg)—0; sodium (mg)—5; fiber (gm)—3; carbohydrates (gm)—7.

• Select mushrooms that are clean, plump, and free of bruises. Check the area where the cap meets the stem very closely. This "veil" area will often be wide for older mushrooms: a sign of rich, mature flavor. However, keep in mind that older mushrooms will also have a shorter storage life.

• Mushrooms are very sensitive to moisture: too much and they decay quickly; too little and they dry out. Store mushrooms on the refrigerator shelf, not in the crisper, which tends to be more humid. They will keep for a few days, packed loosely in a paper bag or covered lightly in a shallow glass dish.

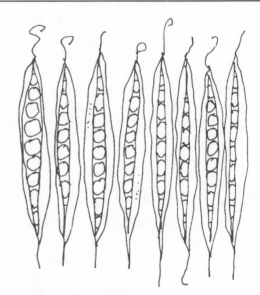

MINTY PEAS

Technically, your friendly green garden pea is not a vegetable at all, but a fleshy seed. Just 3/4 cup of these powerful protein packets—a mere 100 calories—contains more protein than a whole egg, but less than a gram of fat.

Of all the fresh herbs to grow in a home garden, mint may be the easiest to propagate—almost too easy. Many varieties will take root and spread so quickly that they'll occupy the whole garden, so keep your eye on it. Use mint liberally, especially in your summer salads and drinks.

Serves 4

1/4 cup water (59 ml)
2 cups fresh or frozen peas (472 ml)
1/8 teaspoon salt (.6 ml)
1 small sprig of fresh mint
1 teaspoon granulated sugar (5 ml)

In a medium saucepan, bring the water to a boil and simmer the peas, salt, mint, and sugar until the peas are tender—about 5 minutes for fresh, 3 minutes for frozen.

Nutritional Profile per Serving
Calories—53; fat (gm)—0; saturated fat (gm)—0; calories from fat—3%; cholesterol (mg)—0; sodium (mg)—122; fiber (gm)—3; carbohydrates (gm)—10.

STEAMED SWISS CHARD

Swiss chard is actually the top of a variety of beet grown for its leaves not its root. It's valued for the texture of its leaves and stalks; indeed, in European countries, the stalks are considered chard's best part.

A good portion of the nutritional value in greens is released into their cooking liquid, so save it and whenever possible add it to soups, stews, casseroles, and sauces.

Store Swiss chard, and all greens, unwashed, in damp paper towels, placed within plastic bags. They should last well in the refrigerator crisper for three to five days.

Serves 6

3 pounds Swiss chard (1.4 kg)
1/8 teaspoon salt (.6 ml)
1/4 teaspoon freshly ground black pepper (1.25 ml)
1 tablespoon balsamic vinegar (15 ml)

Rinse the chard well. Trim off the red stems; finely chop and place in a steamer tray. Add the whole chard leaves, salt, and pepper; cover and steam for 4 minutes. Sprinkle with balsamic vinegar and serve.

Nutritional Profile per Serving
Calories—57; fat (gm)—0; saturated fat (gm)—0; calories from fat—4%; cholesterol (mg)—0; sodium (mg)—510; fiber (gm)—7; carbohydrates (gm)—12.

ZUCCHINI AND SUGAR SNAPS

Serves 4

1/2 pound sugar snap peas (225 gm)
1/4 cup vegetable stock (59 ml) (see page 144)
1 tablespoon finely chopped fresh basil (15 ml)
2 medium zucchini, cut into matchsticks
1 teaspoon finely chopped fresh mint (5 ml)

Trim the stem ends of the sugar snaps with your thumbnail, pulling the string that grows along the back off with it. Cut in half on the diagonal.

Pour the vegetable stock into a wok or high-sided skillet, add the basil, and bring to a boil. Add the peas and "stir-steam" until they brighten up and are hot all the way through—about 3 minutes. Add the zucchini and continue to stir-steam until just heated through—about 2 minutes. Sprinkle in the mint, toss, and serve.

Nutritional Profile per Serving
Calories—38; fat (gm)—0; saturated fat (gm)—0; calories from fat—6%; cholesterol (mg)—0; sodium (mg)—8; fiber (gm)—2; carbohydrates (gm)—7.

ZUCCHINI CAPELLINI

Serves 4

2 medium zucchini squash, halved and hollowed out
(seeds removed) with a spoon
2 medium yellow crookneck squash, seeds removed
1 teaspoon light oil (5 ml) with a dash of toasted
sesame oil
2 cloves garlic, bashed, peeled, and finely chopped
24 large fresh basil leaves, cut into thin strips
4 teaspoons freshly grated Parmesan cheese (20 ml)

Slice the squash lengthwise on a mandolin to
make long, very thin, pastalike threads.

Heat the oil in a wok on medium heat and
cook the garlic until it just starts turning brown.
Add the squash and basil, stir well, and stir-fry
until just heated through—about 2 minutes.
Transfer to a serving dish and sprinkle with the
Parmesan cheese.

Nutritional Profile per Serving

Calories—70; fat (gm)—2; saturated fat (gm)—1; calories
from fat—30%; cholesterol (mg)—1; sodium (mg)—36;
fiber (gm)—4; carbohydrates (gm)—12.

BAKED FALAFEL

*This is one of those addictive, eat-it-hot-on-the-
run foods. A favorite of Middle Eastern
cooking, falafel is made from garbanzo beans,
highly seasoned, bound with egg, coated with
crumbs, and deep-fried. This lower-fat version,
which is baked instead, has a different
"mouthfeel" but the same great taste.*

Serves 4

15 ounces canned low-sodium garbanzo beans (425
gm), well rinsed
1/4 cup fresh coarsely chopped parsley sprigs (59 ml),
including stems

3 green onions, white and green parts, sliced
2 teaspoons chopped garlic (10 ml)
1/4 teaspoon freshly ground black pepper (1.25 ml)
1 teaspoon cumin (5 ml)
2 tablespoons freshly squeezed lemon juice (30 ml)
1/4 cup liquid egg substitute (59 ml)
3/4 cup yellow bread crumbs (177 ml) (see page 116)
1/4 teaspoon salt (1.25 ml)

Preheat the oven to 350°F (180°C). In a large food
processor, puree all the ingredients except the
bread crumbs until almost smooth.

Spread the bread crumbs on a large plate.
Drop generous, rounded tablespoons of the
mixture into the bread crumbs and roll until
completely covered. Place on a nonstick baking
sheet and bake for 5 minutes to just warm
through. Makes 16 small falafel.

Nutritional Profile per Serving

Calories—263; fat (gm)—4; saturated fat (gm)—1; calories
from fat—13%; cholesterol (mg)—1; sodium (mg)—314;
fiber (gm)—7; carbohydrates (gm)—45

STEAMED SPINACH

Serves 4

20 ounces spinach leaves (567 gm), well rinsed, stalks
removed
1/8 teaspoon salt (.6 ml)
1/4 teaspoon nutmeg (1.25 ml)
1/4 teaspoon freshly ground white pepper (1.25 ml)

On a cutting board, roll the spinach leaves
carefully in small bundles and slice finely (1/4
inch or .75 cm). Cook in a steamer tray, covered,
for 4 minutes. Season with salt, nutmeg, and
white pepper.

Nutritional Profile per Serving

Calories—20; fat (gm)—0; saturated fat (gm)—0; calories
from fat—9%; cholesterol (mg)—0; sodium (mg)—125;
fiber (gm)—1; carbohydrates (gm)—4.

PEARLY MUSHROOMS

Serves 4

1 teaspoon light oil (5 ml) with a dash of toasted sesame oil
10 ounces pearl onions (284 gm), peeled* (if possible, the same size as the mushrooms)
1/4 teaspoon dill seed (1.25 ml)
1/2 teaspoon caraway seed (2.5 ml)
1/2 teaspoon dried thyme (2.5 ml)
2 cups white button mushrooms (472 ml)
3/4 cup beef stock (117 ml) (see page 142)
1/2 teaspoon Dijon mustard (2.5 ml)
1 tablespoon balsamic vinegar (15 ml)
1 teaspoon arrowroot (5 ml) mixed with 1/4 cup beef stock (59 ml) (slurry)

Heat the oil in a large skillet on medium and cook the onions, dill, caraway, and thyme for 5 minutes, shaking the pan every once in a while to turn the onions. Add the mushrooms, cover, and cook for 3 minutes. Pour in the beef stock, mustard, and vinegar, bring to a boil, reduce the heat, and simmer gently until the onions are tender—about 15 minutes.

Add the arrowroot slurry and stir until thickened—less than 1 minute. Serve immediately.

Nutritional Profile per Serving
Calories—71; fat (gm)—2; saturated fat (gm)—0; calories from fat—27%; cholesterol (mg)—0; sodium (mg)—26; fiber (gm)—3; carbohydrates (gm)—12.

*An easy way to peel pearl onions is to pour boiling water over them and let them sit in the water for 3 minutes. Rinse with cold water to cool. Cut off the root (hairy) end and squeeze on the stem end. The "pearl" will pop right out.

STEAMED CAULIFLOWER

Cauliflower contains plant acids that form sulfurous gases when cooked—smells that intensify the longer it's cooked. The solution is quick cooking that not only prevents the smell but also provides a clean, crisp texture, and less nutritional loss.

Serves 4

1 medium head of cauliflower
1 teaspoon paprika (5 ml)
1 tablespoon finely chopped fresh parsley (15 ml)

Break the head apart into similar-sized florets (judicious cutting may help in this process). Place the florets in a steamer tray and steam for 6 minutes. Sprinkle with paprika and parsley before serving.

Nutritional Profile per Serving
Calories—27; fat (gm)—0; saturated fat (gm)—0; calories from fat—11%; cholesterol (mg)—0; sodium (mg)—26; fiber (gm)—2; carbohydrates (gm)—5.

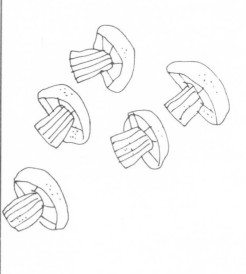

Yellow Bread Crumbs

Makes 1 generous cup (236 ml)

Preheat the oven to 350°F (180°C). In a medium bowl, mix 1½ cups fresh bread crumbs (354 ml) and 1 teaspoon turmeric (5 ml). Spread out in a 9-by-13-inch (23-by-33-cm) baking pan and bake for 5 minutes.

Nutritional Profile per Serving

Calories—31; fat (gm)—0; saturated fat (gm)—0; calories from fat—11%; cholesterol (mg)—0; sodium (mg)—68; fiber (gm)—1; carbohydrates (gm)—6.

Steamed Parsnips

Serves 4

1 pound parsnips (450 gm), trimmed, peeled, and cut into 1-inch pieces (2.5 cm)
1 teaspoon dried summer savory (5 ml) or 2 teaspoons fresh (10 ml)
1/8 teaspoon salt (.6 ml)

Place the parsnips in a steamer tray, sprinkle with the savory and salt, and steam until tender—about 18 minutes.

Nutritional Profile per Serving

Calories—82; fat (gm)—0; saturated fat (gm)—0; calories from fat—3%; cholesterol (mg)—0; sodium (mg)—77; fiber (gm)—4; carbohydrates (gm)—20.

Glazed Potatoes

2 cups fish stock (or chicken stock; see pages 141, 143) (472 ml)
One 3-inch branch fresh rosemary (7.5 cm)
1 pound tiny red potatoes, cut in halves, or quarters if largish (450 gm)
1/2 teaspoon cornstarch mixed with 1 tablespoon cold stock or water (2.5 ml) (slurry)
1/8 teaspoon each salt and pepper (.6 ml)

Pour fish stock into a 10-inch sauté pan. Add the rosemary. Bring to a boil and reduce to 1/2 cup liquid (118 ml). Remove the rosemary.

Place potatoes in steamer tray. Season with salt and pepper. Steam for 20 minutes.

Remove potatoes from steamer and "sauté" (stir-boil) in fish stock. Drizzle cornstarch slurry over top to form a glaze. Toss well to coat thoroughly.

Nutritional Profile per Serving

Calories—112; fat (gm)—1; saturated fat (gm)—0; calories from fat—4%; cholesterol (mg)—105; sodium (mg)—0; fiber (gm)—2; carbohydrates (gm)—24.

Green Mashed Potatoes

Serves 4

4 large russet potatoes, peeled and cut into quarters
1/2 cup nonfat buttermilk (118 ml)
1/4 teaspoon white pepper (1.25 ml)
1/8 teaspoon salt (.6 ml)
1/4 cup finely chopped cilantro (59 ml) mixed with 1/8 cup fresh finely chopped parsley leaves (30 ml)

Boil the potatoes for 30 minutes, drain, and return to the same pot over low heat. Put a kitchen towel over the top of the pot and let them dry out for 15 minutes.

In a medium-sized bowl, mash together the boiled potatoes, buttermilk, pepper, and salt. Stir in the cilantro and parsley leaves and mix well.

Nutritional Profile per Serving

Calories—173; fat (gm)—1; saturated fat (gm)—0; calories from fat—3%; cholesterol (mg)—0; sodium (mg)—111; fiber (gm)—3; carbohydrates (gm)—39.

Steamed Potato Slices

Serves 4

2 large russet potatoes, sliced in 1/4-inch rounds (.75 cm)
1/4 teaspoon freshly ground black pepper (1.25 ml)
1/8 teaspoon salt (.6 ml)

Place the potato slices in first level of the steamer, sprinkle with the pepper and salt, and steam for 8 minutes.

Nutritional Profile per Serving

Calories—79; fat (gm)—0; saturated fat (gm)—0; calories from fat—1%; cholesterol (mg)—0; sodium (mg)—71; fiber (gm)—1; carbohydrates (gm)—18.

Whipped Potatoes

Serves 4

2¼ pounds russet potatoes (1 kg), peeled, boiled, and mashed
1½ cups buttermilk (354 ml)
1/8 teaspoon nutmeg (.6 ml)
1/4 teaspoon white pepper (1.25 ml)
1/4 teaspoon salt (1.25 ml)

Garnish
Fresh chopped parsley
Paprika

In a large saucepan, whip together the mashed potatoes, buttermilk, nutmeg, pepper, and salt and heat slowly to your desired temperature. Transfer to a serving dish and garnish with the parsley and paprika.

Nutritional Profile per Serving

Calories—236; fat (gm)—1; saturated fat (gm)—1; calories from fat—4%; cholesterol (mg)—3; sodium (mg)—241; fiber (gm)—3; carbohydrates (gm)—51.

Potato Casserole

Serves 4

1 teaspoon light olive oil (5 ml) with a dash of toasted sesame oil
1 large onion, peeled and sliced
1 clove garlic, bashed, peeled, and chopped
1 tablespoon fresh finely chopped thyme (15 ml)
1/4 teaspoon freshly ground black pepper (1.25 ml)
1/2 teaspoon salt (2.5 ml)
4 large potatoes, sliced thinly
1/2 cup beef stock (118 ml) (see page 142)

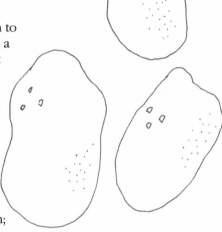

Preheat the oven to 350°F (180°C). In a large skillet, heat the oil and sauté the onion and garlic until the onion is slightly soft— about 3 minutes. Stir in the thyme, pepper, and salt; heat through; and set aside.

Layer the bottom of an 8-by-8-inch (20-by-20-cm) baking pan with a quarter of the potato slices. Spoon a third of the sautéed onion and garlic on top. Continue the layering process, finishing with a neat layer of potatoes on top. Pour the beef stock over the potatoes and bake for 50 minutes.

Nutritional Profile per Serving

Calories—161; fat (gm)—2; saturated fat (gm)—0; calories from fat—9%; cholesterol (mg)—0; sodium (mg)—282; fiber (gm)—3; carbohydrates (gm)—34.

KERR JO'S FRENCH FRIES

The average bag of 30 french fries sports almost 400 calories, and 23 grams of fat.

Serves 4

2 tablespoons light oil (30 ml) with a dash of toasted
  sesame oil
2 large russet potatoes, each sliced lengthwise into 9
  even sticks
1/2 teaspoon salt (2.5 ml)

Preheat the oven to 500°F (260°C). In a large skillet, heat the oil and fry the potato sticks until brown on all sides—about 13 minutes. Transfer the potatoes to a roaster pan and bake for 10 minutes. Remove from oven and sprinkle with the salt.

Nutritional Profile per Serving
Calories—161; fat (gm)—7; saturated fat (gm)—1; calories from fat—39%; cholesterol (mg)—0; sodium (mg)—274; fiber (gm)—2; carbohydrates (gm)—23.

Desserts

BAKED APPLES

Serves 4

4 Granny Smith apples
8 pitted dates, finely chopped
8 dried apricots, finely chopped
4 teaspoons brown sugar (20 ml)
1 teaspoon cinnamon (5 ml)
3/4 cup boiling apple juice (177 ml)
1/2 cup strained yogurt (118 ml) (see page 141)

Preheat the oven to 350°F (180°C). Cut a cone-shaped hole in the top of each apple and dig out the core.

In a small bowl, combine the dates, apricots, brown sugar, and cinnamon. Spoon the filling into the apples and place in an 8-by-8-inch (20-by-20-cm) baking dish. Pour in the boiling apple juice and bake for 45 minutes. Remove from the oven.

Transfer the baked apples to serving dishes. Drain the cooking juices into a small bowl and mix with the yogurt. Drizzle on top of the apples and serve.

Nutritional Profile per Serving

Calories—217; fat (gm)—1; saturated fat (gm)—0; calories from fat—3%; cholesterol (mg)—1; sodium (mg)—51; fiber (gm)—4; carbohydrates (gm)—52.

• Apples are not the nutritional star of this dish: they do supply good fiber; but dried apricots win hands down as a supplier of beta carotene and niacin.
• Granny Smith apples will make a difference in the flavor of your cooking: a complex tart-sweet balance. They're an all-purpose variety that will serve all your baking needs.
• Dried apricots, and other dried fruit, may have been treated with sulfur dioxide as a color preserver. Because sulfites can cause severe allergic reactions in people, check with your guests before you serve them. Untreated apricots are available, but they will be brown, not orange.

BAKED PINEAPPLE

Serves 4

1 ripe pineapple
3/4 cup orange juice (117 ml)
5 nickel-sized slices of fresh gingerroot
1/2 teaspoon arrowroot (2.5 ml) mixed with 1/4 cup
    orange juice (59 ml) (slurry)

Preheat the oven to 350°F (180°C). Cut both ends off the pineapple, slice lengthwise into eighths, and core. Leaving the skin intact, cut the meat off in one long piece, then slice into wedges, leaving them on the skin. Place on a 9-by-13-inch (23-by-33-cm) baking pan and cook for 15 minutes.

While the pineapple is baking, pour the orange juice into a small saucepan, add the ginger, and just heat through.

Just before serving, strain out the ginger with a slotted spoon. Stir in the arrowroot slurry and heat until it clears and thickens slightly. Pour this glaze over the baked pineapple and serve.

Nutritional Profile per Serving
Calories—165; fat (gm)—0; saturated fat (gm)—0; calories from fat—1%; cholesterol (mg)—0; sodium (mg)—3; fiber (gm)—4; carbohydrates (gm)—43.

• Just before a pineapple ripens, starch that has been stored in the stem enters the fruit and turns to sugar. Harvesters try to select pineapples when they're almost fully ripe, with maximum sugar and juice—but not too ripe, or the fruit will spoil before it gets to market. The harvested fruit is rushed to market within two to three days. Check with your produce manager on the shipping method: pineapple flown by jet from Hawaii is the most reliable in terms of good taste.

• Pineapple contains an enzyme, bromelain, that breaks down protein. Not only does bromelain prevent gelatin from setting, it also changes the flavor and consistency of proteins in yogurt or cottage cheese. However, there is a solution: cooking pineapple deactivates the bromelain, so canned pineapple is a safe addition to gelatin; and mix your yogurt or cottage cheese with pineapple just before serving, so the enzyme won't have a chance to act.

SWEET NOTHINGS . . . WELL, ALMOST!

I've noticed that among many people, one reason for large weight gain is the "cookie monster." Cookies are often a holiday treat, a small homemade gift for neighbors, or a little indulgence to celebrate the season. Here are three ideas for low-fat cookies for holidays—or any other time, for that matter.

◆ CHRISTMAS CRANBERRY COOKIES

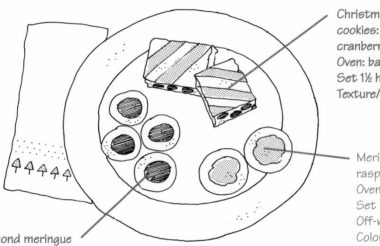

Christmas cranberry cookies: hazelnuts, cocoa, cranberries
Oven: bake 45 mins.
Set 1½ hrs.
Texture/Color

Meringue jam tarts with raspberry jam
Oven: bake 20 mins.
Set 20 mins.
Off-white, dark red
Color/Texture

Chocolate almond meringue mushrooms
Oven: bake 20 mins.
Set 20 mins.
White pale chocolate
Texture/Color

Yields 24

1/4 teaspoon margarine (1.25 ml)
Flour for dusting pan
3 egg whites, at room temperature
1/2 teaspoon cream of tartar (2.5 ml)
1/4 teaspoon vanilla extract (1.25 ml)
3/4 cup confectioners' sugar (177 ml)
2 tablespoons unsweetened cocoa powder (30 ml), preferably Dutch
1/2 cup finely chopped hazelnuts (filberts) (118 ml)
1/4 cup dried cranberries (or dried apricots or chopped dates) (59 ml)

Preheat the oven to 250°F (120°C).

Position a cooking rack in the lower third of the oven. Lightly grease an 8-inch (20-cm) square baking pan with the margarine and dust with flour.

Make sure all your bowls and beating utensils are completely clean and dry. Beat the egg whites at medium speed until frothy. Add the cream of tartar, turn the speed to high, and beat until soft peaks form. Add the vanilla and then gradually beat in the sugar. Continue beating until the meringue is stiff and shiny.

Remove half of the meringue and set aside. Quickly beat the cocoa into the remaining meringue. Spread the chocolate meringue evenly on the bottom of the prepared baking pan and sprinkle with 1/3 of the hazelnuts and the cranberries.

Pipe wide stripes of white meringue over the chocolate. If you don't have a pastry bag, spoon the white meringue on top and smooth carefully into stripes. Dip a rubber spatula in water and gently smooth completely all over the top, striving not to mix the two layers, and sprinkle with the remaining nuts. Bake for 15 minutes.

Remove the pan from the oven and, using a thin, wet knife, cut into 24 squares. Return to the oven and bake for 45 minutes. Without opening the oven door, turn off the heat and let the cookies sit for 1½ hours.

Remove from the oven, let cool completely, and store in an airtight container for up to a week . . . if they last that long.

Time Estimate: Hands-on, 35 minutes; unsupervised, 2 hours, 30 minutes

Nutritional Profile per Serving		
	Classic	**Minimax**
Calories	60	51
Fat (gm)	4	2
Saturated fat (gm)	1	0
Calories from fat	59%	29%
Cholesterol (mg)	6	0
Sodium (mg)	16	8
Fiber (gm)	0	9
Carbohydrates (gm)	6	9
Classic compared: Classic Nut Bars		

♦ RASPBERRY JAM TARTS

Yields 50

3 egg whites, at room temperature
1/2 teaspoon cream of tartar
  (2.5 ml)
3/4 teaspoon almond extract
  (3.8 ml)
3/4 cup granulated sugar (177 ml)
1/2 cup finely chopped almonds
  (118 ml)
1/2 cup raspberry jelly or seedless
  jam (118 ml)

Preheat the oven to 250°F (120°C). Line two baking sheets with parchment paper or aluminum foil.

Make sure all your bowls and beating utensils are completely dry and clean. Beat the egg whites at medium speed until frothy. Add the cream of tartar, turn the speed to high, and beat until soft peaks form. Add the almond extract and then gradually beat in the sugar, until the meringue is stiff and shiny. Fold in the chopped almonds.

Using a pastry bag with a large (#6) plain tip, pipe half-inch-wide (1.5-cm) circles onto the baking sheets. You want to keep them very small so they can be eaten in one bite. You should have 50 tarts. Bake for 15 minutes.

Remove from the oven and spoon or inject 1/4 teaspoon (1.25 ml) of the jam into the middle of each meringue. Return to the oven and bake for 20 minutes. Without opening the oven door, turn off the heat and allow the tarts to sit for 30 minutes. Remove from the oven, cool completely, and store in an airtight container for 3 or 4 days.

Time Estimate: Hands-on, 40 minutes; unsupervised, 1 hour

Nutritional Profile per Serving		
	Classic	**Minimax**
Calories	46	17
Fat (gm)	2	0
Saturated fat (gm)	1	0
Calories from fat	43%	22%
Cholesterol (mg)	8	0
Sodium (mg)	34	3
Fiber (gm)	0	0
Carbohydrates (gm)	6	3
Classic compared: Classic Jelly Tots		

◆ CHOCOLATE ALMOND MERINGUE MUSHROOMS

Yields 50

3 egg whites, at room temperature
1/2 teaspoon cream of tartar (2.5 ml)
3/4 teaspoon almond extract (3.8 ml)
3/4 cup granulated sugar (177 ml)
1/3 cup finely chopped almonds (78 ml)
2 tablespoons unsweetened cocoa (30 ml), preferably Dutch

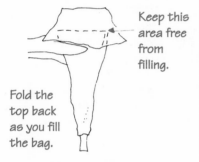

Keep this area free from filling.

Fold the top back as you fill the bag.

Fold to keep sides together.

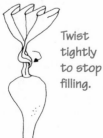

Twist tightly to stop filling.

Preheat the oven to 250°F (120°C). Line two baking sheets with parchment paper or aluminum foil.

Make sure a large bowl and your beating utensils are completely clean and dry. Beat the egg whites at medium speed until frothy. Add the cream of tartar, turn the speed to high, and beat until soft peaks form. Add the almond extract and then gradually beat in the sugar until the meringue is stiff and shiny. Fold all but 2 tablespoons (30 ml) of almonds into the batter.

Remove half of the meringue and set aside. Quickly beat the cocoa into the remaining meringue. Spoon the white meringue into a pastry bag with a large (#6) plain tip and gently squeeze out 50 small button-mushroom-sized caps onto the baking sheets. Clean the pastry bag and refill it with the chocolate meringue. Pipe the chocolate onto the white and sprinkle with the reserved almonds. Bake for 30 minutes. Without opening the door, turn the oven off and let them sit for 30 minutes. Remove from the oven, let the cookies cool completely, then store them in an airtight container for up to a week.

Time Estimate: Hands-on, 45 minutes; unsupervised, 1 hour

Nutritional Profile per Serving		
	Classic	**Minimax**
Calories	30	11
Fat (gm)	1	0
Saturated fat (gm)	1	0
Calories from fat	40%	24%
Cholesterol (mg)	6	0
Sodium (mg)	22	2
Fiber (gm)	0	0
Carbohydrates (gm)	4	2
Classic compared: Classic Pinwheel Cookies		

◆ CRANBERRY DUFF

In my entire career I've never been so inundated by television viewer mail as in the case of "the dreaded marmalade pudding." Could lightning strike twice, I wondered? I now believe that it can: the whole-berry cranberry sauce and hazelnuts produce a lovely texture, good color and great taste. This truly comforting winter dish, made possible by a Minimax treatment, is both cake and hot dessert. Now I'm awaiting the mail!

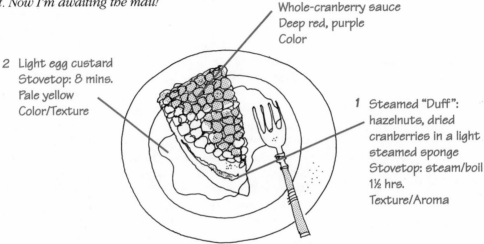

Whole-cranberry sauce
Deep red, purple
Color

2 Light egg custard
Stovetop: 8 mins.
Pale yellow
Color/Texture

1 Steamed "Duff":
hazelnuts, dried
cranberries in a light
steamed sponge
Stovetop: steam/boil
1½ hrs.
Texture/Aroma

Serves 8

Pudding

1/2 teaspoon (2.5 ml) + 1/4 cup (59 ml) +
  2 tablespoons (30 ml) stick margarine
  (not the soft-tub variety)
1/3 of a 16-ounce (454-gm) can + 2 tablespoons
  (30 ml) whole-berry cranberry sauce
1/4 cup brown sugar (59 ml)
1 medium egg
1/2 teaspoon vanilla (2.5 ml)
1/2 teaspoon almond extract (2.5 ml)
1¼ cups all-purpose flour (295 ml)
1½ teaspoons baking powder (7.5 ml)
3/4 cups nonfat milk (177 ml)
1/4 cup dried cranberries (59 ml)
1/4 cup finely chopped hazelnuts (filberts) (59 ml)

Sauce

One 8-ounce or 227-gm container liquid egg substitute
1/4 cup brown sugar (59 ml)
1½ cups 2%-fat milk (354 ml)
2 tablespoons cornstarch (30 ml) mixed with 1/4 cup
  2%-fat milk (59 ml) (slurry)

The steamed pudding: Lightly grease a 6-cup (1.4-l) rimmed bowl, 8 inches (20 cm) across at the top, with 1/2 teaspoon (2.5 ml) of the margarine. Spread 1/3 of the cranberry sauce around the bottom of the bowl (this will be the "crown" of the pudding).

In a small bowl, cream the remaining margarine and brown sugar until light and fluffy and doubled in volume. Beat in the egg, vanilla, and almond extract until well blended and light.

Double-sift the flour and baking powder into a large mixing bowl. Make a hole in the center and pour in the creamed batter. Fold together slowly until about a quarter of the flour is incorporated, then add half of the milk and fold this in with about three stirs before adding the additional milk. The entire mixture should be folded slowly for about 20 revolutions.

Spoon one third of the batter carefully into the pudding bowl on top of the cranberries. Sprinkle with half of the dried cranberries, then half of the chopped nuts. Top with another third of the batter, the remaining dried cranberries, and remaining nuts. Top with the rest of the batter and smooth out. The bowl should be about two-thirds full.

Place wax or greaseproof paper over the bowl and cover with a 14-inch-square cotton cloth. Secure the cloth under the rim lip of the bowl with a piece of string, bring the four corners up to the top and tie them diagonally to form a handle.

Put a wire rack inside a large pot of boiling water. Set the covered pudding bowl on this rack and adjust the water until it comes halfway up the side of the pudding bowl. Cover and simmer 1½ hours. Remove, unwrap, and remove cloth and paper.

Just before serving, make the Custard Sauce: In a small bowl (I find copper bowls work best for this, but a double boiler will do), whisk the egg substitute and brown sugar over a large saucepan of almost boiling water for 5 minutes. Remove from the heat.

In a medium saucepan, slowly heat the 1½ cups milk with the egg substitute–brown sugar mixture, stirring occasionally, until just below the boil. Mix in the slurry made from the cornstarch and extra milk. Keep stirring on medium-low heat until it thickens—about 30 seconds.

Position the whipped egg substitute over boiling water and pour in the thickened milk, stirring constantly with a wire whisk. Remove from heat when it is fluffy and almost doubled in size.

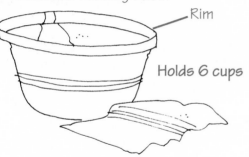

Steamed Pudding Basin

Rim

Holds 6 cups

To serve: Place a serving plate upside down on top of the unwrapped pudding bowl and, holding plate and bowl together with a towel, turn the whole thing over. Carefully lift off the bowl to reveal the crimson-crested pudding, steaming hot. Slice into eight serving portions and top each one with the hot custard sauce. Garnish with the cranberry sauce.

Time Estimate: Hands-on, 2 hours; unsupervised, 1½ hours

Nutritional Profile per Serving

	Classic	Minimax
Calories	428	373
Fat (gm)	18	10
Saturated fat (gm)	10	2
Calories from fat	38%	24%
Cholesterol (mg)	201	31
Sodium (mg)	307	312
Fiber (gm)	1	2
Carbohydrates (gm)	60	62
Classic compared: Steamed Jam Pudding		

ICES

A rich ice cream is maxing-out on temptation: it promises, it delivers, and it is immediately available! I decided to look at the fruit ice as a creative alternative. You'll need a simple ice cream churn to make the Pear Ice, but the Cranberry-Raspberry Ice is so simple all you need to do is plan ahead. I chose pear as the base because it, too, has that dense, smooth . . . even rich . . . mouthfeel of ice cream. As always, I've matched it to some bright notes: ginger, blackberry, and lemon.

♦ CRANBERRY-RASPBERRY ICE

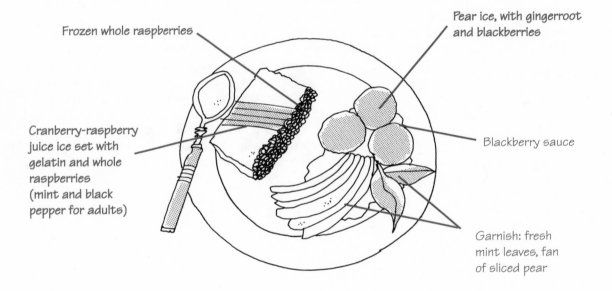

Frozen whole raspberries

Pear ice, with gingerroot and blackberries

Cranberry-raspberry juice ice set with gelatin and whole raspberries (mint and black pepper for adults)

Blackberry sauce

Garnish: fresh mint leaves, fan of sliced pear

Yields 8 cups (1.9 l)
Serves 8–16

One 1½-quart or 1.4-l bottle of cranberry-raspberry juice
2 packets of gelatin
1½ cups whole raspberries (354 ml), fresh or frozen (if using frozen, don't thaw the berries before using, to maintain their shape)

Garnish
4 teaspoons finely chopped fresh mint leaves (20 ml) (optional)
Freshly ground black pepper (optional)

Two days before serving, heat 1 cup (236 ml) of the cranberry-raspberry juice in a small saucepan and stir in the gelatin until completely dissolved. Add to the rest of the juice and mix well.

Pour the juice into a large (15-by-10-inch) (38-by-25-cm) roasting pan to a depth of 1 inch (2.5 cm) and freeze overnight until solid.

The day before serving, take the ice out and let it soften for 15 minutes. Slice it into pieces. In small batches, transfer the ice to a large electric beater bowl and beat until smooth. Continue until all the ice is frothy and light but *not* melted. Use a rubber spatula to work the mixture through the beater blades. The final texture should hold together on a spoon, like wet beaten egg whites.

Cover the bottom of a 2-quart (1.88-l) rectangular plastic container with a single layer of raspberries. Spoon the beaten ice on top, slicing through occasionally with your spatula to get out any major air bubbles. When the pan is filled to the top, drop it several times on the counter to pop any remaining air bubbles. Cover with plastic wrap and freeze overnight until solid enough to slice.

To serve: This is great stuff for the kids, sliced from the loaf or scooped into little paper cones. The adults might enjoy a version mixed with 1/2 teaspoon (2.5 ml) of finely chopped mint per serving and seasoned with freshly ground black pepper.

Time Estimate: Hands-on, 27 minutes; unsupervised, 16 hours

Nutritional Profile per Serving		
	Classic	**Minimax**
Calories	347	124
Fat (gm)	16	0
Saturated fat (gm)	9	0
Calories from fat	41%	2%
Cholesterol (mg)	97	0
Sodium (mg)	50	7
Fiber (gm)	3	1
Carbohydrates (gm)	103	31
Classic compared: Raspberry Ice Cream		

✦ Pear Ice in a Blackberry Puddle

Yields 5 cups (1.2 l)
Serves 6, generously

1½ pounds Bartlett or comice pears
  (675 gm) (2 or 3 pears)
5 (quarter-size) slices unpeeled
  fresh gingerroot
1 cup water (236 ml)
2/3 cup granulated sugar (157 ml)
6 fresh mint leaves, torn into small
  pieces and bruised
1 tablespoon freshly squeezed
  lemon juice (15 ml)
1 teaspoon loosely packed finely
  chopped fresh gingerroot (5 ml)
1 pound fresh or thawed frozen
  blackberries (450 gm)

Garnish
5 large fresh mint leaves
1½ fresh pears

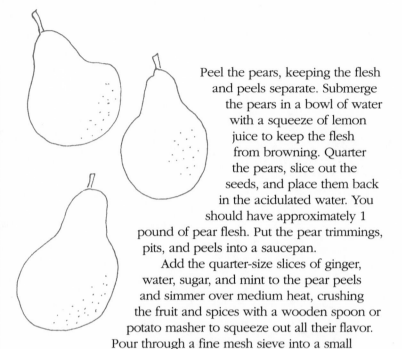

Peel the pears, keeping the flesh and peels separate. Submerge the pears in a bowl of water with a squeeze of lemon juice to keep the flesh from browning. Quarter the pears, slice out the seeds, and place them back in the acidulated water. You should have approximately 1 pound of pear flesh. Put the pear trimmings, pits, and peels into a saucepan.

Add the quarter-size slices of ginger, water, sugar, and mint to the pear peels and simmer over medium heat, crushing the fruit and spices with a wooden spoon or potato masher to squeeze out all their flavor.

Pour through a fine mesh sieve into a small bowl, pressing gently on the residue, without pushing any solids through. Return the liquid to the saucepan, bring to a boil, and reduce to 2/3 cup (157 ml)—about 10 minutes. Remove from the heat and let cool.

Drain the pears, transfer to a food processor, add the lemon juice and chopped ginger, and pulse to a semismooth puree—about 30 seconds. You want to be careful to retain some of the pears' texture for the final dish.

Pour the blackberries into a small, fine sieve and push the berries through into a bowl. You should have 1 cup (236 ml) of blackberry puree. Stir in the pear puree and mix well. Transfer 4 tablespoons of the mixed purees to a small bowl and set aside. Whisk the pear reduction into the pear-blackberry puree.

Ready your ice-cream maker according to the manufacturer's directions. Pour in the pear-blackberry puree and freeze until solid.

To serve: Prepare the garnish by cutting the pears into quarters. Place each pear slice lengthwise on a cutting board, and cut small layers, almost to the end of the pear but not quite. Now spread the layers like a fan. Place a large mint leaf on a small dessert plate and cover the stem end with four small scoops of the ice. Dollop the reserved blackberry-pear puree to one side and place the pear garnish on top of the "puddle."

Time Estimate: Hands-on, 25 minutes; unsupervised, 35 minutes

SUGAR AND ICE

Good ices depend upon the right blend of sugar to the acid of the fruit and the volume of water. The more sugar, the easier it is to spoon. Leave the sugar out, and the ice crystals set up in icy layers without enough *cling* to bind into a scooped ball and almost like solid ice when drawn straight from the deep freeze. In the Cranberry-Raspberry Ice, the gelatin step allows for texture without added sugar.

Nutritional Profile per Serving

	Classic	Minimax
Calories	389	211
Fat (gm)	26	1
Saturated fat (gm)	15	0
Calories from fat	60%	4%
Cholesterol (mg)	305	0
Sodium (mg)	112	1
Fiber (gm)	0	8
Carbohydrates (gm)	44	54

Classic compared: Vanilla Ice Cream

PUDDINGS

Milk puddings are tremendous comfort foods and when made with skim, 1-percent-, or 2-percent-fat milk, they deliver "mouthroundfulness" (smooth texture) as well as good calcium and protein. I've assumed that you may have a basic rice pudding recipe but may not have one for a stirred arrowroot pudding or the famed Indian pudding. Both add variety and delight for those with a sweet tooth who want to eat more than empty shadow calories.

♦ INDIAN PUDDING

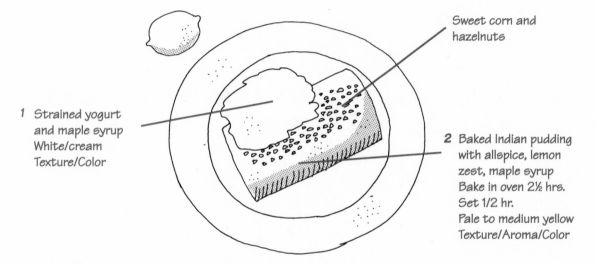

Sweet corn and hazelnuts

1 Strained yogurt and maple syrup
White/cream
Texture/Color

2 Baked Indian pudding with allspice, lemon zest, maple syrup
Bake in oven 2½ hrs.
Set 1/2 hr.
Pale to medium yellow
Texture/Aroma/Color

Serves 8

1/4 teaspoon soft-tub poly-unsaturated margarine (1.25 ml)
5 cups nonfat milk (1.2 l)
1/2 cup (118 ml) + 2 tablespoons (30 ml) fine yellow cornmeal
1/4 cup finely chopped hazelnuts (59 ml)
1/2 cup fresh or frozen corn kernels (118 ml)
1/2 cup maple syrup (118 ml)
1/4 teaspoon ground allspice (1.25 ml)
Zest of 1 lemon, finely grated
One 8-ounce or 227-gm container liquid egg substitute, optional

Maple Sauce
1 cup strained yogurt (236 ml) (see page 141)
2 tablespoons maple syrup (30 ml)

Garnish
2 tablespoons finely chopped hazelnuts (30 ml)

Preheat the oven to 300° (150°C). Grease a 4-by-8-inch (10-by-20-cm) loaf pan with the margarine. Heat the milk in a heavy saucepan over medium-high heat until little bubbles form around the edge of the pan, just before it boils. Be sure to stir it constantly to prevent catching. Slowly whisk in the cornmeal, stirring until it is thick and smooth—about 3 minutes. Remove from the heat and stir in all the remaining ingredients. Mix in the egg substitute at this time for a firmer pudding.

Pour into the prepared pan. Put the loaf pan into a 9-by-13-inch (23-by-23-cm) pan and place both in the oven. Pour water halfway up the sides of the large loaf pan and bake for 2½ hours or until a knife inserted into the middle comes out clean. Remove from the oven and cool on a rack for 1/2 hour.

The sauce: Gently combine the yogurt and maple syrup in a small bowl and set aside.

To serve: Run a knife around the outside of the pudding to loosen, then turn it out onto a serving plate. Pour the sauce on top and sprinkle with the hazelnuts.

Time Estimate: Hands-on, 25 minutes; unsupervised, 3 hours

COMPANION BAKING
In these days of energy conservation, the idea of using the oven for 2½ hours for a single dessert is quite a challenge. This wasn't so in early colonial days, when the wood-burning fire heated hearth, home, and the pudding at the same time. You may want to serve this pudding as a hot dessert alternative to pumpkin pie or Christmas pudding over the holidays, in which case, turkey, ham, or lamb will make a good companion for the cooking at 300°F (150°C) and make you feel like a true green-globalite.

Nutritional Profile per Serving	Classic	Minimax
Calories	406	218
Fat (gm)	13	4
Saturated fat (gm)	8	1
Calories from fat	30%	17%
Cholesterol (mg)	43	3
Sodium (mg)	246	107
Fiber (gm)	1	1
Carbohydrates (gm)	69	38
Classic compared: Indian Pudding		

♦ Arrowroot Vanilla and Orange Pudding

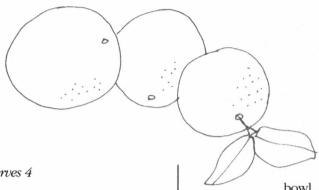

Serves 4

3 tablespoons arrowroot (45 ml)
6 tablespoons granulated sugar (90 ml)
2 cups 2%-fat milk (472 ml)
Zest from 1/2 orange
1 teaspoon vanilla (5 ml)
One 8-ounce or 227-gm container liquid egg substitute

Blend the arrowroot and sugar in a small bowl. Add to 1/2 cup (118 ml) of the milk and stir until smooth.

Heat the remaining milk and orange zest in a heavy saucepan until scalded. Add the arrowroot mixture and stir constantly until it thickens—about 1 minute. Stir in the vanilla and bring to a boil. Remove from the heat and slowly drizzle in the egg substitute, stirring constantly with a wire whisk. Strain into a serving bowl and chill.

To serve: Present in small dessert dishes or ramekins. This pudding goes very well with fresh fruit, such as strawberries.

Time Estimate: Hands-on, 20 minutes; unsupervised, none

Nutritional Profile per Serving		
	Classic	**Minimax**
Calories	233	190
Fat (gm)	8	2
Saturated fat (gm)	5	1
Calories from fat	32%	11%
Cholesterol (mg)	77	9
Sodium (mg)	95	184
Fiber (gm)	0	.3
Carbohydrates (gm)	35	32
Classic compared: Stirred Vanilla Pudding		

FRUIT SALAD SUZANNE

Serves 4

2 navel oranges
5 kiwis, peeled
1/2 cup cranberry juice cocktail (118 ml)
1/4 cup dried cranberries (59 ml)
1 tablespoon honey (15 ml)
1 teaspoon arrowroot (5 ml) mixed with 1 tablespoon cranberry cocktail juice (15 ml) (slurry)

Trim the top and bottom of the oranges and peel, taking off the outer white skin. Cut in half, pull out the pithy stem and navel, and cut into chunks. Cut the kiwis into chunks the same size.

In a small saucepan over medium heat, mix the cranberry juice, dried cranberries, and honey and bring to a boil. Add the arrowroot slurry and stir until the sauce is clear and glossy. Remove from the heat until cool, then pour over the fruit and serve immediately.

Nutritional Profile per Serving
Calories—156; fat (gm)—1; saturated fat (gm)—0; calories from fat—3%; cholesterol (mg)—0; sodium (mg)—8; fiber (gm)—3; carbohydrates (gm)—40.

• The sweetest kiwis will have soft, yielding flesh—similar to that of a ripe peach. If they're very firm, bring them home to ripen at room temperature, away from heat or direct sunlight, for a few days. Once they're ripe, keep kiwis away from other fruits, as kiwis are very sensitive to the ethylene gas that other fruits emit and will go mushy very quickly—even in the refrigerator.

• Be warned: kiwis have an enzyme that prevents gelatin from setting. Cook them for a minute first to deactivate the enzyme. On the other hand, this same enzyme has a tenderizing effect on meat. Just cut the kiwi in half, rub it on the meat, and let it stand for 30 minutes before cooking.

• One large kiwi fruit has more vitamin C than a medium-sized orange or a cup of strawberries, and two large kiwis have one and a half times as much potassium as an average banana and almost as much fiber as a cup of bran flakes.

JAMAICAN FRUIT SALAD

When Treena and I had a glass of Reed's Original Ginger Brew, a Jamaican-style ginger ale, I knew its unique bite and less sweet taste demanded some culinary application. You can use regular ginger ale in this recipe, but if you can find Reed's, go for it!

Serves 4

2 cups watermelon (472 ml), peeled and cut into 1-inch chunks (2.5 cm)
2 cups cantaloupe (472 ml), peeled and cut into 1-inch chunks (2.5 cm)
4 kiwis, peeled and cut into eighths
1/2 cup Jamaican-style or regular ginger ale (118 ml)
Zest of 1 lime
Juice of 1 lime

Place the fruit in a large bowl. In a small bowl, mix the ginger ale with the lime zest and lime juice. Pour on the fruit, toss well, and chill for 30 minutes.

Nutritional Profile per Serving
Calories—115; fat (gm)—1; saturated fat (gm)—0; calories from fat—7%; cholesterol (mg)—0; sodium (mg)—19; fiber (gm)—2; carbohydrates (gm)—28.

STRAWBERRY YOGURT SHAKE, OR ADULT FROZEN POPS

Serves 4

2 pints fresh (1.1 l) or 1 pound frozen (450 gm)
   strawberries
Zest of 1 lime
2 tablespoons coarsely chopped fresh mint leaves (30 ml)
3/4 cup orange juice (177 ml)
One 8-ounce or 227-gm container nonfat vanilla yogurt
1 tablespoon honey (15 ml)

Garnish
Fresh mint leaves (optional)

If you are using fresh strawberries, rinse them well, spread out on a baking sheet, and freeze them for 8 hours or overnight.

In a large blender, puree all the ingredients for 1 minute. Stir well and puree until smooth, but still thick and icy. Taste for sweetness and add more honey if needed. (I designed this to be tart and refreshing, not too sweet . . . *please!*)

Serve in tall glasses, garnished with mint leaves, or freeze in ice-cube trays to make grown-up frozen pops.

Nutritional Profile per Serving
Calories—119; fat (gm)—1; saturated fat (gm)—0; calories from fat—5%; cholesterol (mg)—1; sodium (mg)—26; fiber (gm)—2; carbohydrates (gm)—27.

• Vegetables don't have exclusive claim to anticancer benefits. Preliminary research suggests that strawberries, raspberries, cranberries, and loganberries contain a substance that may help to prevent some cancers: ellagic acid. And the good news is that ellagic acid doesn't seem to be affected by cooking, so you could still reap some of its benefits from processed berry foods, like jams.

• The most popular berry of all, the strawberry, contains more vitamin C than any other member of the berry family; only 1/2 cup (118 ml) will give you more fiber than a slice of whole-wheat bread.

• Raspberries are the most fragile of the berries, with a shelf life of only 1 or 2 days once they reach market. The best way to store them is to spread them out on a plate and cover them with with paper towels and then plastic wrap. Use raspberries within a day of purchase.

• Strawberries can easily turn mushy and moldy within 24 hours if not stored properly. Sort through them when you get them home, discarding any smashed or moldy berries, keeping out the overripe ones for immediate use. Spread the remaining berries out on a shallow pan or plate, cover with paper towels and then plastic wrap.

• Freezing berries is simple: Spread them in a single layer on a baking sheet, pop them in the freezer until they're completely frozen, and then transfer to a good plastic storage bag. They'll keep well up to a year.

RASPBERRY BAVARIETTE

Serves 4

1½ cups strained yogurt (354 ml) (see page 141)
3 tablespoons honey (45 ml)
1/2 teaspoon almond extract (2.5 ml)
3 cups fresh or frozen raspberries (708 ml) (if frozen,
 use whole, unsweetened, and unthawed)

Garnish
Fresh mint leaves

In a large bowl, mix the yogurt, honey, and almond extract. Use a fork or spatula to smooth out the little lumps in the yogurt. Don't whisk—any violent mixing will thin out the texture.

Gently fold in the raspberries. Serve in small bowls garnished with the mint leaves.

Nutritional Profile per Serving
Calories—197; fat (gm)—1; saturated fat (gm)—0; calories from fat—4%; cholesterol (mg)—3; sodium (mg)—141; fiber (gm)—2; carbohydrates (gm)—38.

Basics

BASIC STRAINED YOGURT

Yields 3/4 cup (177 ml)

1½ cups plain nonfat yogurt (354 ml), no gelatin added

Put the yogurt in a strainer over a bowl—or you can use a coffee filter, piece of muslin, or a paper towel and place in a small sieve over a bowl. Cover and let it drain in the refrigerator, for 5 hours or overnight. After 10 hours it becomes quite firm and the small lumps disappear, which makes it ideal for use in sauces. The liquid whey drains into the bowl, leaving you with a thick, creamy "yogurt cheese."

Nutritional Profile per Serving (1 teaspoon)		
	Classic	**Minimax**
Calories	34	51
Fat (gm)	4	0
Saturated fat (gm)	2	0
Calories from fat	99.4%	0%
Cholesterol (mg)	10	0
Sodium (mg)	1	4
Fiber (gm)	0	0
Carbohydrates (gm)	0	0
Classic compared: Butter		

BASIC CHICKEN OR TURKEY STOCK

Yields 4 cups (944 ml)

1 teaspoon light oil (5 ml) with a dash of toasted sesame oil
1 onion, peeled and chopped
1/2 cup coarsely chopped celery tops (118 ml)
1 cup coarsely chopped carrots (236 ml)
Carcass from a whole chicken or turkey
1 bay leaf
2 sprigs fresh thyme
4 sprigs fresh parsley
6 black peppercorns
2 whole cloves

Pour the oil into a large stockpot over medium heat, add the onion, celery tops, and carrots and fry to release their volatile oils—about 5 minutes. Add the chicken carcass and seasonings, cover with 8 cups (1.9 l) water, bring to a boil, reduce the heat, and simmer for 2 to 4 hours, adding water if needed. Skim off any foam that rises to the surface. After 1 hour, add 1 cup (236 ml) cold water—this will force fat in the liquid to rise to the surface so you can remove it.

Strain; use with relative abandon.

BASIC BEEF, LAMB, OR VEAL STOCK

Yields 4 cups (944 ml)

1 pound beef, lamb, or veal bones (450 gm), fat trimmed off
1 teaspoon light oil (5 ml) with a dash of toasted sesame oil
1 onion, peeled and coarsely chopped
1/2 cup coarsely chopped celery tops (118 ml)
1 cup coarsely chopped carrots (236 ml)
1 bay leaf
2 sprigs fresh thyme
6 black peppercorns
2 whole cloves

Preheat the oven to 375°F (190°C). Place the beef, lamb, or veal bones in a roasting pan and cook until nicely browned—about 25 minutes. The browning produces a richer flavor and deeper color in the final stock.

Pour the oil into a large stockpot and fry the vegetables for 5 minutes, to release their volatile oils. Add the bones and seasonings, cover with 8 cups (1.9 l) water, bring to a boil, reduce the heat, and simmer 4 to 8 hours, adding more water if necessary. Skim off any foam that rises to the surface. Strain and you've got a marvelous Minimax tool.

QUICK BEEF STOCK IN A PRESSURE COOKER

Yields 4 cups (944 ml)

Same ingredients as for Basic Beef Stock, minus the carrots

Brown the bones in the oven as for Basic Beef Stock.

Pour the oil into a pressure cooker over medium heat and fry the onion and celery tops for 5 minutes. Add the browned bones and the seasonings, cover with 6 cups (1.4 l) of water, fasten the lid, bring to steam, lower the heat, and cook for 40 minutes from the time when the cooker starts hissing.

Remove from the heat, leave the lid on, and let cool naturally—about 30 minutes. Strain; you will have about 4 cups (944 ml) of stock.

Note: Whenever you're using a pressure cooker, check your manufacturer's instruction book for maximum levels of liquids, etc.

Basic Ham Hock Stock

Yields 6 cups (1.4 l)

One 1-pound ham hock (450 gm)
1 bay leaf
3 whole cloves

In a pressure cooker, cover the ham hock with 2 quarts (1.9 l) cold water, bring to a boil, remove from the heat, and drain, discarding the water. Put the ham hock back in the pressure cooker, add the bay leaf and cloves, pour in 2 quarts (1.9 l) water, fasten the lid, and put over high heat. When the cooker starts hissing, turn the heat down to medium-low and let simmer 30 minutes. Strain and have at it.

Classic Fish or Shrimp Stock

Yields 4 cups (944 ml)

1 teaspoon light oil (5 ml) with a dash of toasted sesame oil
1 onion, peeled and coarsely chopped
1/2 cup coarsely chopped celery tops (118 ml)
2 sprigs fresh thyme
1 bay leaf
1 pound fish bones (no heads) or shrimp shells (464 gm)
6 black peppercorns
2 whole cloves

Pour the oil into a large saucepan and sauté the onion, celery tops, thyme, and bay leaf until the onion is translucent—about 5 minutes. To ensure a light-colored stock, be careful not to brown.

Add the fish bones or shrimp shells, peppercorns, and cloves, cover with 5 cups (1.2 l) water, bring to a boil, reduce the heat, and simmer for 25 minutes. Strain through a fine-mesh sieve and cheesecloth.

Basic Vegetable Stock

Yields 4 cups (944 ml)

1 teaspoon light oil (5 ml) with a dash of toasted sesame oil
1/2 cup coarsely chopped onion (118 ml)
2 cloves garlic, bashed and peeled
1/2 teaspoon freshly grated gingerroot (2.5 ml)
1/2 cup coarsely chopped carrot (118 ml)
1 cup coarsely chopped celery (236 ml)
1 cup coarsely chopped turnip (236 ml)
1/4 cup coarsely chopped leeks (59 ml), white and light
   green parts only
3 sprigs fresh parsley
1/2 teaspoon black peppercorns (2.5 ml)

Pour the oil into a large stockpot over medium heat, add the onion and garlic, and sauté for 5 minutes. Add the rest of the ingredients, cover with 5 cups (1.2 l) of water, bring to a boil, reduce the heat, and simmer for 30 minutes. Strain, and great flavor is at your fingertips.

Easy, Quick Enhanced Canned Stocks

Canned stock (low-sodium if possible)
Bouquet garni

Pour the canned stock into a saucepan, add the appropriate bouquet garni, bring to a boil, reduce the heat, and simmer for 30 minutes. Strain and move forward, enhanced, of course.

Basic Bouquet Garni: For ease of operation, I suggest you use our basic "bunch of herbs": 1 bay leaf, 2 sprigs fresh thyme (1 teaspoon dried), 6 black peppercorns, 2 whole cloves, 3 sprigs parsley.

For poultry: Add a 4-inch branch (10 cm) of tarragon (2 teaspoons or 10 ml dried) or 6 sage leaves (1 teaspoon or 5 ml dried).

For fish; Use either a few small branches of fennel or of dill, incorporated into the basic bunch of herbs.

For beef: Use a few branches of marjoram or rosemary incorporated into the basic bunch of herbs.

I let my herb bunches go around twice when I use them to flavor a canned broth. In this case, I simply simmer for up to 20 minutes and then put the bunch of herbs into a sealable plastic bag and keep it deep-frozen until its next appearance. Do be sure to label it: a frozen herb bag could be a disappointing late-night microwave snack for twenty-first-century teenagers!

How to Get In on the A.C.T.

Welcome to the section on A.C.T., an acronym for Aromas, Colors, and Textures. In Minimax cooking, food ingredients that provide these sensuous experiences must be marshaled to counterbalance the reasonable reduction of fat, salt, refined starches, sugars and large meat servings.

I've listed dozens of ingredients that are outstanding contributors to aroma, color, or texture, under the heading most appropriate to their contribution to a recipe. **In each description you'll find a portion of text in bold type, just like this sentence.** The boldface section will give you one or two ways in which that ingredient can be used in the Minimax kitchen.

My hope is that you'll use these lists to give you the tools to start springboarding into your own kitchen experiments. Remember, when you make the decision to Minimax a recipe, you need to be familiar with the A.C.T. ingredients that you think will both distract and delight your family and friends.

So the first step is to think through your personal A.C.T. ingredients likes and dislikes. Never use something just because I suggested it in a recipe or because it's the culinary trend. If you don't fancy it, replace it with a vegetable, seasoning, or garnish you do like.

I look forward to hearing how your experiments go. Who knows: Could you be the one to invent a new culinary classic? Of course, I shall be experimenting in my own kitchen, looking for great new alternative recipes made possible by the need to live creatively within limits.

A.C.T. Contents

Allspice

"All for one, one for all."

Allspice is a combination of warming spices found mixed together in one seed. Its flavor is pungent: a combination of cinnamon, nutmeg, and clove.

You can buy allspice either as a whole berry or already ground. Two general rules apply to all the solid spices: allspice, clove, nutmeg, cinnamon, black and white pepper, cardamom, and cumin seed. First, they all keep better in their whole form. Second, the moment a spice is converted to powder, it begins to release its volatile oils. Over time, these oils lose their effectiveness, even develop "off" flavors.

So for Minimax seasoning, where aroma means so much, I suggest you purchase whole spices and make fresh powders as needed. You can pulverize the spices by hand with a mortar and pestle or whiz them in a small high-speed coffee grinder or food processor.

One word of caution about the coffee grinder: Because you will always find large pieces of unprocessed spice after grinding, I recommend that you tip the whizzed spice into a bowl through a small, fine-mesh hand sieve.

Freshly ground allspice can be used as a great accent in meat loaves or dark brown stews, or scattered over freshly steamed greens, carrots, or beans. I use the whole berry as part of a pickling spice for either canned or fresh pears, peaches, and apricots (recipe follows).

SPICED PEARS

1/2 cup de-alcoholized red wine (118 ml)
1/2 cup apple-cider vinegar (118 ml)
6 whole cloves, freshly ground
6 allspice berries
One 3-inch or 8-cm piece of cinnamon stick
2 pears, peeled, halved, and cored (or peaches or apricots)
1 cup water (236 ml), or enough to cover

In a medium saucepan, heat the wine and vinegar. Stir in the cloves, allspice, and cinnamon stick. Add the pear halves, pour in enough water to cover, and poach for 30 minutes. Remove the pears and serve as a side dish for venison or pork. The poaching liquid can then be thickened and used as a sauce: just mix 1 tablespoon arrowroot (15 ml) with 2 tablespoons water (30 ml). Remove the poaching liquid from the heat, stir in the arrowroot slurry, return to medium-high heat, and stir until thickened—about 30 seconds. Serve immediately.

Almond Extract

"A wee drop of the good stuff"

This is high drama: the aroma released by almond extract is powerfully attractive, an easy rival to vanilla and cinnamon for the title of most popular spice on the block.

Use almond extract mixed with cocoa powder as a substitute for chocolate in cakes, cookies, custards, and ices. You do have to be careful not to overshadow the other flavors. Start with 1/8 teaspoon (.6 ml) and sniff the result. Almond extract can give the simple sweetness of meringue additional depth. I also add a few drops to the cooking water when making saffron- or turmeric-colored rice.

As with any of the aromatic oils, you will be better off buying the pure extracts. There are numerous artificial flavors that are produced in test tubes by scientific geniuses. They will be less expensive, but some develop really "off" flavors during storage. I believe it's always better to pay a little extra for pure almond extract. Protect your investment by keeping it in a dark, cool place.

Anchovy Fillets

"The enchanted savior of the banal"
—Christian Glynn

These dark orange-brown, finely boned, tiny fillets of small fish that inhabit the Mediterranean Sea and the English Channel provide a strong, salty, decidedly fishy, and unmistakably aromatic quality. Now, I know anchovies can be an acquired taste. However, for every critic there are dozens of devotees for whom a touch of anchovy does wonders.

They can be bought as fillets in very small cans (because they are, after all, a very concentrated flavor) or ground into a paste and packed into convenient tubes or bottled sauces. I prefer the whole fillets because they allow me maximum flexibility to use them coarsely chopped or smeared into a paste with the back of a knife against a board.

The fillets that are packed in oil can be soaked in milk to relieve a certain amount of the saltiness. I usually cut them in half, lengthwise, to decorate somewhat bland dishes. They blend well with seafood, poultry, and melted cheese in all forms, especially on pizza.

The aggressive saltiness of anchovies should be utilized as pockets of sodium, rather like capers; in which case, eliminate all other salt. They're really good stuff, and I urge you to give them a go as soon as possible.

I teaspoon (5 ml): 188 mg sodium

Basil

Thank God for the seasons.

When spring gives way to summer the basil plants in my garden—all five varieties—are at their very best and remain so into the late fall. It's one of those climatic rights of passage that make me delight in the seasons year after year.

Basil, regardless of its exotic varieties, is one of the most profound and flowery aromas. It's hard to call an aroma delicious, yet basil has a scent that trumpets the arrival of taste.

I use fresh basil on tomatoes and in dishes with a tomato-based sauce. In salads, especially ones with dark greens, it's great. Finely sliced it's a lovely garnish for white yogurt sauces and a good accompaniment for fresh oregano in many pasta dishes. Fresh basil outdistances dried basil by a mile! It's one of those fleshy-leaved plants whose flavor does not last long after picking. Because of this seasonal succulence, there have been several attempts made to trap its qualities for off-season use.

The best is pesto, an Italian invention that combines basil, oil, cheese, garlic, and pine nuts into a very potent semisolid seasoning that keeps well under refrigeration. Each tablespoon (15 ml) packs 23 calories and 2 grams of fat, so use it sparingly. Make a Minimax version by following the Cilantro Pesto recipe on page 155, substituting equal amounts of basil leaves for the cilantro. A second method of preservation is in the new volatile oil-suspension form sold in small bottles and found in better supermarkets under the brand names Dilijan and Rayner's.

Bay Leaf

The pick of the bunch

This evergreen leaf from the laurel family, a native of Southern Europe, Northwest Africa, and Southwestern Asia, is absolutely essential in the famous French bouquet garni, quite literally the bunch of herbs that finds its way into so many great European dishes.

Wherever you have moist heat and a savory conclusion, such as in the Hearty Vegetable Stew with Beef (see page 52), you need to consider an herbal bouquet that can be very varied. In its classic general form, the pick of the bunch is the bay leaf; and here it is better to use the European variety than the California one, which tends to develop a rather medicinal flavor. Add to this some thyme, fresh or dried, celery, parsley, especially the stalks, peppercorns, and a few cloves. Tie them all in a muslin bag or bruise them with the back of a knife and pop them into a stainless-steel mesh ball. This keeps the

finer pieces from being lost amid a recipe and cropping up unexpectedly!

Bay leaves add greatly to rice: use one leaf for every uncooked cup measure (236 ml). I always drop one in soup stock and fish-poaching liquids. They are especially good for adding flavor to nonfat milks used to make sauces and for upgrading canned bouillon in moments (see page 144).

Canadian Bacon
Not a rasher decision

Canadian bacon is a perfect example of Minimax: Start with a loin of pork that is brined and smoked. Now cut away all the fat and rib meat for bacon slices, or what the Brits call rashers, leaving only the lean eye meat.

Producers reduce the fatty risk and enhance the lean center with a mild smoke and salt seasoning. Of course, there's still the nitrate added to keep the pink appearance. My view of this as a risk is that I seldom use more than 2 tablespoons (30 ml) finely chopped per portion, and the amount of nitrate in this is literally minuscule.

There are many recipes that call for salt pork or bacon, usually in fairly substantial amounts. I've found that 1 or 2 tablespoons (15 or 30 ml) added at the end of cooking, just before serving, will certainly establish that delicious smoky presence with far less risk.

Let me explain "risk": bacon and all salted and smoked foods have a very high return appeal. Once you've decided upon a platter of crisp bacon slices for breakfast, or a plump smoked pork sausage for lunch, you may feel a strong desire to repeat the experience. The nature of the risk is in its repetition. In this case the risks are saturated fat, sodium nitrate, and smoke, which have been implicated in Japan's high rate of stomach cancer.

So rather than ban Canadian bacon, be sparing; enjoy its fragrance without letting it become repetitive.

I buy it in a block, about 8 ounces (227 gm), and keep it in a sealed plastic bag in the refrigerator.

1 tablespoon (15 ml): 16 calories; 1 gm fat

Caraway Seed
One bite, and you're in Eastern Europe.

Nothing moves me closer to Eastern Europe than caraway. This tiny seed is soft enough to chew and remarkably intense. You may have encountered it (with some surprise) in a slice of rye bread and may not have wanted a return visit because anise (licorice) in bread is not exactly usual in our white-bread world.

On the other hand, you might have eaten cabbage, gently steamed or perhaps braised with caraway—how could you not come back for more?

I always give caraway a try in dishes with a reasonably high onion content. I make an adaptation of the famous French onion soup in which I reduce the broth and add arrowroot to thicken as a sauce. To this I add caraway in very small amounts, 1/2 teaspoon (2.5 ml) at a time, tasting at each addition to make sure that I've added just enough to be aware of—wonderful when served with roast pork tenderloin.

I have also experimented with 1 teaspoon (5 ml) in a whole-wheat, low-fat pastry crust for a chicken pie. It looks quite odd but has an elegant taste.

Cardamom
Move over, mints!

Indian restaurants often have a bowl of cardamom where other restaurants have a dish of mint candies. Cardamom is a good breath mint but it's also quite strong—almost peppery-tasting, with a dash of ginger.

Because of its natural warmth and pronounced aroma, cardamom is a perfect ingredient in curries, especially when made with fresh tropical fruit (see page 74). Even if you buy a ready-mixed curry powder as a convenience, you can still add an extra 1/4 teaspoon (1.25 ml) of cardamom for each tablespoon (15 ml) of powder to add depth and mellowness. There's lots of potential for experiments here, especially with winter squash and sweet potatoes. In Scandinavia, it's a favorite spice to add to cookies, cakes, and breads.

Cardamom can be purchased as small round pods that look like tiny heads of garlic. If you press the husk, it will easily crush and expose its very small, dark brown seeds. These can be separated and then crushed in a mortar and pestle or whizzed in an electric coffee mill until powdered. It can also be purchased already powdered. In some cases the outer pod and the seed are ground together, but this method takes away from the freshness of the flavor.

Cayenne Pepper
Asbestos-tongue time

Cayenne has aroma and color, but its use and reputation come from its heat—which is more a matter of touch than taste.

Taste is quite clearly defined as salt, sweet, sour, and bitter. Some authorities have added the word *piquant,* or *spice-hot,* to the list because it is discerned in the palate where the rest are grouped. Certainly cayenne peppers, ground to a fine pink-red powder, must have pride of place in the piquant category—more for recognition than degree of heat, however, because the habanero and Scotch bonnet are considerably hotter.

I have found that when fat is removed from a recipe, there are several major enhancement opportunities, all connected to taste. I use sour as in lemon or lime, bitter as in radicchio and almonds, or spice-hot as in jalapeño, black peppercorns, or cayenne. Each of these primary tastes works well to draw attention away from the loss of fat and its way of fixing flavor on the taste buds; but I must say that spice-hot is the clear winner in the attention-getting stakes.

Please don't recoil at the idea of painful heat. It is possible to introduce an effect slowly: a scattering of as little as 1/8 teaspoon (.6 ml) in a casserole or a stew of four servings may simply begin to feel warm; at 1/4 teaspoon (1.25 ml), it begins to feel hot; and at 1/2 teaspoon (2.5 ml), it becomes a major contributor; 1 teaspoon (5 ml), and I'm reaching for the water.

Try it now. If cayenne is not available, then look for ground red pepper, which is actually a blend of peppers. Use it in any savory dish that has had its fat content reduced.

Chili Powder
Culinary fusion: 1+1=2.3!

Because chili powder is a classic blend, achieved with various degrees of success, of cayenne pepper (ground red chilies), and ground cumin seed, I need to refer you here to two other Minimax heroes for background. What makes this combination so brilliant is its use in the world-renowned dish chili, in which ground beef and pinto beans make their bow with these two perfectly matched seasonings: cayenne for the beef and cumin for the beans. Combine all four and, bingo, you've come up with a kind of gastronomic royal flush.

It's because of this achievement that I believe that chili powder should be reserved for dishes that are composite and include beans. I would even propose a fusion of cultures and add a very light dusting of chili powder to a minestrone when that Italian classic is made with tender white fagioli (beans), to Boston baked beans, and even to the French cassoulet. But please, in every case the idea is first to lower fat and salt and then increase creativity by using just enough of an unusual seasoning to create a surprise.

I would never, in a fit, propose such an unorthodox innovation if these classics were to be served in their original form or under their classic menu names. When fusions take place, the diner must always be advised.

And now I bow my head and await the judgment of my peers in at least three nations . . .

Cilantro
The alias plant

Welcome to my pick of the pack as the "International Herb of Many Names." Cilantro is the flat leaf of the coriander plant, from which we get coriander seeds.

A native of southern Europe, Africa, and Asia, it's also called Chinese parsley and fresh coriander.

Cilantro has a great affinity for Mexican and other South American dishes. Freshly chopped in salsa, sprinkled on egg and egg-substitute dishes, or as a garnish to most bean dishes, it seems to love to share its aroma happily with cumin. One primary and delicious Minimax use is in Cilantro Pesto (recipe follows).

One word of warning: if you have not as yet ventured into the use of cilantro, you need to know that, at first, it must be used sparingly. If you eat it as liberally as watercress, it will seem soapy; but when you ease it up to a jalapeño, green tomatillo, and tomatoes, it adds a zing all its own—and frankly, I love it. Try 1 teaspoon (5 ml) chopped for a four-person salsa or just a sprinkle on tomato soup or plain steamed rice.

You should find it in parsley-sized bunches right next to the fresh parsley in the produce department. Unhappily that's far too much, so share the experience with a friend.

CILANTRO PESTO
Makes 3 cups (708 ml)

3 cups packed cilantro leaves (708 ml)
1/2 cup light oil (118 ml) with a dash of toasted sesame oil
5 garlic cloves, bashed, peeled, and chopped
2 jalapeño peppers, cored and seeded
1 cup walnuts (236 ml)
1 cup very mild feta cheese (236 ml)
Juice of 1 lemon
1/4 cup ice water (59 ml)

Place all the ingredients in a food processor and puree into a thick paste. Refrigerate in a tightly covered container until ready to use.

Cinnamon
King of the spices

In all the approval ratings, cinnamon is the number-one spice in terms of both use and appreciation. It's powdered as a topping for frothy coffee, it's an essential in sticky Danish, and it moves mightily at many other less extroverted levels, for instance as a background aroma in ketchup and barbecue sauces.

I strongly recommend buying cinnamon in its stick form rather than preground. I have a fine stainless-steel grater that I use for grating nutmeg and cinnamon on the spot, because there is just no substitute for the fresh aroma. Try the comparison sniff test sometime and see for yourself. I recommend the fine, slender sticks with a light orange color. These sticks are, by the way, the curled dried bark of an evergreen tree native to Ceylon.

In the Minimax kitchen, I also use cinnamon for POPs, or perfumes of the palate. POPs are spice mixtures that recall the garam masala of Indian cooking; these mixtures, made from warm, aromatic spices pounded in a pestle or otherwise pulverized to a powder (I've wanted to use that sentence for years!), are sprinkled over dishes in much the same way as we use salt and pepper. Try my basic Minimax POP below. Another interesting idea is to add a 1-inch (2.5-cm) piece of cinnamon stick to wood chips when you prepare a smoked dish.

BASIC POP

(PERFUME OF THE PALATE)

One 1/2-inch (1.5-cm) piece of cinnamon stick
3 whole cloves
1/4 teaspoon freshly grated nutmeg (1.25 ml)

Place the spices in a small coffee mill or grinder and grind to a fine powder. Strain through a fine-mesh sieve to remove large pieces before using. Great sprinkled on fresh fruit with a little nonfat sweetened yogurt.

Cloves
A budding star of stage, screen, and springboard

Someone had to pop it into an apple pie as an experiment—would you have thought of that? A dried flowering bud from a Southeast Asian tree seasoning a temperate climate fruit!

Such is the experimental joy of springboarding, especially with the powerful aromatics, and clove is right up there with nutmeg and cinnamon (it even temporarily cures toothache).

I use cloves primarily in garam masala (see page 160) and in all my stocks (see page 141–44). I'm very careful not to overdo it. When I call for two or four in a recipe, I really mean it. There is no point in punching someone in the eyes with a singular herb or spice. The true artistry of A.C.T. is to layer aromas, colors, and textures, letting them interweave so subtly that it's hard to sort out exactly what has been used.

Coconut Essence
The lure of the Pacific islands

Coconut milk is a wonderful liquid seasoning; and coconut cream, made from the freshly grated, simmered, and pressed nut meat, is highly aromatic, soft, and velvety smooth. It's also heavily laced with saturated fat and, when added to the simplest of fare, makes the fat percentages look like a triple-stacked hamburger and french fries.

It is for such moments of culinary trial that Minimax was born. How to minimize the risk from the fat and still preserve the dynamite appeal?

I discovered the answer is to squeeze it until you've got what the trade calls a WONF (with only natural flavors). A natural essence extraction traps flavor and removes fat. Ask for it at your supermarket as a natural coconut essence.

But what of the soft and velvety-smooth texture? The answer is add it to strained yogurt (see page 141).

I use cocoyog (it will never catch on as a word) in southern Indian, Indonesian, and Pacific island recipes as an absolute last-minute finisher. As with any nonfat yogurt sauce, it cannot be boiled without breaking; so bring the dish to the boil, remove it from the heat, stir in the cocoyog gently, and then serve immediately.

It actually does the trick for aroma and part of the texture without a speck of fat.

Coriander
Knock-'em-down, drag-'em-out seasoning

Often found in southern Mediterranean dishes, all the way down into northern Africa, coriander is the seed from which we get fresh coriander, alias cilantro alias Chinese parsley.

It is essential in the famous "knock 'em down, drag 'em out" hot relish of North African cuisine called harissa, which is often served with couscous. The recipe follows.

Apart from this adaptation, you might like to experiment by using coriander as a seasoning, along with salt and pepper, in lamb and poultry dishes.

HARISSA SAUCE

Serves 6

6 dried red chili peppers
1/4 teaspoon caraway seed (1.25 ml)
1/4 teaspoon cumin seed (1.25 ml)
1/2 teaspoon coriander (2.5 ml)
1 clove garlic
Olive oil as needed

Whiz all ingredients in a small coffee grinder or food processor. These semimoist spices can be combined with a little olive oil until you get a mustard-sauce consistency.

Cumin

Seasoning bedrock

Here is a seed that, because of its appearance, is easily mistaken for caraway; its taste, and especially its aroma, however, couldn't be more distinctive.

Cumin and coriander form the seasoning bedrock of any good curry powder. They're best when whizzed in the seed form into a fresh powder and passed through a fine-mesh sieve before using. Try a good pinch of cumin in any pasta dish in which tomatoes are present. Ground cumin, lemon zest, and freshly squeezed lemon juice will lift the pleasure of a bean dip where you've lowered the oil content. In fact, cumin is a powerful addition to any bean dish, and complements well any use of lemon—this could develop into one of your very best experiments.

Curry Powder

An aromatic train of thought

First of all, there is no such thing as a premixed "curry powder" in a good Indian kitchen. Perhaps the only place it's found is on the Indian railways, where a degree of convenience is apparently essential. Of course, in this country, we have dozens of premixed powders available that vary in their degree of spice/heat.

Let me encourage you to experiment and make your own curry powder. Here are a few clues on how it's assembled: the overall aroma, color, and touch are made up from a flavor base, like cumin

or coriander, to which is added color— yellow turmeric; then heat—cayenne pepper; and, finally, aromatic individuality—ginger, cardamom, cloves, cinnamon, fenugreek, garlic, allspice, or zests of citrus. For an example, see page 74, where I've made up a list of spices that go well with a fresh fruit curry.

Once you've made a few discrete tests, you'll quickly get the hang of it and will be developing your own individual powder. Who knows: You could end up selling it to the Indian railways.

De-alcoholized Wine

Enjoy it all!

When you want to cook, drink, and drive, you can enjoy it all with de-alcoholized wines. These wines are distinguished by the fact that they are made from classic grapes, by classic methods, and only then subjected to the removal of the alcohol—by a system of cold filtration called reverse osmosis. This method preserves the natural esters and essences that are lost when the wine is heated in traditional methods of alcohol removal. De-alcoholizing also

allows the juice to retain grape varietal characteristics. The bite and bouquet developed by alcohol are, of course, missing; but this isn't a problem when it comes to cooking, because heating dispels most, but not all, of the alcohol and floral benefits anyway.

Over the years I have found that the Ariél vineyard in Napa Valley, California, produces the most consistently attractive de-alcoholized wines. It's now only a matter of time before other growers recognize the potential and begin to compete in this rapidly expanding market.

I use de-alcoholized wines to bring the aroma (not bouquet) and color of wine to food. In casseroles I split the amount, adding half at the beginning of the cooking process and half to freshen at the end. I also deglaze sauté pans with it in order to lift off the meat residues that stick to the pan before making a sauce. I use it, too, in marinades, sweet berry sauces, and sophisticated fruit ices.

I really value de-alcoholized wine in my kitchen. I deeply appreciate being able to offer a creative alternative both for myself and my friends.

Dijon Mustard
The Rolls-Royce of seasonings

Fatty spreads like margarine, mayonnaise, or butter can contribute up to one-quarter of the recommended fat intake per day. In an effort to back off from their huge consumption, many folks have taken to using mustards—especially the one that you get from passing Rolls-Royces—now available in every supermarket.

The city of Dijon is the center for dominant French-style mustard: a light grayish-yellow combination of mustard powder and *verjus* (grape juice). Mustards are also made elsewhere in France but are usually blended with various herbs. Dijon mustard has only 4 calories in each teaspoon (5 ml) and carries enough flavor impact to equal a tablespoon (15 ml) of butter.

Because 1 tablespoon (15 ml) of butter has about 14 grams of fat and Dijon mustard has no fat content, it seems like a generally good idea to use it as a spread for savory sandwiches and salad dressings. Try blending Dijon mustard into strained yogurt (see page 141) to replace mayonnaise in your next sandwich. In 80 days, you could have consumed more than 17,000 fewer calories than you would from fat, with this one simple step!

Dill Weed and Seed

Here are two very different uses, but the same essential flavor: much lighter in the weed than the seed.

Dill is one of those herbs that carry a true fresh flavor into their dried form; in fact, you may find that fresh dill in a stock-based sauce or soup has too light a flavor. If this is the case, you can always reinforce the flavor by simmering 2 tablespoons (30 ml) of crushed dill seeds in 1 cup (236 ml) of stock.

I use finely chopped dill, fresh or dried, scattered as a seasoning and garnish over virtually any fish, shrimp, mushroom, or egg dish. It's also a super flavor with vegetables, especially ones that use Minimax yogurt sauces as a topping.

The seeds have considerable bite and do well in the same categories as caraway (see page 152).

Fish Sauce

An open mind before an open mouth?

Welcome to the kitchen of the brave! Fish sauce is the ketchup of the Southeast Asian kitchen. If at first glance the idea of eating the juice strained from small fish packed in salt and fermented for several months in the sun does not tempt your taste buds, keep an open mind. I must tell you that fish sauce is an essential Asian ingredient and that the better brands are really wonderful.

Look for it packaged in glass, not plastic, from companies based on the west coast of Thailand. It will be considerably more expensive than the average fish sauce, but well worth it.

Wherever you use soy sauce, try using fish sauce in its place. Start with a tablespoon (15 ml) for a four-person soup or entree, taste it, then continue adding 1/4 teaspoons (1.25 ml), tasting after each addition, until you reach your level of acceptance.

Believe it or not, you may soon double your tolerance level. Fish sauce is, of course, high in sodium, but you don't need to add a lot to make a difference.

---

1 tablespoon (15 ml): 10 calories; 0 gm fat; 681 mg sodium

Garam Masala

Perfume of the palate (POP)

Just like curry powder, the traditional Indian spice mixture garam masala is made up from the spices on hand according to the nature of the dish being presented. **This Indian condiment of mixed, warming spices is sprinkled on just like salt and pepper, to give a great last-minute kick to curry or any strongly flavored vegetables, like braised onions or baked parsnips.**

A typical selection of garam masala spices would include nutmeg, cumin, cloves, allspice, cinnamon, and black pepper. The mixture does not include the coloring of turmeric or the heat of cayenne because its sole purpose is to enhance aroma.

Because of its aromatic focus, I always

make mine fresh and "to order." Try this simple recipe as a start: In a small coffee grinder whiz until finely powdered one 2-inch or 10-cm piece of thin cinnamon stick; 6 allspice berries; 1/4 teaspoon freshly ground nutmeg (1.25 ml); and 4 whole cloves. Push the mixture through a sieve onto the surface of the food just before serving.

Garlic

One fresh clove at a time, please.

Garlic is a compound bulb made up of numerous bulblets, or cloves, enclosed in a papery sheath. I mention this only for anyone who thinks that the desiccated, powdered, pureed, extracted, or encapsulated products are the real thing. Each of these commercial products is designed to save you the time of preparing fresh garlic—and to steal from you the essence of the garlic experience.

I believe that garlic in small quantities is the perfect aromatic. I use it in dozens of dishes, but only in small quantities. Although some cultures love huge amounts of garlic, I happen to believe that any dish with one pronounced seasoning is actually out of balance.

You might like roasting garlic and spreading it on toasted bread. Its taste is actually quite delicate when cooked this way (see the recipe below).

I always buy garlic that's firm to the touch, its paper husk free from mold or discoloration, in small quantities. I keep it in a clay pot with small breathing holes, not in the refrigerator. I never buy one of those ropes of garlic to hang on the wall because I just can't use them fast enough.

I peel each clove when I need it. Years ago, I gave up peeling the whole head and submerging the cloves in oil to keep. It sounds good but can lead to botulism—not a great idea.

GARLIC SPREAD

This is a robust alternative to butter and a great hors d'oeuvre dip.

Serves 8

1 whole head of garlic
1 cup strained yogurt (see page 141)
1 tablespoon fresh chopped parsley (15 ml)
1/4 teaspoon coarsely ground black pepper (1.25 ml)
1/4 teaspoon salt (1.25 ml)

Preheat the oven to 375°F (190°C). Slice about 1/2 inch (1.5 cm) off the top of the garlic, wrap it in aluminum foil, and bake for 35 minutes. Remove the foil and press until all the flesh squeezes out. You should have 1 heaping tablespoon (15 ml) of puree. Mix it with the yogurt, parsley, black pepper, and salt.

Gingerroot

Bao syang went the strings of my heart.

This is splendid stuff, and it's cropping up all over the place in produce departments that care about cooks.

Ginger "root" is actually a rhizome, or creeping stem, that lies horizontally along the ground's surface. It's become such an important part of my Minimax cooking that I believe that, without its strong, bright note, most of my whole concept of "above-the-line cooking" would fail (see page 10)!

I use gingerroot with green onions (scallions) and garlic; they have become the essential three musketeers of my Asian recipes. Tossed into a hot frying pan, they explode with unparalleled fragrance—what the Chinese call *bao syang*. They are the basis for innumerable stir-fries.

Powdered ginger has a taste quite different from that of the fresh root. It's hot and dry, and great for muffins or cookies, but it can never be used in lieu of the fresh root. Try crystallized ginger as a superb taste counterbalance to the sweetness in low-fat ice cream. Ginger syrup is a triumph of "mind over melon," especially honeydew.

Look for a fresh gingerroot in the produce section of your grocery. It should weigh about 1/4 pound (113 gm). A young root, characterized by a small diameter, doesn't need to have its paper-thin skin removed before cooking. Sealed in plastic and refrigerated, fresh ginger should keep for 3 to 4 weeks.

Ham Hocks

Stock up!

I've long pondered how to bring home the bacon and ham (flavors) to Minimax cooking without the fatty risks. Well, if you love the smell of bacon frying, or freshly baked ham, you'll love the aroma of simmering ham hocks. I actually think you'd have to get your nose removed in order truthfully to disclaim its impact.

But what is a ham hock? It's a large lump of mahogany brown skin and bones that come from the leg, between the foot and knee. The hock  is salted, smoked, and packaged for sale, right there among the hams at your supermarket.

A ham-hock stock has become a staple of many Minimax dishes (see page 143), especially any dish that involves cooking dried beans. Be sure to pour the stock through the fat-separator cup before using. The cooked hock can be stripped of its lean meat, which can be chopped and used as a garnish. Start off trying it simmered with some black-eyed peas, shredded kale, and leeks, garnished with the meat—you've got the idea.

Juniper Berries
Flavor of the forest

Juniper is the primary flavoring of gin; its piney, peppery taste makes it the perfect complement to wild game, robust marinades, and forest mushrooms. The berry is actually a small, dark cone from a bushy evergreen tree, just a little larger than a peppercorn, but not as hard.

I often use a few juniper berries in marinades for depth (see page 60). Be sure you remove them from a dish before serving; they are chewable—but not at all a pleasant surprise!

Kaffir Lime Leaves
Turning over a new leaf?

When the people from Southeast Asia and Thailand arrive in the United States, chances are they'll plant a Kaffir lime tree as soon as they're able to. This tree is a native of Asia and grows an ugly-looking citrus fruit. The leaves, which look a little like a common bay leaf, are sometimes used as a shampoo rinse by Thais to ward off evil spirits. But my interest lies in the leaves' aromatic, lemony quality.

I use Kaffir lime leaves primarily in a spicy "hot and sour" chicken soup. It's also an excellent addition to basic stocks (see page 141), where it can be stirred in with the bay leaf in equal measure. It always brings a bright background note of citrus.

Lemon Grass
Is that a stalk in my soup?

Lemon grass, sun-dried tomatoes, yellow raspberries all belong to a valuable gastronomic genre that I call "above-the-line seasoning": bright aromas, colors, and textures that serve to distract and bring pleasure in place of high-fat ingredients (see page 10).

Lemon grass is, in fact, a rushlike grass with quite a woody stem. It has a fresh, lemony flavor that does well in all broths and bouillons (see page 141) and, traditionally, the classic hot-and-sour Thai soup. I like to use it when cooking rice; an inch or two (2.5–5 cm) to 2 cups (472 ml) of uncooked rice will provide a welcome edge. Try serving a stalk of lemon grass as a spoon with your tea.

You can grow this grass yourself; just harvest it when it's young. It's a great garnish for seafood or salads. It won't live through a frost but will continue to grow indoors in a south-facing window. You can also buy lemon grass fresh at very good supermarkets. I don't recommend the dried varieties, which, in my judgment, aren't worth anything. If you can't locate the real thing, you can substitute lemon zest in a pinch.

1 tablespoon (15 ml): 1 calorie; 0 gm fat

Maple Syrup
Tapping the right source

Maple syrup is made from the sap from the sugar maple tree, a native of North America. When nothing has been added, it's labeled either "grade A" or "pure." This is very important, because all kinds of additives are used to aid in its harvesting and extend the real stuff with artificial colors and flavors.

I use maple syrup to sweeten strained nonfat yogurt for dessert. I also use it to add depth when I sweeten my egg-substitute custard. At breakfast, it's wonderful drizzled on apple pancakes with a sprinkling of finely chopped Canadian bacon.

It's a good idea to keep maple syrup in the refrigerator after it's opened, to prevent mold. If it becomes crystalline, simply set the jar in a pan of warm water and heat it gently; it will soon become pourable.

1 tablespoon (15 ml): 52 calories; 0 gm fat (compare with same amount of refined sugar: 48 calories; 0 gm fat)

Mints
The royal mint was once a penance.

Peppermint, spearmint, orange mint . . . the list goes on and on—and every herbalist has his or her favorite. All the varieties have a basic minty flavor, with subtle variations.

Way back in Elizabethan England, in an effort to slow down the consumption of lamb for at least one season of wool gathering, the Queen decreed that every English man and woman who ate lamb had to eat a bitter herb as penance. Mint was chosen, and laced with vinegar, to make the first mint sauce. It is still used today to overwhelm the flavor of young lamb, but it is ideally suited to yearling, hogget, or mutton.

Mint is actually bittersweet and, with all its crossbreeding, has become a mighty salad herb—provided it isn't overdone. I happen to like a Thai-style mix of spearmint, hot red chilies, mint, and either lemon grass or lemon juice—great for salads. Slip a few crushed leaves into green beans; or try, perhaps, a dusting of finely chopped peppermint or apple mint over a fresh-fruit salad mixed with low-fat vanilla frozen yogurt.

By all means, grow mint yourself, but box it in because it grows like mad in all directions. It will also dry quite well.

Nutmeg
Grate flavor!

This spice is the relatively large seed culled from a tree that is native to Southeast Asia. I have little doubt that it's better . . . no, best . . . no, absolutely essential to buy the whole seeds and grate them freshly for each use. I think preground nutmeg tastes like liquid detergent when it hangs

around for a few weeks. Because so little effort is required to grate it fresh, there should be no contest.

I use nutmeg to season all dark green leafy vegetables, along with a little salt, some freshly grated pepper, and a squeeze of lemon. Test it on carrots glazed with a little reduced stock that has been thickened with a touch of arrowroot. Try it on green beans with a little fresh garlic. In each case, you'll see how the seasoning makes it possible to do without adding butter.

You can also add just a whisper of nutmeg when dusting a dish with a small amount of Parmesan cheese—not too much, just enough to enhance the cheese. It works wonders.

Oregano
Oil of the mountains

This could be the reason why you like Italian food. You might have thought it was the pasta, the cheese, the tomato, but no: I believe it's the oregano, "oil of the mountains."

It seems that *Origanum vulgare* is actually wild marjoram, characterized by purple-spiked bushes. The true kitchen oregano, *Origanum heracleoticum*, has white flower spikes. If you're going to plant it in your herb garden, remember always to buy it as a plant because, apparently, the seeds revert back to the wild variety through cross-pollinating when in flower. True mountain-grown oregano probably does not undergo this reversion because of its remote location.

Now all this may seem somewhat obscure, but let me assure you that the flavors are quite different. *Origanum heracleoticum* has a superb fragrance that will convert you from herb "user" into herb "fancier"—maybe even herb "lover"!

In your first experiments, please use only two or three whole leaves. Try them with stewed tomatoes or a homemade vegetable soup. If you like green salads that bite back, try chopping two or three leaves very finely and sprinkling them on the salad the moment before you toss and serve.

Parmesan Cheese
Good-hearted cheese

You may be used to buying Parmesan cheese from the store already grated and shaking it dustily from its carton onto your food. Did you ever wonder why the cheese smelled like a ship on its first day out in a storm, before the new passengers had found their sea legs? You may, as a result, have asked yourself, "What's all the fuss?" and gone back to the ever elastic mozzarella or cheddar.

Stop! You must try a piece of good Parmesan cheese and grate it freshly onto your Minimax meals. **I use it, along with dry Monterey Jack cheese, scattered on the surface at the last moment. Purchase the**

Parmesan cheese

best you can find, grate it only when needed, and use a single level tablespoon (15 ml) for each serving. This gives you the aroma, appearance, and taste of much more cheese with far less weight.

The world's best Parmesan cheese, from the cows around Parma in Reggio Emilia, Italy, is called Parmigiano-Reggiano. It is semisweet, slightly salty, and has the dry, crumbly heart found in the cheese of the Grana family. It is also made from skim milk, which helps lower its fat content.

1 tablespoon (15 ml): 23 calories; 2 gm fat

Peppercorns
Jacob's seasoning?

Peppercorns come in a variety of colors from a single plant, a creeping Indian native (which sounds altogether too ominous).

The green peppercorn is harvested early and either disappointingly dried until simply hot and ordinary or pickled in brine for a wonderful "above-the-line seasoning." **It has a salty taste like a caper, a bite like a pepper, and the texture of a pine nut. I use them in white sauces and in salsas.**

The black peppercorn is next in line, picked just short of full maturity. **They are dried and have become my constant seasoning companion.** I usually treat them to a rough grind at the last moment. I prefer to season at the end of moist-heat cooking rather than at the beginning.

The white variety is left on the vine until fully mature. It's then steeped in water to soften and remove the husk. Some amount of fragrance is lost in the process,

and without the husk the inner core is hotter. **I use white pepper in light-colored sauces and mashed potatoes.**

Rosemary
A myth about the Mrs.?

Myth has it that when rosemary grows well, the woman of the house is in charge. I've tried to let mine die, but it continues to flourish in my garden! As good dried as fresh, rosemary is one of my top favorites; in fact, if I had to choose between basil and rosemary, I'd wind up in severe procrastination.

I love to braise vegetables in a stock, with one 4-inch (10-cm) branch of fresh rosemary added for each 2 pounds (900 gm) of vegetables, lightly wrapped in muslin to prevent the hard leaves from floating around in the sauce. A short branch laid in a roasting pan with a leg of lamb is wonderful. If you are a barbecue fan, try slapping a dried branch under your grilled entree (hamburgers, chicken, salmon steak, or sausages) just before serving and wait to

hear the cries of delight. In addition, a branch of rosemary in the steaming water or bottom tray of a Stack 'n Steam pot will add an agreeable light perfume to seafood or vegetables.

Do try to get a plant growing at home. Rosemary loves the sun. It's a semihardy perennial that needs to be brought indoors if you experience cold winters.

Sage
Abounding with summer's fragrance

You'll want this large herb in your garden, with its proud purple flowers and powder-pale velvet leaves.

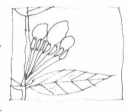

Its classic use is in sage-and-thyme bread stuffings for poultry. I employ a Minimax version of this, using 2 to 3 fresh sage leaves and a 2-inch (5-cm) sprig of lemon thyme inserted into a turkey breast before roasting. The flavors infuse into the meat during cooking. Sage is also great with veal and pork. I like a branch of 5 to 6 leaves tossed into a chicken stir-fry. Just remember to remove it before serving.

One spring I planted a couple of sage plants and the following summer had a 4-by-2-foot stand that flourished all summer long. It doesn't weather extreme cold well but does come back valiantly in the spring, flowers and all, if kept indoors over the winter.

Sea Salt
Beating to windward across the kitchen floor

A look at its label reveals that strange companions are running with table salt these days: cornstarch and talcum powder, to name just the ones I recognize by name. That's one of the reasons I prefer to season with sea salt, which is quite literally evaporated seawater complete with all its natural span of minerals. It seems that, for my taste, I need to use less than ordinary table salt.

I keep the sea salt crystals in a salt grinder, which is much the same as a pepper mill, but with nylon cogs that can't corrode. Then I freshly grind 1/8 teaspoon (.6 ml) into dishes I'm cooking to serve four people. When the dish is finished, I taste it again and sometimes add another 1/8 teaspoon (.6 ml), depending on the power of the other flavorings.

One-fourth teaspoon of sea salt contains 533 milligrams of sodium. Remember that the daily allowance for a nonhypertensive person is 2,400 milligrams, and adjust the salting of your meals accordingly.

Sesame Oil
My favorite daydream

I have a favorite daydream in which I discover that the entire secret behind the huge hamburger chains' success is the sesame seeds on the bun. Then I awaken to return to the task of finding a successful alternative to the "all-beef patties, bacon-lettuce-cheese–secret sauce, with fries and milkshake."

One way to counter risky fat-laden foods is with a less risky fat, such as aromatic toasted sesame oil. I do this by adding one part toasted sesame oil to fifteen parts plain oil, such as canola or light-flavored olive oil. The sesame aroma is powerful and distinct, and it counters the fact that I often use only a teaspoon (5 ml) of oil in my sautés and stir-fries. Unfortunately, the sesame fragrance is quickly lost when heated, so I also keep a small bottle in the refrigerator and shake on a few drops just before serving a stir-fry or rice pilaf.

Shallots
Beyond bromide and breath mints

Do you suffer from indigestion when eating onions? Do you view garlic as antisocial? If the answer to any of these questions is yes, then you might be ready for the shallot.

The taste of a shallot falls neatly between onions and garlic without the side effects (for most people). Quite apart from its social convenience, the shallot is the perfect Minimax seasoning. **I use shallots wherever I've got a delicate, light-flavored sauce, soup stock, or poaching liquid for all seafood recipes. Make a great vegetable side dish or garnish by slicing them very finely, tossing them in a little oil and adding thinly sliced mushrooms, lemon juice, cayenne pepper, and dill weed.**

Shallots are part of the onion family, but they are much smaller than the average onion and their flesh is white tinged with purple. The dry skin is usually a golden brown, and they're often sold in small mesh bags. Granted, it's a bit of a fiddle getting the skin off, but the gentle aromatic rewards are plentiful.

1 tablespoon (15 ml): 3 calories; 0 gm fat

Soy Sauce
A deep, dark Asian classic

Now here's a classic if there ever was one: the deep dark brown, salty liquid obtained by fermenting soybeans. **Besides the traditional use of soy sauce as a seasoning for Asian stir-fries and other dishes, I have found that its rich color and salty taste complement almost any dull-colored, bland-tasting sauce or soup. You will have to taste carefully after each addition, making sure that you like its unique, fermented flavor. You should also avoid the addition of any other salt, to keep within sane limits of sodium use.**

Using the Minimax frame, I'm trying to keep within an intake of 1,800 milligrams of sodium a day because my wife, Treena, is hypertensive and must restrict her use of salt. If you, or anyone you cook for, suffers from high blood pressure, please exercise care when using soy sauce. Check the label, noting the serving amount upon which the nutritional analysis is based. It's often much smaller than you think, maybe even needing to be doubled to get the amount typically used in cooking.

You'll find a whole range of soy sauces in the specialty section of your supermarket; but if you want a real eye-opener, check the yellow pages for an Asian market. Make an appointment and ask to be shown around so that you can begin to understand some of the basics. I'm told this is a high compliment to people from Asia. If you strike it lucky, you'll develop a relationship right in your own neighborhood that will profoundly expand your culinary horizons

Summer Savory
A savory savior

Early converts to agricultural pest control by natural means noted that beans survived the black fly when savory was planted in their midst. In time, summer savory followed the bean from the field into the kitchen, where it did equally as well.

I share the bean farmers' enthusiasm for summer savory's use in plain, comforting country kitchen food. If you can carry the idea of thyme in your mind for a moment, and imagine slightly larger leaves with a peppery aftertaste, then you've got summer savory. Add a sprinkle to any bean dish

along with a pinch of cumin. The combination will make you a bean and legume devotee, I promise.

Tarragon
Napoleon didn't win, but tarragon did.

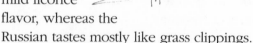

First of all, make sure you're using French tarragon rather than Russian. The French has a mild licorice flavor, whereas the Russian tastes mostly like grass clippings.

I use tarragon with robust chicken dishes. A 6-inch (15-cm) sprig can be placed in the cavity of the bird before cooking. I also scatter 6 to 8 leaves into the roasting pan—it makes a great gravy (see page 66 for making pan gravies with less fat). A few leaves on steamed root vegetables are wild when matched with nutmeg and lemon juice. Because its bite is so pronounced, tarragon makes a great seasoning for wine vinegars (see page 171).

French tarragon is an annual, but mine has often survived a mild winter in a small window box. With lots of sun, it's a great producer.

Thymes

A new contender for the herbal hall of fame

There has been a lot of activity lately in the herb field, crossing one plant with another to get apple mint, pineapple sage, and even caraway thyme. I'm fascinated with flavors and thoroughly enjoy playing with them in my kitchen.

One variety of this herb I must tell you about is lemon thyme. I'm letting it replace basic thyme in my bunch of herbs for bouquet garni (see page 144) and in the general seasoning of a wide variety of vegetables. I can see lemon thyme rising to become a constant companion to my all-time favorites, basil and rosemary.

You can easily purchase a good starter plant from a garden nursery. It's wonderful to go there and meet people who grow herbs—they're unique personalities.

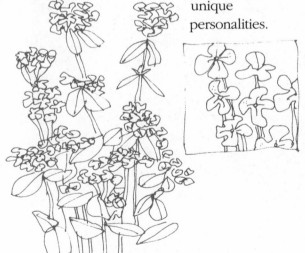

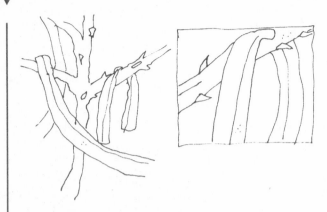

Vanilla

Not-so-plain vanilla

There is a disparaging phrase: "plain vanilla," absolutely basic, nothing new—but so popular.

I suppose a lot depends upon how you buy and use it. Vanilla labeled "artificial" is a tribute more to man's ingenuity than his taste, and I'd prefer you passed it by. Instead, look for vanilla labeled "pure." This means it's an extract or essence obtained by fermenting the pod of a climbing orchid that grows in tropical areas. The extract is a great flavoring for cookies, meringues, and yogurt.

You may also find vanilla packed individually in fine glass tubes as the original dry black pod. This is more than a gourmet curiosity. Pick it up and inspect it carefully. If you can see fine white whiskers, don't think it's gone bad; you just happen to have stumbled on the highest-grade vanilla. But even without the hair, these pods are still a good value. **I use vanilla pods to season nonfat milk for custards and sweet sauces. The pods can be used over and over again, as many as**

twelve times, with each use delivering wonderful flavor. Try cutting the pod open and scraping the fine-as-dust seeds onto ice cream and folding them carefully in or onto a maple-syrup-sweetened strained yogurt (see page 141).

Plain vanilla? Hardly!

Vinegar
A vital counterbalance

This is an item of great value to the Minimax kitchen. In fact, I believe vinegar is vital to every cook who is trying to counterbalance responsible reduction of fat, salt, and sugar on the modern table. Its value lies in linking acidity, the taste of sour, with both aroma and color.

Vinegar is an essential for salad dressings. It's also great for sharpening broths used for poaching seafood. Depending upon its flavoring and degree of acidity, it can be used as a marinade or as a splash finish for a bland casserole or stew. Try only 1 tablespoon (15 ml) at a time and taste before adding a second.

Each variety also has its own benefits. Balsamic is an incredibly complex vinegar that's great in salads and for finishing steamed vegetables—a sprinkle is enough. It comes from northern Italy where, by law, it must be aged for at least ten years. Balsamic vinegar goes through various barrels made of oak, chestnut, mulberry, and juniper, picking up the flavors of each. Some are very old and expensive. I suggest you buy a mid-priced variety that doesn't need to rely upon a fancy label for status selling.

Wine vinegars are delicate and best used in sauces and salad dressings. The best is made by the slow, aromatic Orleans process—a bit expensive, but you should at least sample it once. Look for "Orleans" on the label.

Seasoned vinegars come in a vast array of flavors. Buy them prebottled, or create your own. Start with wine, cider, or a rice-wine base, then add your own fresh herbs. Perhaps some branches of French tarragon or basil leaves? You can also add top-quality berries of all kinds, especially raspberries, red currants, even blueberries. Try 2 cups (472 ml) fruit to 2 cups (472 ml) vinegar in a wide-mouthed jar. Let the mixture work for a week on a sunny window ledge, then replace the fruit and let it sit for a second week. Besides the great seasoned vinegar, the fruit will be pickled in the process and can be used as a relish with cold meats and fish. Keep the seasoned vinegar in clean bottles, corked and cool.

I like the sweet-and-sour taste of cider vinegar for poaching peaches and pears (see the Spiced Pears recipe on page 149). Mild rice-wine vinegar is wonderful in a crisp Asian-styled marinated-vegetable salad. It can be found in the specialty section of your supermarket.

Worcestershire Sauce
Fluent fusion

This is one of the most successful bottled sauces ever made. Challenged in the West only by tomato ketchup and mayonnaise, it has two secrets to its popularity: one known but not discussed; the other known only to a few.

We do know that the liquid base is much the same as that of Asian fish sauce (see page 160): small, salted fish that are fermented in the sun until they've decomposed (see why this secret isn't discussed?). There was a version of this in culinary use as far back in time as the Roman era, called *garum.*

Somewhere along the path, the Roman *garum* fused with the Asian fish sauce; bitter tamarind, sweet molasses, sour vinegar, and aromatic garlic were added, plus the second secret, which gives the modern Lea & Perrins Worcestershire sauce its unique twist.

Recently this traditionally dark sauce went pale, almost white, and virtually doubled its potential uses.

I use Worcestershire sauce to perk up blandness in virtually any dish. (The new, pale version is wonderful in New England Clam Chowder!) It's important to shake the bottle very well before using and to add only 1 tablespoon (15 ml) at a time, tasting after each addition and being very sure before adding more.

Zests of Citrus
Free flavor from frugal fruit

This is a great example of natural "value-added" merchandise! Commonly with many fruits it's "off with the peel and on with the eating." Oranges, lemons, and limes are squeezed and discarded. Grapefruit is prodded, scooped, pummeled, and gouged as an aerobic breakfast exercise and then hurled out. In every case, the zest went out with the pith—sound like a mid-life crisis?

Now you need never waste the free flavor hidden in the skin of citrus fruit again. I use the flavor-packed zest to season nonfat milk for custard and sweet sauces. I also make a crème caramel with orange zest, rosemary, maple syrup, and egg substitute. The zest and herb combine to distract attention from the withdrawal of 58 grams of fat per serving. Fine zest matchsticks can be put in a little cold water, brought to the boil, and then poured into ice water to "blanch" before being added as a garnish to sauces served with bland dishes.

The trick is to take only the outer skin and leave the bitter white pith behind. I peel the zest from brightly colored, blemish-free fruit when I need it, using either a potato peeler, a special notched "zester," a sharp fine-holed grater, or a very sharp knife and a steady hand.

Achiote Powder
Brilliant yellowy red

Butter bright when just a touch is used, gradually decreasing to orange reds when applied with a slightly heavier hand, the seeds of the annato tree, native to tropical America, have long been used to brighten dishes in the Philippines and Mexico.

Achiote powder does have a degree of mustiness to it, so please be sure that any other seasonings are reasonably pronounced. I would never, for example, use it to color a light fish fumet (a clarified reduction of good fish stock). For that delicate purpose I would use powdered saffron.

Use it to color rice or to provide the red in Asian red sauces. Where a sauce is both strongly flavored and dark brown, it can be added to bring about warm mahogany tints.

You can find achiote powder in Asian markets or specialty supply houses that provide Latin American foods. It is packaged as a powder or paste, or in a solid cake. I prefer the powder.

Beet or Beetroot
Definitely purple

Lots of creative opportunity here: this root vegetable packs the highest natural sugar content of any vegetable but must be handled carefully because its purple color bleeds.

Because of a beet's sweetness, you can experiment by contrasting it with various vinegars, from the heady depth of Balsamic, through cider, white, or red-wine, to the pale mild rice-wine vinegars. All work well because of the attraction of opposites: sweet to sour.

You can find fresh beets with bright green tops in the produce department or may purchase them in cans or jars. If you want to cook them yourself, you must be careful not to cut into the root in any way. Trim the leaves (which are also delicious) at least 1 inch (2.5 cm) away from the root, then boil gently for 40 to 45 minutes; or steam the small ones (2 inches, or 5 cm, in diameter) for 25 minutes. When they're cool enough to handle, peel and slice. All this care prevents loss of color and flavor from bleeding.

When using prepared beets, drain off the juices, add just enough vinegar to moisten, and then garnish with fresh chopped parsley, chives, or finely sliced fresh basil and a little cracked black pepper.

One great dish is whipped potatoes with 1/4 cup of beets (59 ml) added to every 1 cup of potatoes (236 ml), together with black pepper and parsley. Drizzle with your choice of vinegar and serve steaming hot—ah, shades of my youth!

1 cup (236 ml) cooked: 49 calories; 0 gm fat

Bell Pepper
The Model-T pepper goes Hollywood

Undoubtedly the star color, texture, and taste garnish of the present generation of cooks, this South American native pepper is mild and sweet without being sugary.

Once upon a time it came like the first Ford car: in one basic green color. But now, like the automotive industry, the pepper has been coaxed to perform remarkable feats of coloration: How about a sunny yellow? Traffic-light red? Tropical orange? Or darkest purple? I'm almost sure they'll be doing polka dots any day now!

All bell peppers, regardless of color, have one fabulous characteristic: You can roast them. Just cut off the top and bottom, de-seed, lay the pieces flat, brush them with very little olive oil, and place under a broiler until the outer skin chars black. The skin is easily removed; and the flesh, which is now supremely moist—almost oil-like—can be used to garnish pasta, white sauces (where its color doesn't bleed), fish, poultry, or salads.

Roasted peppers, often called pimientos, can also be purchased in jars. They range from very small and expensive containers from Spain to jars of a rough-roasted black-flecked California variety, a great value that look just as if you'd made them yourself.

---

1 tablespoon (15 ml) roasted: 2 calories; 0 gm fat

Carrot
All in the family

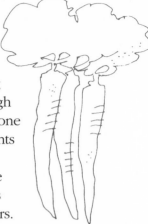

What sets the carrot apart is its strong orange color and its high level of beta carotene, one of the potent antioxidants that help the body to defend itself against the effects that free radicals have upon some cancers.

Somehow, in any effective food presentation, there needs to be a central color; and although the red-to-orange range is not obligatory, it certainly helps. Carrots make a most attractive garnish, especially because they are easily sliced into fine matchsticks, heavier "batons," discs, diagonals, and the interesting roll-cut shapes of Chinese cooking.

The convenience of the current miniature, prepeeled fresh or frozen packs has greatly increased consumption, but so has the arrival of organically grown European varieties that have considerable crisp sweetness. These tend to be fairly short and stubby, almost cylindrical.

Freshly ground nutmeg does such a great job as a carrot seasoning that it prompts experiments with other freshly ground spices, such as allspice, cinnamon, and cloves. Whatever you do, use very small quantities of these warming spices; their purpose is to get up under the carrot flavor, never to overwhelm it.

---

1 cup (236 ml) cooked: 70 calories; 0 gm fat

Cocoa

An answer for my chocolate-coated dreams

A confession: I'm addicted to chocolate and all its cocoa-butter, sugar-sweetened smoothness. In fact, any chocolate in my house must be kept under lock and key.

I have found that cocoa powder provides the much-loved color and aroma of chocolate without the fat. It's the residue made during the early processing of the cocoa bean when there is a pressing to remove a good deal of the cocoa butter. Thus cocoa powder contains only a small amount of fat. It's bitter, strongly chocolate-flavored, and very dry—so dry that it must be handled carefully to prevent it from lumping.

Cocoa has natural acids, and that can pose some taste problems. Some brands neutralize this acidity by adding an alkali. When this is done it carries the word "Dutch" or "dutched." If you have had an acid-tasting cocoa in the past and decided to keep using chocolate because of it, you might enjoy the switch.

I use cocoa whenever chocolate is named . . . but I still have dreams.

Corn

Pure Minimax Gold

Corn is also called maize, and its effect on food can be literally a-maize-ing! A clear and beautiful butter-yellow in appearance, wonderfully sweet, it is also a textural masterpiece when cooked until it just resists and then "pops" in the mouth. Take it another stage as the main ingredient in the classic dish polenta, and it becomes one of the great texture/color garnishes.

I use corn as a central color and enjoy matching it with bright greens, like broccoli, chard, or collards. When you slip it into a "Boston-styled" seafood chowder, it does wonders. I also use it as a creamy, golden topping for a smoked salmon-fish cake (see page 42). Because of its sweetness, corn literally begs to be matched with sour and bitter seasonings and does very well as a salsa-styled salad.

If you've never experienced fresh corn on the cob at its peak, you may want to have a quiet word with your produce manager at your supermarket (remember it is *your* market) and ask when he expects to get fully ripened corn. Make a note, purchase it on the day it arrives in the store, and cook it that night, to enjoy its full sweetness. Better yet, find a local farmer or even grow your own. It traditionally gets smothered in butter, but frankly, at its peak ripeness, corn only needs to be steamed for 8 minutes and served without adornment—you will be in gastronomic heaven.

Cranberries

A berry by any other name . . . wouldn't!

As a jellied sauce, this tart red berry, native to North America, has graced countless tables as a holiday condiment for turkey. May I now suggest that it's time to update the cranberry's image in your cupboard?

I use whole-berry cranberry sauce as a colorful and piquant layer in a fabulous dessert, Cranberry Duff (see page 126). Layered in a loaf pan with carrots, parsnips, whole-wheat bread, sage, and thyme, cranberry makes a colorful and tangy addition to a Thanksgiving feast as a Minimax alternative to stuffing.

Perhaps most exciting is the appearance of cranberries as dried fruit. The marketing industry has come up with some pretty fanciful titles: "Crannies," "Craisins," and even "Unraisins," to name but three. Don't let the hype cover the fact that dried cranberries are literally packed with what I call "bright notes." In the drying process, the cranberries lose a good deal of their fresh color, but even a dull ruby red is great when it's so full of flavor and texture. **Wherever you would use raisins, try dried cranberries as an alternative.**

I make a satisfying snack from fresh cranberries in season: simmer 2 cups (472 ml) with 4 whole cloves for 4 minutes, spread them out to cool, and then oven-dry to preserve.

1 cup fresh berries (236 ml): 47 calories; 0 gm fat

Edible Flowers

A meal for Mother's Day?

I'm certainly prepared to accept that some folks will never, ever eat flowers. It's a shame, but it's their perfect right. If you, on the other hand, are ready for an adventure, this is your A.C.T. ingredient.

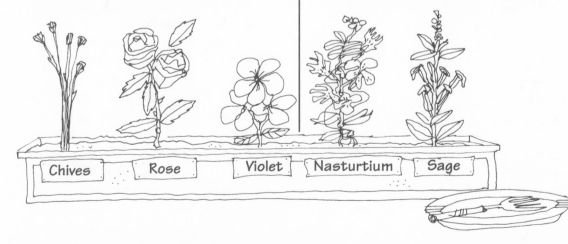

Chives   Rose   Violet   Nasturtium   Sage

The colors added by edible flowers can be dazzling, but there are a few other issues that must be considered. First, let's settle the issue of blossom size: the smaller the better seems to be a good rule, especially with nasturtiums and their leaves.

Second, of critical importance is your supply source. You must be sure that they have not been sprayed with systemic pesticides. There are growers who guarantee on the label that their flowers, herbs, and other edibles are chemical free.

Third, don't expect terrific flavors except from the white-flowered garlic chive, the nasturtium, sage blossoms, and other flowering herbs. The rest of the pack are either tart, as in the tuberous begonia, or plain nothing, valuable only for their appearance, such as violets, pansies, rose petals, and fruit-tree blossoms. There are also some garden flowers that can be toxic, and so I really don't recommend indiscriminate floral experiments. Get a reference book to find a complete list, but here are a few you should avoid: lilies of the valley, sweet peas, oleander, and foxglove.

Use flowers as a garnish for salads and for any nonstewed main dish. Some flowers go very well with desserts and can be brushed with egg white, dipped in fine sugar, placed on greaseproof paper, and oven-dried at about 200°F (96°C) for 1 hour, with the door slightly ajar to prevent any moisture accumulation.

Molasses
The browning version

Molasses comes from the first extraction of sugar cane. Each time the very dark brown treacly syrup is boiled it becomes lighter and sweeter. At this early stage, the taste is slightly caramel/burned, heavy and butter/sweet. **Because the flavor is so strong, I use it sparingly as a coloring in muffins and soda cakes. I've also used it drizzled lightly over frozen low-fat yogurt, with some almonds to partner the bitter side of its dual personality.**

Molasses keeps well if tightly capped and left in the refrigerator. Watch out for mold: if it develops, toss it. There is some iron, copper, calcium, magnesium, and potassium in molasses, which is one reason why it winds up in some pretty disgusting health-food shakes.

1 tablespoon (15 ml): 55 calories; 0 gm fat

Paprika

The paprika punch line

"Paprika and parsley": it's almost a Minimax test-kitchen joke. Whenever a light-colored dish is completed and we consider a garnish, there is a chorus of "paprika and parsley," followed by general laughter.

The fact is that parsley's bright green and paprika's brilliant red do go very well together, have a subtle flavor that doesn't overwhelm the main dish, and make a stunning appearance. Try it yourself over a white-sauced fish or poultry item—it really does make a difference in eye appeal, especially when, in an effort to reduce fat, you've taken out the cheese that would otherwise have made a light-colored dish go "au gratin golden" under the broiler.

Paprika is made from small bell peppers that are dried and ground. If it comes from Spain, it's slightly sweet but a great color. Hungarian paprika is more complicated: both sweet and somewhat hot, resulting from the inclusion of the seed pod in the powder.

In dishes such as goulash, I like to add two-thirds of the paprika at the beginning of the stewing process and stir in the rest just before serving to give an added blush and a pleasant, sweet aroma.

Parsley

My faithful culinary companion

Parsley has been a constant companion over my forty-seven-year culinary journey. My first book, published in New Zealand in 1960, was dedicated to "parsley and my wife." (Treena graciously allowed me to live through that!)

So, why write a word about such a common garnish? What's so wonderful about this herb is its brilliant color, yet restrained taste; its quite mild, slightly peppery crispness never, ever seems to fight even the most delicate dish.

The first thing I do with a fresh bunch of parsley is to separate the tops from the stalks and finely chop the leaves. Then I pile the lot into a corner of a clean linen towel, fold the cloth into a ball, rinse well under cold water, and then twist it vigorously, so tightly that the linen is stained green. I keep these well-dried parsley clippings in a clay jar in the refrigerator to use as sprinkles. Because of the dehydrating influence of modern refrigeration, the herb partially dries and keeps well.

The stalks are another matter. I use these in salsa, sauces, and many other seasonings. They have great flavor and texture—bite one and see. Chopped into small pieces they can add a special bite to omelets, tomato sauces, and, well, almost everything except ice cream . . . Well?

Radicchio
A colorful counterbalance

One would never think that taste went much further than sweet, salt and the mouthroundfulness of fat. These are the most commonly used "blunt instruments" of cooking with which we are most familiar or to which we are even addicted. But there are two other sensations that are less "blunt": sour, as in lemon; and bitter, as in radicchio.

Radicchio is an Italian cabbagelike vegetable with a deep purple-red hue and a somewhat hot taste. I chop it finely and use it as a surprise in salad, where its color brings balance to greens without my having to resort to tomato. It's also a fine addition simmered in stock, then strained out and discarded, just to create a pale pink color and mild bitterness (see Sweet Lime and Broiled Seafood Salad, page 46).

One brief word on the value of sour and bitter: we often use these words to describe aspects of human nature that are negative. Their contribution to cooking, however, can be quite positive, counterbalancing sweet, salty, and fat, which are definite nutritional negatives. Sour and bitter are powerful tools, and there is much room for experiment. I look forward to hearing your creative ideas.

Raspberries
Summer sensory sensation

Another seasonal blessing! Although they will make their expensive way into supermarkets off season, there is no comparison to the taste of summer-ripened raspberries, picked at a local field, that slide gently into your hand at the easiest tug—and more than once directly into the mouth!

Fresh raspberries have a sweet-and-sour balance with a velvet touch. **Toss them in a fruit salad with other fresh berries and a sauce of low-fat vanilla yogurt, sweetened with a little honey. You can use fresh or frozen berries as a seasoning sauce by pushing them gently through a fine-mesh stainless-steel sieve to remove the seeds and mixing them with low-fat or nonfat frozen yogurt.**

Red Cabbage
Pickle me purple

I suggest three major ways to bring the dark red purple color and sweet taste of red cabbage into your cooking: One is to pickle it, with the result a zingy and crunchy purple (recipe follows); the second is to cut it into very fine shreds and steam it; and the third is to use it raw.

I suggest you use very fine shreds, especially when raw, in salads, but try to keep them 2 inches (5 cm) long for ease of eating. The same fine shreds steam perfectly in just 2 to 3 minutes and only need a scattering of fresh

herbs (parsley, dill weed, basil, etc.) and some freshly ground black pepper. For a great color idea, cut Swiss chard in the same-size shreds and mix them together for a brilliant green and red/purple. I use this mixture to create nestlike wreaths around light-colored stews or "sauced" sautés.

RED CABBAGE

Serves 6

1 dried red chili, diced
6 allspice berries
6 whole cloves
One 1/2-inch (1.5-cm) piece cinnamon stick
6 black peppercorns
1 bay leaf
1 teaspoon light oil (5 ml) with a dash of toasted sesame oil
2 cups red-wine vinegar (472 ml)
1/2 cup water (118 ml)
1 medium head red cabbage (1½ pounds or 675 gm), cored, quartered, heavy veins removed, and shredded

Whiz the chili, allspice, cloves, cinnamon, black peppercorns, and bay leaf in a small coffee mill for a few seconds until finely powdered. Pour the oil into a large saucepan on medium heat, add the ground spices, and cook for 2 minutes, or until it forms a paste. Add the vinegar and water and simmer, covered, for 10 minutes. Stir in the cabbage, cover, and cook for 6 minutes, until just tender but not limp. Transfer to a bowl, making sure the cabbage is completely submerged in the liquid, cover tightly, and chill in the refrigerator until cool.

Red Currants

A call to arms

Red currants are not that common in produce departments. They have a short but blissful season, damage easily, and enjoy only a brief shelf life. Also, you can purchase red currant jelly anytime (which I prefer to serve with roast lamb instead of mint sauce)—four good reasons for their scarcity.

But let me tell you why you should start demanding their seasonal appearance: they're brilliantly colored, tart/sweet berries, terrific for garnish as well as a sauce for frozen yogurt. Just poach them in a little sweet wine and thicken with a little arrowroot.

If growers and supermarkets fail to respond to my call to arms, may I suggest that someone start freeze-drying them as a competitor to raisins and dried cranberries?

1 cup (236 ml) raw: 66 calories; 1 gm fat

Saffron

Sauce for the nineties

Imagine what 70,000 crocuses must look like. Then imagine plucking their stigmas. Assuming extremely nimble fingers, say picking thirty a minute, that means thirty-eight hours of crocus plucking occurs for each pound (450 gm) of saffron—no wonder this is the world's most expensive culinary spice!

Fortunately, you need only a very little to make saffron's buttery yellow contribution to your cooking. I use it to bring the appearance of butter to dishes

that are traditionally served in pools of butter, like pan-fried or broiled fish, or the classic kedgeree. Just a knife point of saffron powder added to a crystal-clear stock, thickened with a bit of arrowroot, gives you a beautiful butter yellow sauce. It doesn't taste like butter but acts as a colorful creative alternative that matches the diner's past memory and moves him or her into a more positive frame of mind to encounter a fat-free sauce.

You can also buy saffron in threads, exactly as it came from the crocus, in tiny compressed cakes, or as a bright red powder. I prefer the powder, provided it's sealed by a reputable company that doesn't mix it with turmeric, which seriously alters the taste toward the peppery side.

Strawberries
Everything has its season.

The warm, red, natural packaging of strawberries is almost as inviting as a brown-speckled egg; the contents, of course, are much more attractive from the cholesterol standpoint.

It seems that in these days of high-technology transportation, you can always find the glossy-red-lipstick color of strawberries at the supermarket; highly uneven in quality, this fruit will really lack taste. Instead, I wait until their natural season brings them to full ripeness at local farms; then I have my fill for a month or two. **Dusted with black pepper and brown sugar, dunked in honey-sweetened nonfat vanilla yogurt, they**

are a sublime dessert. I also make a "chocolate" (cocoa powder) angel-food cake, layer the strawberries inside, and ice it with a maple-syrup-sweetened strained-yogurt frosting—a Minimax version of strawberry shortcake.

If you have any garden space open to the summer sun, I highly recommend growing at least a pound (450 gm) of your own absolutely chemical-free berries. And take advantage of the peak-of-season taste and abundance. This year I'm going to make strawberry jam for my neighbors for Christmas.

I cup freshly chopped: 45 calories; I gm fat; 94 mg vitamin C

Summer Squash
Awaiting discovery

Often growing sheltered by large green leaves, summer squash lies in warm garden beds awaiting discovery. (Now I'm sounding like a promo for the Monday-night movie!)

Light and delicately flavored, they come in an array of shapes, colors, and sizes. Draw up a list: Crookneck is buttercup yellow, almost designed to be hung on the wall and admired, were it not better to cook it fresh off the vine; the hunter green zucchini; plump, sage green pattypan with crinkled edges.

All the summer squashes steam beautifully, especially when picked at the beginning of their ripe cycle (not too young—let's say adolescent). Please experiment using your favorite fresh

snipped herbs. I believe French tarragon is a must, but you might like summer savory, dill, or pineapple sage. With freshly ground black pepper and just a touch of salt, you're off and running—come on, it's time to get out there and do it (unless of course, you're reading this in winter, in which case turn to page 184 for winter squash).

1 cup (236 ml) cooked: 36 calories; 1 gm fat

Sun-Dried Tomatoes
The sun-dried sea

When I left the public stage in 1974 for a fourteen-year sabbatical, I left a kitchen that hadn't yet heard about sun-dried tomatoes. On my return in 1988, they had become quite the thing, and today as I write, you almost have to wade into the modern kitchen through a vast sun-dried sea.

I use them in Minimax for their surprising, concentrated flavor and chewy but crisp texture. Stay away from the nutritional pitfall inherent in the oil-packed versions. Buy them sun-dried and packaged in plastic. They are easily resuscitated by soaking in boiling water for two minutes, then draining. Chop them up and start springboarding—mixed into mashed potatoes, perhaps?

I've used sun-dried tomatoes (which are actually oven-dried) for added depth without fat in a number of sauces. Their dark red color and crinkled flesh are an especially welcome boost to pasta sauces where I've reduced the volume of extra-virgin olive oil.

Sweet Potato
My favorite root

I obviously enjoy all the root vegetables, but this is my favorite. Beyond the lovely orange color and balanced sweetness, what makes sweet potato extraordinary is its smooth, creamy texture and, last but not least, its remarkable storehouse of nutrients, including beta carotene, vitamin A, vitamin C, and calcium.

Sweet potatoes make a great side dish. I sprinkle them with freshly grated nutmeg, black pepper, lemon juice, or chili powder. They await your invitation, and are perfect baked or steamed. Avoid the candied version, in which the natural sweetness is obscured. Whenever I'm baking something in the oven at 350°F (180°C), I always slip in a sweet potato or two. The dry heat of my wall oven convection unit decreases moisture and concentrates flavor. I keep them in their skins in a covered bowl, to be mashed well and added to soups and sauces as a thickener and color enhancer—it's time to springboard.

When storing fresh sweet potatoes, remember they spoil quickly at temperatures above 55°F (13°C).

1 cup (236 ml) cooked: 181 calories; 0 gm fat

Tomato

Any vegetable as fruitful?

This fruit is so important that an entire chapter should be devoted to it. There are few foods that attract as many fanatical followers. It seems some people almost worship, in a backyard-barbecue kind of way, the huge beefsteak variety of tomato. Others hunt through their supermarkets for the plum-shaped Italian roma tomato, for its denser, less watery flesh—a good quality for Italian cuisine.

I like a small-sized tomato, picked vine-ripe from the garden, fresh-smelling as a geranium, busting crisply in the mouth with its sweet acidity. You can find so many varieties—tiny yellow and bright red cherry tomatoes—that I'm sure you could grow right where you live!

Before you drown them in prepackaged salad dressings, try your fresh tomatoes sprinkled with fresh basil and drizzled with a little of my oil-and-vinegar dressing (see page 30)— fresh, fresh, fresh all the way. If you must use canned, I recommend the low-sodium Italian variety.

1 cup (236 ml) fresh: 38 calories; 1 gm fat

Tomato Paste

Mr. Maillard, I presume?

Whenever a sauce or casserole is dark, its taste is often "deep": full of the complex and stronger flavors you associate with marinades, braising, game, and the classic Creole and Cajun dishes of the southern United States.

I achieve this color depth and complexity without fat throughout my Minimax recipes by cooking tomato paste. Just spread it out in a skillet, with a teaspoon (5 ml) or less of oil over medium-high heat, and cook it until it turns a dark brown color. This is the Maillard reaction, named for the scientist Camille Maillard, who discovered that high temperatures cause browning of proteins. As this coloring process occurs, hundreds of modified flavor molecules are developing: hence, color, complexity, and depth. Please see page 52 for the detailed method as used in a simple stew. You'll also see my constant use of tomato paste for deep mahogany brown sauces that I believe go so well with all meats.

You can buy tomato paste in a range of sizes and even relatively expensive tubes. My choice is always the 6-ounce (170-gm) can. Open them and use them quickly; I've found that they quickly turn "tinny" if left in the fresh air.

Turmeric
Yellow Desert Storm

A spice powdered from the aromatic root of an Indian plant, turmeric is largely responsible for the bright yellow coloring and frank, musty aroma in curry powder.

I find its peppery taste appealing, especially in spiced yellow rice dishes. Just add 1/4 teaspoon of turmeric (1.25 ml) to 1 cup of uncooked rice (236 ml). Enhance this colorful garnish with textural additions like green pistachio nuts, chopped raisins, figs, crystallized ginger, or dried mango. You can make it a complete meal with some cooked chicken breast (see Yellow Rice, p. 89) and Harissa Sauce (see p. 157).

All you need to complete the experience is a black tent, a Rudolph Valentino video, and a copy of General H. Norman Schwarzkopf's military memoirs.

Winter Squash
Winter mouths a-waterin'

If summer squash's taste is like the twirl of a Victorian parasol in the sun, light as air and delicate, then winter squash is a full, vibrant yellow raincoat, speckled with ocher, red and green. Winter squash's sugar starches mature to an intense sweetness under toughened outer skins, ready to protect them against coming frosts, perfect for storing through the cold months until spring.

Whether they are baked or steamed, the kitchen warms to their aroma. Dusted with favorite spices, squash means comfort, color, and fewer calories in your cooking. Dust butternut, Hubbard, and acorn squash with nutmeg, allspice, or lightly with cinnamon, and watch winter mouths begin to water. Their use can be as varied as your imagination: I use spaghetti squash in a vegetable ragout, and butternut to make a grand cheesecake filling in a fig crust for winter holidays. They can also be the base for a smooth pasta sauce (see page 83).

1 cup (236 ml) cooked: 94 calories; 0 gm fat

Agar Agar
"Mouthfeel" without fat

Vegetarians and some religious people don't use gelatin, which comes from pig skins that are slowly simmered, strained, clarified, and dehydrated. After that description you, too, might be looking for an alternative.

Agar agar is certainly an acceptable substitute. It's made from seaweed that is boiled, filtered, and then freeze-dried. It is odorless, colorless, gels swiftly, and holds its shape longer at higher temperatures than gelatin. You can find it sold in very light bundles of long thin strands or as a packet of fine sticks. Asian markets always stock it. It's a bit more expensive than gelatin.

Now, how would you use it?

Both gelatin and agar agar deliver mouthroundfulness: that elusive, often fatty, reaction that happens in the mouth and gets confused as taste when, in fact, it's touch. When agar agar is added to fruit juices, it helps to smooth out the crystals in the freezing process. It sets custards in pies or cheesecakes from which you've removed the egg yolks. Agar agar can also add substance to an otherwise-thin broth or bouillon.

1 ounce (28 gm): 67 calories; 0 gm fat; 6 gm protein

Arrowroot
All that glistens isn't oily!

Arrowroot is a pure starch thickener that comes from the root of a Central American tree. This fine, white powder is so fine that it's used as the base for many facial powders.

Arrowroot's most exciting quality is that it thickens in hot liquid (195°F or 91°C) without the need to boil for 30 seconds to remove starchy flavor, as is the case with cornstarch (see page 189). The general formula is to make a slurry with 1 tablespoon arrowroot (15 ml) and 2 tablespoons cold liquid (30 ml) to thicken 1 cup of hot, thin fluid (236 ml).

The sauce that results is done when the slurry turns clear. With arrowroot, it clears completely and glistens on pasta—reflecting light just as oil or butter would; in fact, when used with a pinch of saffron in a good clear broth, it can look just like melted butter, yet it has absolutely no taste of its own.

Arrowroot's biggest drawback is that it doesn't thicken dairy products well, especially yogurt—or, for that matter, very crisp stir-fried vegetable sauces. It goes slippery, rather than smooth like cornstarch. When it cools, it gels, so always stir it in at the last moment and serve very hot.

Be sure that you buy it by the pound (like cornstarch) and not in the tremendously expensive glass herb jars. Health-food stores and food cooperatives stock it in bulk.

1 tablespoon (15 ml): 29 calories; 0 gms fat

Barley
Grain food as beef?

Properly cooked barley has the characteristics of good ground beef: slightly chewy, just the right size, mild, earthy, but clean. Just shut your eyes, hold your nose, and try it—preferably not when eating out.

But not all barley is created equal. As part of the mad scramble to make whole foods convenient, we have robbed pot barley of its outer nutritious husk and turned it into pearl barley. What an achievement for mankind: we save ourselves about 15 minutes (45 minutes for pot barley compared to 30 minutes for pearl)!

I use barley whenever I want to reduce the quantity of ground meat, of any kind, in any dish: meat sauces for Italian dishes, Sloppy Joes, lasagna, meat loaf, meatballs, even hamburger. In recipes that call for 45 minutes or more of moist heat (stews, casseroles, etc.) you can use it raw. In quicker dishes, parboil it first until just tender (30–45 minutes). Ratios change, but in general I use up to one-third barley, e.g., reduce hamburger from 4 ounces (113 gm) to 2 ounces (57 gm) and add 1 ounce uncooked barley (28 gm), which will expand in volume.

You can find pot barley at health-food stores and food cooperatives where grains are sold in bulk. Yes, you can use pearl, but it won't have quite the texture.

1 cup (236 ml) cooked: 192 calories; 1 gm fat

Beans
Delicious depth charges

Depth is important when you're diving, but even more so when you're cooking. Depth is a hard concept to describe except to say that it's the opposite of thin, watery, insipid, or pale. Depth brings substance to a dish and is usually a combination of several techniques and ingredients. For example, in classic cooking, a roux (flour and butter cooked together) mingles with ham-hock broth and cayenne peppers to give depth to Cajun dishes. Olive oil, onions, Roma tomatoes, and oregano give depth to Italian food. Unfortunately, the perception of depth is usually provided by ingredients with fat. So, I'm always experimenting to find alternative methods of providing depth in Minimax.

A great ingredient to provide depth without fat is beans. Serve them whole as a smooth garnish or blend them into a soft, velvety paste with some good reduced stock (see page 141), and stir them into casseroles, stews, and soups to provide depth without fat.

Many people shy away from beans because they are relatively high in calories and because they take time to cook. It's true that 1 cup of beans (236 ml) has about 234 calories; but there is only 1 gram of fat, and that's great news when beans are used to replace fat-laden depth charges.

Cooking times can be substantially reduced when you invest in a pressure cooker (a vital piece of equipment for the Minimax kitchen). Just look at these numbers:

Cooking Times		
	Boiling (hours)	**Pressure Cooking (minutes)**
Black turtle beans	1½–2	15
Garbanzo beans	2–3	18
Kidney beans	1½–2	11
Pinto beans	1½–2	6
Navy beans	1½–2	5

If the thought of a pressure cooker makes you turn pale, then there're always canned beans—literally "ready to go." I always have two cans on hand in my cupboard. You do have to be careful about the sodium content of canned beans, though. Rinse them well with water if you are salt sensitive.

Beans, my friends, are great food and will become increasingly popular as we approach the year 2000.

Bean Sprouts
Germination can be fun!

Want to get your children more involved with their food—to even eat vegetables? Here's a starting point that will also deliver an extremely fast-cooking stir-fry vegetable or a great crisp salad garnish: the sprouted mung bean. It isn't chock-full of nutrition, but it does have a fresh and clean taste, a wonderful texture, and—perhaps best of all—it fills the plate visually for next to no calories.

Most supermarkets now provide fresh sprouted beans, often several varieties, including lentils, which have more flavor

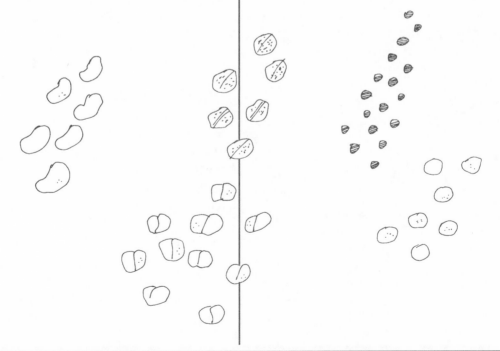

and nutrition. When buying, watch out for faded, limp, pale green shoots and give them a quick sniff test. Fresh sprouts should smell like fresh rain just fallen on a vegetable garden. If they smell even a little like a dumpster, then buy dried (raw) mung beans from a health-food store, food cooperative, or good supermarket and germinate your own (see below). I do not recommend canned bean sprouts.

I use bean sprouts in salads for added *crrrisp*, but I'm always careful to add them after I've put on the dressing because it doesn't take long to turn crunchy sprouts into a sodden sponge. In stir-fry dishes, they must be added last; literally seconds in the pan will warm them through and not spoil their texture.

Sprouted mung beans, 1 cup (236 ml): 15 calories; 0 gm fat; 2 gm protein

Sprouted lentils, 1 cup (236 ml): 32 calories; 0 gm fat; 4 gm protein

Sprouted peas, 1 cup (236 ml): 179 calories; 1 gm fat; 13 gm protein

GROWING YOUR OWN BEAN SPROUTS
You will need 1/3 cup edible seeds (78 ml), a large jar, a piece of cheesecloth, and a rubber band. Place the seeds and 3 cups of water (708 ml) in the jar, cover the mouth with the cheesecloth, secure with the rubber band, and soak overnight, unrefrigerated. Drain the seeds and rinse with fresh water. Drain well and lay the jar on its side in a dark place.

Rinse and drain the seeds twice a day. Most sprouts will be ready in two or three days. The sprouts will turn green if you place them in direct sunlight on the last sprouting day.

Bulgur Wheat
"Gimme cracked wheat and I don' care."
— *Ancient Egyptian folk song*

This must be one of the oldest forms of convenience food in the world. It's quite simply wheat kernels that have been boiled, dried, and then cracked. Wheat stored in this way keeps very well and is quickly prepared with the minimum amount of heat.

Bring 2 cups of water (472 ml) to a boil, pour in 1 cup of bulgur (236 ml), cover, and leave for 15 minutes; without any other heat, it will be ready. The resuscitated wheat will be nutty with a crumbly texture: an excellent addition to smooth vegetable-based soups and sauces (see page 144). Simmered in skim milk, with almonds scattered on top, and bathed in a little maple syrup, it's a fabulous hot breakfast. Cool and mix it with minced onion, garlic, oil, parsley,

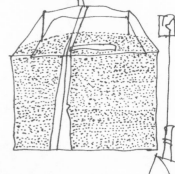

Bulk Bulgur Wheat

lemon juice, mint, tomato, and cucumber, and you've got Tabouli Salad, one of the all-time great Middle Eastern classics.

Minimax uses bulgur to replace ground meats in much the same way as it uses barley. With barley, you can use up to one-third the volume (2 ounces or 57 gm ground meat to 1 ounce or 28 gm barley), but I prefer not to add more than *one-quarter* the amount of bulgur because of its more discernible cereal taste.

Bulgur wheat comes in either cardboard boxes or bags, and is usually found near the rice in supermarkets.

1 cup (236 ml) cooked: 149 calories; 1 gm fat

Capers

Pleasure pockets

They spread out in a dish, each one carrying a dynamite concentration of sour, bitter, and salt. If you haven't experienced a caper, this description may sound unappealing, but once you've cooked with these "pockets of pleasure," you'll never look back.

Capers are the unopened buds of a flowering, trailing Mediterranean or North African bush. The immature buds are pickled and packed in small bottles. Watch the prices, as they vary considerably. If you keep the level of the pickling above the capers and the bottle tightly capped, they should last in the refrigerator for several weeks. If a mold forms on the surface, risk not; toss them out.

Because capers are, of course, highly salty, I recommend 1 tablespoon (15 ml)

per serving as quite enough. And when they are present in a dish, there is no need to add salt as a seasoning.

Deglaze a sauté pan in which you've cooked meats, chicken, or fish and blotted up the fat with a paper towel. The residues can be lifted off the pan by adding either a little wine or reduced stock. Toss in some capers, parsley, or dill weed, heat through, and maybe thicken with a little arrowroot/wine slurry (see page 185)—you have a terrific coating sauce for meat, chicken, or fish.

Capers are a champion bright note for above-the-line cooking (see page 10).

1 tablespoon (15 ml): 4 calories; 0 gm fat; 123 mg sodium

Cornstarch

The plot thickens, but how?

Throughout the book, I use pure starch thickeners rather than the classic flour-and-butter combinations that require extended cooking time to lose their raw starchy taste.

I gain speed with cornstarch and superspeed with arrowroot, but the two are not equal in quality.

Arrowroot (see page 185) is perfect for clear sauces and the gloss finish that makes a pasta-and-vegetable dish look as though it's been bathed in oil. Cornstarch is always slightly cloudy and is better used in lightly colored sauces that are not translucent. Cornstarch is also better than arrowroot for mixing with dairy products, such as strained yogurt (see page 141).

Mix 1 tablespoon (15 ml) cornstarch with 2 tablespoons (30 ml) liquid to form a slurry, or thin cream. Remove the pan with the liquid to be thickened from the heat, stir in the slurry, return the pan to the heat, bring to a boil, and stir until the mixture clears, about 30 seconds. The boiling removes the raw starch taste. It's important to do this just before serving, because cornstarch gradually loses its thickening ability when held at serving temperature.

Finally, a word about goopiness. This occurs when the starch is overused; the sauce ends up resembling axle grease. The rule to follow: "Less is best." Creep up on your task 1 teaspoon (5 ml) at a time, until everything just holds together.

Couscous

True grit

Couscous is another modern culinary battleground where the war is over texture and time.

If you love to handle food and delight in classic kitchen labors, go the second mile and get all steamed up about the traditional method for cooking couscous. Tiny beads, or grits, of precooked hard (durum) wheat semolina paste are first rinsed and then spread out to plump for 10 minutes. They're then broken up into fine even-sized pieces. The premoistened pasta is now steamed over a hot bubbling stew (tagine) in a special colander (couscoussière) for 30

minutes. Time to toss them again to break up the lumps and then back for a second steaming for 30 minutes. **They're now ready to serve plain or very well garnished with dried fruits, nuts, or vegetables and seasoned with saffron or turmeric, ginger, cinnamon, citrus zest, orange flower water—the list is endless. Total elapsed time is 80 minutes.**

Now, in comes modernity, in which the identical semolina pasta grits are precooked twice and then dried for instant use. Just pour on boiling water and, bingo, it's all done in 5 minutes—very similar to bulgur wheat.

Which method suits you? Either way, you'll have a well-seasoned grain without the use of oil and flesh proteins (meats). I favor the classic method for its smooth, plump, almost satinlike texture. However, I'm also ready to accept the instant provided that it's cooked in very well seasoned reduced stock and not water. It is less than the best, but in real terms the classic does involve a substantial time element.

1 cup (236 ml) cooked: 210 calories; 0 gm fat

Nuts

All nuts provide crunchy textural enhancement to your cooking.

Almonds, pistachios, hazelnuts, and pine nuts go well with cereals, seafood, and salads.
I like pine nuts scattered sparingly on top of pasta dishes.

They provide pockets of monounsaturated oil, much the same way as a few capers provide bright areas of saltiness.

Because of their higher fat content, walnuts go well in salads with fruit, deeper-flavored meat, and game dishes.

Pecans are surprisingly high in fat and should always be used sparingly. I utilize them in composed salads made with strong dark greens and marinated chicken.

The high oil content of nuts will cause them to go rancid quickly, as will light. Buy small quantities and keep them in airtight containers—dark glass or plastic jars are good—in the refrigerator. If you buy them prepackaged, check the label to make sure that no oil or salt has been added.

Seeds and nuts can be purchased in a variety of packages and a variety of processing. The more processed, the higher the price and the lower the nutritional value. Choose nuts and seeds that are firm and smooth. If they are in the shell, they should be heavy for their size (the sign of a meaty nut). Always avoid nuts and seeds with mold, even if the mold wipes away easily.

MINIMAX SEED MIX

A very nutritious way of adding crunch to a meal. It's quite tasty and high in protein. Combine equal measures of sunflower seeds, unhulled sesame seeds, green pumpkin seeds, and flaked almonds. Combine with a half measure of flax seeds.

Oats

Some of us grew up terrorized by lumpy, pale, salty oatmeal. Even though oats are a part of my Scottish cultural roots, I, too, would back off into a dark corner if I were ordered to "open wide" for such gruel—a grueling experience!

Because we all need high-carbohydrate calories at the start of the day to fuel our activities, I believe oats are vital in the Minimax process. In addition to having no fat, they're high in soluble fiber, have 50 percent more protein than wheat, and are a source of iron, manganese, vitamin E, zinc, and folacin.

So let me reintroduce you to the wonderfully soft, comforting texture of oats. I eat oats for breakfast almost every day, hot in winter, cool in summer, topped with grated apples, raisins, Minimax Seed Mix (see the Nuts section above), honey, and yogurt. Try stirring in a small bit of aromatic spice: cinnamon, nutmeg, allspice, or cloves. You may like sweetening it with applesauce or a puree of prunes. Mixing oats with these accompaniments will quickly elevate their status at the family breakfast table.

Old-fashioned Rolled Oats

1 cup cooked (236 ml): 146 calories; 0 gm fat

Pasta

The world's most popular carbohydrate

One way or another, I believe pasta has achieved the reputation of overwhelming favorite. Inexpensive and convenient to cook, it's widely available, in myriad shapes and colors. I think it's greatest attribute is a relatively neutral taste that allows it to absorb and complement flavors from virtually any source (or sauce).

I use all pastas as satisfaction foods (see page 8). There are many techniques, and huge amounts of mystique associated with pasta cooking. In general, pasta is well cooked when it remains "firm to the bite," or in Italian, *al dente*—to suit the tooth (see cooking chart at right). This firm texture means it must be chewed more completely, and mixed with mouth enzymes that make it easier to digest. Fresh pastas take only minutes to cook; dried varieties take anywhere from 7 to 14 minutes. Look at the package for specific directions.

To lighten the popular cream-sauced pastas, I make a cornstarch-thickened strained yogurt sauce (see page 141). Where there is a need for butter or oil on the pasta to make it glisten, I use a good stock reduction, with a little arrowroot to provide mouthfeel.

Perhaps the only problem comes with managing the longer-strand versions of spaghetti and fettucini: if eaten with flair rather than caution, they demand a marinara-colored wardrobe. In all cases, I dust the top with a tablespoon (15 ml) of freshly grated Parmesan cheese.

Italian pasta uses semolina, a hard (durum) wheat with a high gluten content. In the more prosperous northern parts of Italy, the flour is mixed with eggs and the pasta usually served fresh. In the south, the flour is moistened with water and then thoroughly air-dried until brittle. There are also Asian pasta-type noodles made mostly from rice flour.

Plain pasta, 1 cup (236 ml) cooked: 224 calories, 0 gm fat

Egg pasta, 1 cup (236 ml) cooked: 213 calories; 2 gm fat

Pasta Cooking Times

(for dried pastas, in minutes)

Spaghetti	10
Lasagna	10–12
Linguini	6–8
Fettuccine	6–8
Capellini	4
Macaroni	8–10
Orzo	7–9
Penne	10–12
Farfalle	10–12
Radiatori	8–10

Quinoa

A springboarder's delight

Quinoa (pronounced kee-NO-ah), native to South America, is an oval grain about the same size as millet. Its flavor is mild and almost fresh compared with that of other grains. Quinoa cooks quickly and is perfectly done after 15 minutes of simmering. It's usually a very pale yellow, but can be reddish and even black when raw.

I use quinoa in rice pilaf to a major extent, as much as 50 percent of total volume. It's also a great grain for tabouli-type salads (see page 34) or as a garnish in place of pasta, rice, or potatoes. Use your creativity to come up with new ways to complement its delicate texture and flavor. Perhaps a little ground cumin, a touch of cayenne, some dill weed or saffron—it's a springboarder's delight.

You can purchase quinoa at health-food stores. It is a little more expensive than other grains, but the nutritional content is high, providing very good plant protein, more iron than other grains, copper, manganese, folacin, potassium, riboflavin, magnesium, and zinc.

A reliable supply house for quinoa is Naturally Yours in Erie, Pennsylvania (telephone 814-474-3828).

I cup cooked: 178 calories; I gm fat; 22 gm protein

Radish

Hot crunch appeal

Here is great crispness, with just enough bite to let you know it didn't give up without a fight. The radish is a traditional accompaniment to salads, where its bright red color is a welcome contrast to greens. **Try cutting radishes into tiny squares and stirring them into a sauce at the very last moment. Their tart, hot taste will easily blend with the most delicate flavors, while adding an unusual textural crunch. They remind me of water chestnuts or raw celery.**

The point is that radishes will get you thinking about what you are eating, and that, to some extent, can take the attention you might give to salt, fat, sugar, and large portions.

I tablespoon: I calorie; 0 gm fat

Rice

Life itself for multiplied millions

Rice, in all its wonderful variety, is still the simple seed of semiaquatic grass that comes from common roots, in the Far East. I use all the varieties for textural reasons, but one type simply cannot be all things to all dishes.

Brown rice is the seeds with their overcoat left on and their valuable bran intact. It takes longer to cook, but the nuttiness and moistened chewiness is

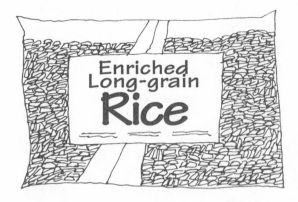

well worth it, especially for binding lower-fat, lower-meat-content hamburgers and meat loaf.

White long-grain rice is used when you want grains to be fluffy and separate, as a garnish. I use pearl or short-grain rice for dessert rice puddings or when I want rice that sticks together well. Arborio rice is the rice of choice for risotto (a creamy Italian rice dish).

Basmati and texmati rice are very slender and fine-grained and also quite aromatic. They've become my favorite as a full accompaniment. Multicolored mixed long- and short-grain rices are a blend of different colors and textures that, for a comforting, attractive pilaf, are hard to beat. Check your supermarket for premixed blends.

1 cup cooked: 126 calories; 2 gms fat

Strained Yogurt
Fresh cheese

Strained yogurt is my unabashed textural signature in white dishes. Providing both texture and color **I use it as a basic spread to replace butter or cream cheese, and in recipes to replace cream, sour cream, and crème fraîche. See page 141 in the Basics section for its very simple method of preparation and then have it on hand in the refrigerator for constant use.**

Now a few words of encouragement:

Even if you have decided that you don't like yogurt, give strained yogurt a try. When left to strain overnight, yogurt loses half its volume (the liquid whey). This makes a considerable difference to the taste and texture and wins over many previous critics.

After an overnight of straining, the yogurt will develop small, soft lumps that need to be smoothed out with the back of a spoon. If left for 12 more hours, it thickens even more, and the lumps mostly disappear—a desirable quality for coating sauces.

When you add strained yogurt to reduced starch-thickened aromatic stocks (see pages 141–144), be careful to have the liquid just below simmering. Drizzle the stock into the yogurt slowly, stirring gently. Because it's nonfat, the yogurt has nothing to hold it together and it breaks easily into tiny flecks.

Once you've got the hang of it, I think you'll find strained yogurt is a firm favorite—and remember, it has virtually no fat.

1 cup: 273 calories; 1 gm fat

Wheat Germ

Freckles for pie crust

Wheat germ is the embryo of the wheat kernel and comes with some very important nutrients: thiamin, vitamin E, iron, and riboflavin. It has more food value in its raw state than when it's toasted.

I stir a tablespoon (15 ml) or so into my pie crusts for a freckled finish and to replace nutrients that have been removed from plain white flours. I also spoon 1 tablespoon (15 ml) into 1/2 cup (80 ml) nonfat vanilla yogurt with 1/4 cup grapes (59 ml) and 1 tablespoon honey (15 ml). It's a satisfying, fast, healthy, and enjoyable dessert.

Because wheat germ's calories come from monounsaturated fat, it goes rancid quickly, especially when raw. I strongly suggest you buy it from a store that keeps it under refrigeration. I store mine in the deep freeze and never buy more than 1 pound (450 gm) at a time.

1 tablespoon (15 ml): 27 calories; 1 gm fat

Wild Rice

A top-seeded American player

I kept this specialty separate from the types of rice discussed earlier (page 193) because it is not, in fact, a rice, even though it too is the seed from an aquatic grass. The seed of wild rice is native to North America and is easily recognized for both its relative length and its color, which is almost black.

I use wild rice as a garnish and in mixed rice pilaf. Cooking times equal those of brown rice: between 40 minutes and 1 hour in a saucepan or 12 minutes in a pressure cooker. I prefer to cook mine at a slow boil and stop at 35 minutes. Remove from the heat and drain the water, put a metal colander over the saucepan, cover with a towel, and allow the rice to finish cooking by steaming in its own heat for 10 to 15 minutes. This method keeps the essential earthy chewiness, stops sog, and preserves color by keeping most of the black shells from breaking open to reveal the white interior.

1 cup cooked: 166 calories; 1 gm fat

Index

Achiote powder, tips on
    selecting/preparing, 173
A.C.T. (aroma, color, texture),
    2–3, 15–17, 93, 145
    list of ingredients, 147
Agar agar, tips on selecting/
    preparing, 185
Allspice, tips on selecting/
    preparing, 149
Almonds
    Chocolate Almond Meringue
        Mushrooms, 125
    tips on selecting/preparing
        almond extract, 150
Anchovy fillets, tips on
    selecting/preparing, 150
Apple(s)
    Appley Brussels Sprouts,
        108–9
    Baked, 120
    Roast Turkey with
        Apple-Orange Gravy,
        Swiss Chard, and Sweet
        Potatoes, 66–67
    Salad, 27
    tips on selecting/preparing,
        27, 120
Apple Salad, 27
Appley Brussels Sprouts, 108–9
Apricots, tips on selecting/
    preparing, 120
Arrowroot
    Arrowroot Vanilla and
        Orange Pudding, 134
    tips on selecting/preparing,
        185
Arrowroot Vanilla and Orange
    Pudding, 134
Artichokes, Jerusalem. *See*

    Sunchokes
Asparagus
    Steamed, 106
    tips on selecting/preparing, 106

Bacon, Canadian, tips on
    selecting/preparing, 152
Baked Apples, 120
Baked Falafel, 114
Baked Herb-Garden Salmon,
    36–37
Baked Pineapple, 121
Baked Sweet Potatoes, 104
Bananas
    Sautéed, 77
Barley
    pot, tips on selecting/
        preparing, 63
    Pot Barley A-2-Vay, 88
    tips on selecting/preparing,
        185–86
Basic Beef, Lamb, or Veal
    Stock, 142
Basic Chicken or Turkey Stock,
    141
Basic Ham Hock Stock, 143
Basic POP (Perfume of the
    Palate), 156
Basic Strained Yogurt, 141
Basic Vegetable Stock, 144
Basil, tips on selecting/
    preparing, 151
Bay leaf, tips on selecting/
    preparing, 151–52
Beautiful Red Sauce, 90
Beans
    tips on selecting/preparing,
        186–87

Graham Kerr's Creative Choices Cookbook

A collection of distinct methods and recipes that minimize the risk and maximize the flavor in everything you cook!

Graham Kerr's Kitchen

(G. P. Putnam's Sons)

Home cooks and professional chefs from across the country join Graham Kerr to offer original recipes, tips, and inspiration for making positive, creative, and delicious changes in the way you cook and eat.

These books are available at your bookstore or wherever books are sold, or, for your convenience, we'll send them directly to you. Call 1-800-788-6262, (press 1 for inquiries and orders) or fill out the coupon below and send it to:

The Berkley Publishing Group
390 Murray Hill Parkway, Dept. B
East Rutherford, NJ 07073

	U.S.	Can
Graham Kerr's Creative Choices Cookbook	$14.00	$18.50
ISBN 399-52135-6		
Graham Kerr's Creative Choices Cookbook (hardcover)	$21.95	$28.95
ISBN 399-13896-X		
Graham Kerr's Kitchen (hardcover)	$21.95	$28.95
ISBN 399-13989-3		

Subtotal $ _____

Postage and handling* $ _____

Sales tax (CA, NJ, NY, PA) $ _____

Total amount due $ _____

Payable in U.S. funds (no cash orders accepted). $15.00 minimum for credit card orders.
*Postage and handling: $2.50 for 1 book, $.75 for each additional book up to a maximum of $6.25.

Enclosed is my ❏ check ❏ money order
Please charge my ❏ Visa ❏ Mastercard ❏ American Express
Card # _____ Expiration date _____
Signature as on card _____
Name _____
Street address _____
City _____ State _____ Zip _____

Please allow six weeks for delivery. Prices subject to change without notice.
Source Key #72